BEHIND THE MASK

THE EXTRAORDINARY STORY OF THE IRISHMAN
WHO BECAME MICHAEL JACKSON'S DOCTOR

PATRICK TREACY

LIB
ERT
IES

To my friend Frances Kenny, who co-authoured part of my story, giving me the inspiration to keep writing on days when my passion ebbed, and, on many nights, taking pen to paper and helping me to document the painful memories of the deaths of my mother and father and, more so, of my lost love

And to Trish, for the wonderful days we spent together, and without whose love this book would never have been written

TABLE OF CONTENTS

FOREWORD

I first met Dr Patrick Treacy in February 2010, shortly after the dreadful earthquake that nearly destroyed a great part of Haiti. I was blown away by this total stranger's kindness. Dr Treacy stood in the midst of the debris of what once was our school and our home, holding an envelope. My heart opened to him immediately. I was amazed by the powerful speech he was making about the natural disaster that had struck the country.

My wife and I only knew that he was an Irish doctor. We stood there in disbelief when he simply presented us with a cheque. We didn't know what to say. In his eyes, we saw hope. He was ready to offer himself to humanity. Walking with him in the neighbourhood, I was filled with joy to see him comforting, touching, loving all these unfortunate people left with nothing. Dr Treacy made them laugh.

Soon after that, he invited us to come to his country to walk in the path of many great men by commemorating the annual Doolough Famine Walk with the people of Ireland. He said: 'Archbishop Desmond Tutu walked with us and three years later South Africa was liberated! Come and walk in his path for Haiti.' I strongly believe that the compassion and the love he has for the poor, the weak and the unfortunate would impress anyone on this planet, because he carries the world's problems on his shoulders.

It is a great honour to have been asked to express myself in the foreword of this book written by this remarkable man. Dr Treacy is a faithful servant with a strong personality, a friend of humanity. He is without borders and sees everyone in this world with one colour: the colour love. Yes, he is colour-blind.

I am proud to present *Behind the Mask*. I trust it will speak to millions of hearts, as it did to mine.

—Pierre-Pressler Dorcilien
Presiding Bishop
Restoration Ministries

INTRODUCTION

I have a story to tell, and if you follow me to the end of this book you will understand why I have decided to write it down. It is a story that exposes many personal intimacies, from my financial struggles as a young doctor, to my time as the personal dermatologist of the most recognised face in the universe, Michael Jackson. It is the story of how I got to know the singer as a friend and witnessed the personal agonies he suffered during the treatment of his vitiligo, of watching him cry as he took off his wig and showed me his scarred scalp. It is the story of how I smuggled cars to Turkey to finance my college studies and had to have a piece cut out of my leg to debride an HIV needle-stick from a Dublin heroin addict, in the days before there was any treatment for AIDS.

I never speak publicly about my patients, but in Michael's case, I have decided to make an exception, because I want to defend him from his detractors. I want to show you the humane side of Michael Jackson, a person who always cared deeply about others – it's a side of him that is not seen often enough in the media.

This story begins with my childhood in Garrison, a small village in rural County Fermanagh. In the early pages, I nearly lose my life in Northern Ireland's ethno-political conflict, and I witness the death of our bread-delivery man, Jack McClenaghan, one spring day in May 1979. Retired from the Ulster Defence Regiment (UDR), he was out making deliveries when the IRA motorcyclists fired their bullets. His next stop would have been our house.

From my earliest childhood, I dreamed of travel and adventure, of living amongst the Marsh Arabs that Wilfred Thesiger wrote about, of experiencing the thrill of flying with the Royal Flying Doctor Service, like on the TV series from Broken Hill in New South Wales, Australia. If life is about living out your childhood dreams, then I have long since achieved that ambition, lived those adventures. I will tell you how I was captured by Saddam Hussein's army near the town of Halabja, while working as a doctor in Iraq.

As my story unfolds, you will see how my parents were influential in determining my decisions. My mother instilled in me a passion for education. She had achieved one of the highest mathematical examination results in Ireland, but had been unable to go to college. She was determined that her children would all go to university, and encouraged me to study medicine at the Royal College of Surgeons in Dublin. I could probably give her credit for my first meeting with U2 when they were just a fledgling band playing in the flea market outside the college, and my later sitting with Bono at the 2003 United Nations Association of the USA Global Leadership Awards in New York.

My father, meanwhile, had a gift for making me believe in myself. He had a variety of passions, including local history, and together we would spend our Sundays exploring the megalithic tombs and Mass rocks in the west Fermanagh area. In those historic places, if we listened closely to the wind, we could almost hear the spirits of our ancestors and the heartbeats of the generations of people who came before us. My father showed me where teachers had once run hedge schools, and nearby holy wells that the saints of Ireland once visited. My teacher brought life to these monuments and told me stories about a Catholic people who had to practise their religion in secret, away from the prying eyes of murdering English soldiers.

My father also loved music and mechanics, and his energetic attitude made me believe there were no limits to what I could achieve. You will understand my gratitude to him when I tell you about the night he cut down the expensive billboard outside our garage and used it to build some sound-proof boxes that I needed for my research but couldn't afford to buy; they helped me win both the British Amateur Young Scientist of the Year title and the Irish Aer Lingus Biochemist of the Year title. I treasured these memories and later recounted them to Michael Jackson after he told me of his very different childhood, when his father beat him with a belt until he cried.

This is not meant to be an autobiography, but a memoir. As you read it, we will stand together at the Berlin Wall on the night it falls, and in Moscow on the night the Soviet Union ends. You will see how I helped start a whole new field of medicine from a small room in an apartment in Dublin's embassy belt, and how the rich and famous of the planet eventually came to that small room. You will hear how cosmetic medicine developed into its own speciality and how, within ten years, I was invited to lecture to doctors worldwide about techniques I had pioneered in Dublin. Later, you will hear how I weathered the Great Recession.

As Ben Franklin said, 'Out of adversity comes opportunity,' and I wrote this book largely as a means of filling the time that the recession created for me. It has been cathartic, cleansing my mind of some memories that had been haunting me. This is the story of my personal journey, of surviving life, of how I got to where I am.

1.
THE EARLY YEARS

Garrison, the picturesque little fishing village where I grew up, lies perched on the border of the Republic of Ireland, snuggled into the scenic shores of Lough Melvin and is favoured by tourists from all over the world. The older boatmen told stories of famous people, like Charlie Chaplin, having once visited the locale to fish for salmon and trout. The regular influx of different nationalities to the area meant that, although it had a distinctly rural character, it wasn't insular. I learned my first Bob Dylan songs on guitar when I was twelve, from some long-haired Americans who stayed at the local youth hostel. The village had a caravan park, two hotels and a smattering of public houses, so when I was young, the place was a hive of activity in summertime.

The conflict in Northern Ireland, which we euphemistically called 'the Troubles', pitted neighbour against neighbour. Since our garage served both sides of the community, our family tried to remain impartial. In fact, we would sometimes have a known IRA volunteer standing with a UDR reservist, waiting for my father. That was the nature of the conflict: the fields had to be tilled, the broken harvesters repaired, but when twilight came the guns were loaded. The cultural differences could be seen and heard all around us. They were in the colours of our school jackets, which newspapers we bought and, sadly, the games we played. Sometimes difference was more subtly felt – an intangible, steely force honed by years of hatred and mistrust. My father's favourite piece of advice was: 'If you have to say something, say nothing.'

As young children, the conflict skimmed above our heads like the stones we threw across Lough Melvin, and Garrison was a wonderful place to grow up. There were seven in our family: four boys and three girls. When we were young, we had the freedom of the nearby lakes and green fields, our daily adventures limited only by our rural imaginations. We spoke a dialect all our own. *'Bad cest to you, ya havral!'* was a common expression that evoked misfortune on another and was probably only understood within a twenty-mile radius of Garrison. Our country naïveté was offset by a wonderful sense of community spirit; neighbours looked out for one another and helped those who needed it, whether with food or labour. Of course, the price of this was a loss of privacy, but that didn't particularly bother us. Everybody knew – and *wanted* to know – everybody else's business.

My parents were devout Catholics and both had taken the 'Pioneer pledge', promising that they would never drink alcohol. They were decent, industrious people who worked long hours to provide for our family. We weren't given to open displays of affection in our house but I knew I was well loved – it was shown in other ways, like in the small hand-crafted toys my father spent hours making, or the long, unsociable hours my mother worked in her shop, saving all she could for our education. The shop supplied the villagers with their daily needs, but because it was attached to our home, it was really more like a prison for my mother as people came from seven in the morning and thought nothing of knocking on the door for a packet of cigarettes on their way home from a dance in Bundoran at three in the morning.

On weekends, our father would take us to the local cinema in Ballyshannon and sometimes, on Sundays, to the dodgem cars in Bundoran or the nearby unspoilt beaches in Rossnowlagh. He excelled at telling stories and had an unending repertoire of legends about our forefathers and how they had lived hundreds of years earlier. I loved these stories, as they belonged to the atmosphere of the village and, more importantly, who we were as a people.

My father, Pat, was a mechanic by trade and, as such, was

involved in the daily affairs of the local community – fixing the out-dated cars and machinery which were the economic lifeblood of our neighbours' lives and harvests. He had been raised in Corramore, a townland about two miles up the road from our house, and had spent his entire life in the village, so everyone knew the 'seed and breed' of him, as they say. Similarly, my mother, through her grocery shop, knew the financial circumstances of our neighbours; every year she waited until they sold their livestock at the harvest fair in Ballyshannon before receiving payment for the provisions of the previous year. I remember her working late into the night, adding up lists of debtors, too tired to say the rosary. She often fell asleep during the Joyful Mysteries, giving me and my brother Raymond an opportunity to sneak upstairs and listen to the latest hits on Radio Luxembourg. In those childhood days before the Troubles began, the sounds of the Beatles and the Rolling Stones led us to believe that England was a wondrous Shangri-La across the Irish Sea.

Everyone in our family was expected to help out in the business after school. My sisters – Anne, Bernadette and Caroline – mainly helped my mother in the shop. The boys – Sean, Raymond, Brian and I – usually helped in the garage, often working late into the evening if my father's workload was particularly heavy. These roles were not set in stone and we all helped out wherever we were needed.

When I was very young, I loved to spend the long dark winter evenings with my father by an open fire in his old bicycle shop, built before the garage opened. He and his friends gathered around a brown HMV valve radio, listening to what was happening in the outside world. These were the days before television, and I remember how the neighbours told each other stories and laughed away the winter nights. The shop was filled with broken gramophone springs, brass carbide lamps and the warm tones of the old radio. Some of the news from the radio, like the assassination of President John F. Kennedy in 1963, was very sad and I still remember how they all fell silent. Almost every Catholic household in the locality had a framed photo of JFK, twinned with one of the Pope, hanging in their living room. Kennedy was considered an honorary Irishman and a decent human being who was going to set the world right. The memory is deeply ingrained because I had never heard of anyone dying like that – assassinated – but, more importantly, because it was the first time I had seen my father cry, so I cried too.

Sometimes, he and his friends stayed up until the early hours of the morning listening to heavyweight boxing matches like the big Cassius Clay v. Sonny Liston fight in 1964. On nights like this, the bicycle shop was charged with excitement, the men jumping to their feet and punching the air at imaginary opponents. When Sonny Liston withdrew, they became even more excited and the voice of the man who claimed to float like a butterfly and sting like a bee crackled into our shop: 'I *am* the greatest!' Shortly after that fight, he changed his name to Muhammad Ali.

When I was eight, my father decided to expand his business by building a dedicated garage and having petrol pumps installed. This required local contractors to dig a large hole in front of our house to accommodate two fuel tanks. The JCB digger operator was called Danny Keown, and he was helped by a local man who was nick-named 'Big Bad John' after a Jimmy Dean hit. We kids enjoyed chatting to them while they worked, as they were the first adults we'd spoken to outside of our own family circle.

Such was the excitement on the morning the petrol pumps arrived that I decided to skip school and hide in my bedroom. I wanted to be with my father and my Uncle Johnny, who was helping to install them. My mother was furious when she discovered me, and insisted that I go to school immediately. My father, sensing my disappointment, took a different view. 'Sheila, it's a big day for all of us, he just wanted to be here to see it,' he said. 'Tell Master Regan he's sick – he'll remember this day long after that old school is gone.' I couldn't articulate it at the time, but this felt like a rite of passage, as if my father was treating me as a grown-up for the first time. It later transpired that he was right: Devenish No. 2 Primary School closed in 1972, but the old petrol pumps are still standing.

I remember every detail of that day, including the proud look on my father's face when the electricity supply to the Regent Super pump was connected and he filled his black Austin A40 Devon with his own petrol for the very first time. He shook the droplets from the nozzle, put the hose back in position, then scooped me up, placed me in the open boot of the car and drove the short mile into Garrison to buy me a celebratory ice cream. Those were the days before health-and-safety regulations gained a stranglehold, when childhood was full of excitement and wonder.

My father didn't always agree with my antics, however. One day, when I was about ten and my brother Raymond was six, an elderly farmer called Johnny Keenan arrived at the garage driving a light-blue A30. Johnny was small and stubby, with patchy white hair. His car had been Austin's answer to the Morris Minor when it was launched in 1951, but fifteen years had passed since then and it had aged and rusted. My father was out on a job so the old farmer addressed himself to me.

'Would you be able to fix that hole in her, Sonny?' he said.

Johnny pointed to a large rusty perforation that had recently grown in the front wing on the passenger side. To others, I was called P.J., to distinguish me from my father, Pat. But Johnny Keenan always referred to me as 'Sonny'.

'Sure, I can fix it with Isopon filler, Johnny. Do you know what the colour of her is on the log book so I can get an exact match?'

'It says sky blue on the tax book, Sonny,' he replied, tightening the rope belt around his coat before leaving. 'I'll pick it up in the morning.'

Although we had a new DeVilbiss paint spray-gun, Raymond and I decided the job was too small to warrant using it or even going to the bother of mixing paint from our suppliers in Enniskillen. Cans of spray paint hadn't been invented, or if they had been, they hadn't reached Garrison. After a little deliberation, Raymond remembered that our mother had tins of sky blue gloss household paint on sale in the shop, and he ran off to fetch some while I began to fill the hole.

We worked late into the evening and, in a magnanimous gesture, when the wing was completed, we decided to balance the slightly different colours by painting the entire car. Raymond climbed onto the roof to apply some finishing touches, and we had a struggle to get him back down without ruining the job or getting him covered in blue paint. When we were finished we stood back to admire our handiwork. It had been no mean feat for two small boys armed with paintbrushes and two cans of gloss paint, but we had pulled it off. Exhausted but happy with our night's work, we went inside and fell into bed.

The next morning my father called us into the garage. He was standing, hands in pockets, staring open-mouthed at the elderly gentleman's car. For a moment, I thought he was awestruck by our work of art. He wasn't.

'What did yous pair do to Johnny Keenan's good car?' he roared as he paced alongside the offending vehicle, shaking his head. 'Yous have destroyed the man's car and he's coming for it this morning!'

My father was a mild-mannered man who dreaded any type of confrontation with his customers and was sometimes known to hide in the house when the more challenging ones arrived. There was George Blair from Garrison Post Office, with his continually revving engine; Fonsie McGovern from the Melvin Hotel, with his broken outboard motors; and, to top the lot, Vincent Kennedy from Glen Cross, with his disassembled lawnmowers. Each of them was one of God's children, and part of my father's never-ending technical nightmare. To be honest, I enjoyed their company, especially Fonsie, who always treated me as an adult. They were all characters who used our garage as an extension of their own workshops, but their endless trivia often got in the way of our other, paying customers. My father, thinking he would have to face Johnny Keenan's fury, politely sought refuge in the village for half an hour while his two prepubescent sons were left to deal with the problem.

True to form, Johnny Keenan arrived exactly when he said he would, to collect his car.

'That's a newer model than mine,' he said, looking with rheumy eyes at the sparkling blue vehicle which my father had parked at the back of the garage. 'Where's my own?'

'Daddy went out to Garrison in it,' I replied, unable to make the confession.

'Will he be long, Sonny?'

'I don't really know – he was gone before I got up here,' I mumbled.

As is the custom of rural farmers, Johnny started to explore. He proceeded to get into the car, and found his prayer book and rosary beads in the front pocket of the dashboard.

'He must have taken all my stuff out of the car before he left. I wonder why he did that?' he said, still not making the connection.

A difficult fifteen minutes of shrugging shoulders and skirting the issue passed before my father returned and parked his car down the road at the petrol pumps, still not daring to come into the garage.

'Your father is in a black car, Sonny – he just pulled up at the pumps,' Johnny said, perplexed.

After a while, my father relented and slowly made his way back up to the garage to join us.

'Well? Did you tell him yet?' Dad asked.

'No, not yet,' I muttered, my eyes fixed on the toe of my shoe.

'That's a newer model than mine Pat,' Johnny said to my father as he got into the front seat. 'Is it an A35? Naw, it couldn't be – they'd have trafficators!' he mused, referring to the little orange stalks which used to pop up in the centre of the door frame before electric indicators were invented.

I couldn't take it any more.

'Johnny, that's your car,' I blurted out. 'Me and Ramy painted it for you last night.'

'My car?' He scratched his head slowly as he took another look. '*My* car?'

'Well, if that's my car, I'm a very happy man and yous can have a fiver each for the bother you put into it!'

He took his wallet from his pocket and handed my brother and me £5 each.

Of course, it didn't really cover the filler and labour we'd put into it, or my mother's paint, or the possible repercussions of having such an advertisement driven around the countryside, but Ramy and I didn't care – we were in the money!

I learned a valuable lesson that morning: own up to your actions, however hard it may be, because nothing is worse than waiting for the hammer to fall. I have often wondered whether Johnny later spoke to my father in private about the incident.

★

The state I grew up in had only been in existence for a few generations. Although children didn't actively participate in the politics of the day, the fact that Catholics and Protestants were segregated in Northern Ireland's school system meant we were taught two very different versions of history. This left marks on us, much like the thumbprints the priest left on our foreheads on Ash Wednesday, but not as easily washed away.

The problems between our communities started after the partition of Ireland in 1920, when a small group of Irish Republican Army members in the North dedicated themselves to achieving a united Ireland. The new Northern government passed the Civil Authorities (Special Powers) Act (Northern Ireland) 1922, giving the Protestant police force power to do almost anything they deemed necessary to eradicate this danger. Unfortunately, long after the threat had been dealt with, the Act was still used against ordinary Catholics. Many Catholics were not allowed to hold jobs in the public service, and Protestants were given priority on housing lists. The new brand of democracy was not 'one man, one vote', but 'one house, one vote' and, as Protestants generally owned more property than Catholics, their community held the reins in politics.

Despite this discrimination, two significant events had taken place in the social upheaval of post-war Britain that favoured the Catholics: the introduction of social welfare and free university education. The poor of Britain no longer needed to send their children out to work to help support the family, so they sent them to school instead. In this new socialist world, the Labour Party had unknowingly sown the seeds of a new, well-educated generation of Irish

Catholics, who would no longer be willing to accept the status quo. Indeed, my generation was the first to benefit from the new, 'fairer' scheme.

★

My primary school teacher, Master Regan, lived next door to us. He was in his late fifties, with a shock of white hair, and he brought us to school in Garrison each morning in his brown-and-white Hillman Minx car. This didn't entitle us to any special treatment; in fact, sometimes, after my older brother had been mischievous at school, we had to endure the odd silent journey the following morning.

In those days at Devenish No. 2 Primary School, I would imagine the world outside of our village. The world map on the wall was like a door to another universe, one where they spoke those strange languages I'd heard on the wooden short-wave radio in my father's bicycle shop. At break time, I would carefully take down the large school atlas from the top of Master Regan's cupboard and then the very essence of my day would change. My finger would run across the red expanse of the Soviet Union, following the snaking route of the Trans-Siberian Express from Minsk to Tomsk and beyond. The imaginary train's whistle would blow in short, steady blasts, telling me it was arriving at a station in a place far away from Garrison. Images of snowy Siberian landscapes, of red setting suns that cast long shadows along the carriages, filled my boyhood imagination. By the time the train reached Irkutsk, it was usually time to leave the atlas aside for another day.

One day, a missionary priest visited our school and I remember how his eyes hardened, almost glazed over, as he told us how the pagan Russians had no religion and were destined to go to hell. He was taken aback when the teacher allowed me to mention the towns on the route of the Trans-Siberian Express. When my mother seemed to agree with the missionary, I discovered there were lots of people out there who were destined for damnation and felt lucky to be born into the one true faith.

Mr Regan was one of the best teachers I have ever met. He had a great love of life and was passionate about nature and about our cultural heritage. He taught us the old language, Gaelic, and all things Irish. In class, he explained that our family names were important parts of our heritage, and taught us local history. 'P. J.,' he told me once, 'your townland is called Knockaraven, a word that comes from the Gaelic "Cnoc an Aifrean", which means "Hill of the Mass".'

We learned about our religion, and about how the English had banned our forefathers from practising their Catholic faith and had executed our priests for performing the sacred ritual of the Mass. Master Regan told us about the lookouts who watched from rocky vantage points to warn of approaching English troops and that one of these was located near Glen Cross, close to where my father was born. He taught us to be proud that our ancestors had stuck to their religious convictions amidst such adversity, and that we should be thankful to have a proper school, as Catholic education in that period had been carried out in secret hedge schools, groups of students hiding from view behind large hedges.

Master Regan explained to us that the village's name, 'Garrison', was a reference to a barracks erected by the Protestant King William of Orange when he halted in the village before the Battle of the Boyne in 1690. William's victory in that battle had secured the Protestant ascendancy, and British rule in Ireland. The local Orange Order provoked much antagonism when they marched in his memory through the village of Garrison each year.

★

In 1967, I passed the entrance exam to St Michael's Grammar School. I was to be plucked from the innocence of childhood and sent to a far-off boarding school in the market town of Enniskillen. This was normal for a rural student from my area, as there was no secondary school close to our village at that time. Although the seminary-type school I was headed to had a wonderful academic reputation, the prospect of leaving my parents behind at such a young age unnerved me.

My brother, Sean, who was four years my senior, was already at St Michael's, but mostly I felt that I was now on my own, fending for myself in a strange world where I was subject to loneliness and, often, cruel bullying. I knew that I had to come to terms with my new situation, but, although I never doubted the pedagogical prowess of the priests to whom my education had been entrusted, theirs was a strict style that could never inspire the same sense of wonder and desire to learn that Master Regan's approach had.

I often lay awake in the dormitory and listened to others crying softly late into the night. We lived a regimented existence, rising at eight every morning to attend Mass in the chapel and taking breaks throughout the day for prayer, the Angelus at noon and the rosary every night. Although I came from a very religious home – my father went to Mass every morning – this religiosity was overwhelming. During weekly confession, we sat in the large wooden pews waiting our turns, watching as the other unfortunates walked up behind the main altar to tell the priest their sins. Everybody immediately knew if a student had admitted to masturbation as the priest loudly chastised him in front of the rest of us. The humiliated boy would then have to walk all the way back to his seat amidst the hushed chorus of his friends. It was public mortification without a right to defend oneself. I hated it.

Corporal punishment was legal in Ireland at that time and we were regularly strapped for very small infractions of the rules. The instrument used was made of compressed leather, which was brought down hard across the palms of our hands. The dean, whom my older brother had nicknamed 'Stokey', was particularly cruel. He had us choose which colour leather we'd like used on us – black, brown or white – increasing the time we spent in anticipation of our punishment. After school hours, boys debated which colour was the best. Tactics were discussed too, such as dropping our hands slightly when the leather was about to make contact. That required perfect timing and, in my opinion, didn't really work, although some boys swore by it. It took a lot of willpower not to withdraw your hand as you saw the strap coming. If you did so, the punishment would perhaps be doubled and dished out by an even angrier man.

We were also subjected to ear- and hair-pulling and the occasional

knuckle to the shoulder or side of the head. This wasn't really considered a punishment, more a reinforcement of whatever point the
teacher was making to a boy he didn't think was paying enough
attention. I'm sure one Irish teacher, in particular, was responsible
for many later cases of baldness. Some of the boarders couldn't take
the school's strict regime, and ran away – a futile exercise, which
only made matters worse for them when they returned. It was difficult for some young rural boarders because, in those days, if they
went home and told their parents the teacher had hit them, they
were often informed that they must have done something to deserve
it. Although some of the priests were later accused of abuse, I never
witnessed any during my time at this school.

Life at the seminary followed regular patterns and, every month,
we were allowed to see a film in the recreation hall. I looked forward
to this, and fondly remember the black-and-white 1938 biographical
drama about Father Edward Flanagan's work with disadvantaged
boys in *Boys Town* and the 1953 colour epic *Shane*, starring Alan
Ladd. From time to time, we were also allowed downtown to the
Ritz Cinema to see recent Hollywood films such as *Butch Cassidy
and the Sundance Kid*, *Doctor Zhivago* and *The Sound of Music*, films
that reinforced a sense of decency and social mores that I had
learned at home and still carry with me to this day.

★

My father couldn't come to collect me every weekend. It was a fifty-
mile round trip from Garrison to Enniskillen. On top of the time the
journey itself took, he was likely to be stopped by the British army
and asked a series of tedious questions about the nature of his trip
while his car was searched. Apart from this ordeal, there were still
five children at home, and my mother had her hands full. At times,
I remained at school for as long as three months without seeing my
family and, eventually, I learned to get over the separation.

On weekends at the school, we amused ourselves by playing
soccer, which I wasn't very good at. It was annoying to be picked sec-
ond-to-last for the team and, for a while, I took up hurling, eventually

becoming a reserve on the Fermanagh team. There was no rugby at our school, but, for Gaelic football, we had a new pitch, which we were all very proud of and enjoyed playing on. Sometimes we went to the handball alley, but what I most enjoyed were the few occasions when we were allowed down town to Enniskillen, where I had the opportunity to meet with my old Garrison neighbours – mostly farmers who came to the weekly mart on Belmore Street. It was always a real pleasure to meet them and hear all the news from home that hadn't been included in my mother's letters.

In the summer months, many of the younger students went to the Donegal Gaeltacht to live for a while amongst native Irish speakers and hopefully improve their native tongue. It was a wonderful opportunity to meet girls from Mount Lourdes Convent in Enniskillen, and many friendships forged amongst the wild hills of Loughanure, Annagry and Ranafast in west Donegal still survive to this day. While there, we'd jump on the backs of bread-delivery vans and hitch lifts to the nearby villages. This is how I first met the Irish traditional group Clannad, who were performing in their father's pub in Crolly, mixing cover versions of the Beatles and the Beach Boys with traditional music. We continued our friendship in later years, when we met again in the clubs of Dublin.

After the Gaeltacht, I went home to spend the rest of the summer helping my father in the garage. He was old-school, having trained as a mechanic in the days before cars had microprocessors and computer sensors. He always left the more complex technical problems to me and Sean, who was naturally talented and became my mentor in the garage during my teenage years. There was nothing he didn't know about car engines and, much to the consternation of some of our neighbours, he loved to race cars along the local roads. Despite that, the villagers really missed him when he left Garrison and moved up to Lisburn to start a family of his own.

At sixteen, I won a number of awards, including Northern Ireland's British Amateur Young Scientist of the Year and the Republic of Ireland's Aer Lingus Biochemist of the Year. My winning biochemistry project showed the effects of different sound waves on plant growth. Many of the judges thought it was ahead of its time. My research secured me a personal introduction to British Prime Minister Harold Wilson, when he opened the London International Youth Science Fortnight in 1974. My parents were proud of my academic achievements when they were later printed in the *Fermanagh Herald* and, if any remarks were passed in the village about a young Catholic boy meeting a British prime minister, I was never made aware of it.

Throughout these years, I lived in two totally different worlds – the rural and the academic – and it seemed as though I had a foot in each.

2.
THE TROUBLES BEGIN

The world I was growing up in began to irrevocably change in 1968, when the newly formed Northern Ireland Civil Rights Association (NICRA) began a series of peaceful protest marches against discrimination, calling for 'one man, one vote' and the repeal of the Special Powers Act. The members of the organisation used the language and symbolism of Americans who followed Dr Martin Luther King. In October of that year, a march in Derry was met with a violent backlash from the largely Protestant police force, the Royal Ulster Constabulary (RUC). Three days of rioting followed and many Catholic homes were burned to the ground.

Undaunted, in January 1969, thousands set out on a peaceful march from Belfast to Derry and were attacked by loyalists and off-duty policemen who carried bricks, bottles and iron bars. The marchers retreated to Catholic areas, where they erected barricades to stop the police from entering. Police were seen to side with loyalists and the rioting got worse over a period of two days, spreading to other towns across Ulster. There were murmurings of rebellion when we watched the news and saw the burnt-out houses and the horror these riots had left in their wake. Fifteen hundred refugees were moved across the border and took up residence in the Republic.

Irish Taoiseach Jack Lynch said he could no longer stand by and see nationalists under attack in Northern Ireland. He deployed the Irish army to the borders of the six counties with medical aid and a plan called Exercise Armageddon. The planned invasion of the six counties was halted when the British army arrived and ring-fenced Catholic areas in Derry and Belfast, protecting them from further attack. Catholics who believed the presence of the British army would bring stability, though, were in for a rude awakening. Soon after the army arrived it became obvious that most of its men held the same views as their RUC counterparts, and one was as likely to be stopped, questioned – and often abused – by somebody with a Liverpool or a Leeds accent as by someone with an Enniskillen accent.

This was a new age of television journalism, and little could be hidden from the eyes of the world. Even though I was still a teenager and unable to assess the situation properly, I was incensed at the treatment of the protesters and the brutality of the Northern Ireland security forces. Although I had been exposed to some conflict in my early life, I had never experienced anything on this scale. I saw a creeping coldness replace the warmth that had long characterised the people of Northern Ireland. Neighbours who had been friends for many years now began to take a different attitude towards each another and even schoolchildren were careful about who they spoke to.

★

It was during this increasing tide of turmoil that a new church was consecrated in Garrison. Along with Patsy Tracey, the son of the local contractor who had installed our petrol pumps, I was let out from St Michael's for the day to attend the ceremony. Although he was younger than me, we were great friends and I was delighted when he joined me as a boarder in far-off Enniskillen. One of the most popular pastimes there was to take the red phosphorous material from three or four match heads, pack it into the hollow barrel of a key, tamp it down with a nail, tie it with string and bounce it quickly against a wall, making it to explode with a 'bang'. It was a childish game we played to see who could make the loudest noise, but I suppose if we had been picked up by the British army with these 'bangers' in our possession, we might have been perceived as the IRA bomb-makers of the future.

The old stone church in Garrison, where Patsy and I had served together as altar boys, had outlived its usefulness and residents had been collecting money for a long time to replace it with a new structure, even seeking donations from as far away as America. When the goal was finally achieved, we were all invited to attend the grand unveiling. Residents were bursting with pride, and local women had festooned the altar with bouquets of fresh flowers, ready for Canon Hackett to arrive and preside over the inaugural Mass.

All the villagers were dressed in their Sunday best. Patsy sat behind me as Canon Hackett started his welcoming speech from the lectern. We had been messing around with bangers on the way, and I had slipped mine into my pocket as we went in to attend the ceremony. At some point Patsy must have become bored because he slid his hand into my pocket and retrieved the banger. He was trying different nails for size when the banger exploded in his hands. Canon Hackett teetered sideways in shock, and a group of men who thought he was injured ran to form a protective circle around him.

Smoke and a sulphurous stench filled the air, children began to cry and someone in the congregation shouted that the Canon had been shot! For a few moments I believed he had been shot too, because I hadn't felt Patsy take the banger. It was only when I turned and saw the horror on his face that I realised what had happened. I remember my mind whirring through a list of excuses that might save him from discovery, but nothing materialised in time. As the last wisps of smoke cleared it was obvious who the culprit was.

The whole village was in an uproar and, once they got over their shock, the priests vented their anger on Patsy and his extended family. As the weeks and months wore on, I genuinely thought that the incident would be forgiven and forgotten. But that wasn't the case. It was a harsh reaction and totally undeserved – it was indisputably an accident. With the wisdom of passing years, though, I suppose the reaction has to be seen in the context of the changing circumstances in the previously tranquil village.

★

My father played the box accordion and during the summer we would attend *céilís*, small social gatherings where people perfected their Irish dancing to the musical accompaniment of jigs and reels. In hindsight, he was very good, and the sessions were always enjoyable, but my musical tastes were maturing and veering more in the direction of T. Rex and David Bowie. This began to separate me from some of my childhood friends in Garrison, who were listening to the country music that the showbands played in the Astoria in Bundoran. Musical tastes in rural Ireland were important as they defined where one went to dances, what one talked about and probably even who one would eventually marry.

At fifteen, I started going to dances. One of the first bands I followed was the hard-rock band Thin Lizzy, which had formed in Dublin a few years earlier. Their lead singer, Phil Lynott, was a tall, thin black man with a huge Afro and a strong Dublin accent. This was unusual, as not many black people lived in Ireland at the time. Thin Lizzy later found fame on *Top of the Pops* in the UK with their hit single 'Whiskey in the Jar', but on the night I first saw them, they were just another fledgling band.

It was a slightly older friend, Thomas Maguire, who brought me to see Thin Lizzy in the Holyrood Hotel in Bundoran. When Phil took to the stage, he had a great personal presence, performing with a bottle of champagne in one hand and a microphone in the other. Tommy and I decided to grab a bit of Thin Lizzy memorabilia. As the singer raised the bottle to his lips, I ran forward and made a grab for it, but he moved his body sideways and I accidentally ended up with the gold chain from around his neck dangling in my hand. I didn't know what to do with it, so I looked at Tommy and we both ran and hid behind the bar at the back of the hall.

Phil stopped playing and demanded the return of the chain, which he said his mother had given to him. Anyone who was a fan of Phil Lynott knew how precious his mother was to him. The dancing crowd parted before me like the Red Sea but, unlike Moses leading the Israelites, I was completely in the wrong and had to make my way back up to the stage to return the item. Phil took the chain, smiled and handed over the rest of the bottle of champagne for Tommy and me to finish, despite the fact that I was too young to drink.

★

That summer, I started a little business from home, fixing radios and televisions. One of my first customers was an aged bachelor called Paddy McGuinness, who was a great lover of *The Gay Byrne Hour* on RTÉ. He told me his radio was broken and asked if I could fix it. It was a 1959 Bush transistor model with a dial that moved a red line across the different stations to the right wavelength. Paddy was accustomed to finding his favourite presenter at a particular point on the dial, which he had marked on the side of the radio with a red pencil line. During the repairs, I had to retie the old, tethered cord over the tuning spindles, and Gay Byrne was inadvertently moved further along the bandwidth. No matter how hard I tried, I couldn't convince him that he was still listening to RTÉ. Even though I waited until it was time for Gay Byrne to come on, and brought the radio to Paddy's house to let him hear the show, he still wouldn't believe me – he accused me of tuning in some English station where he wouldn't be able to hear the Sunday Gaelic Athletic Association (GAA) football game. I eventually had to send across to Manchester for a new tuning cord before he would take the radio back from me. The characters in the village pubs, Gilroy's and Casey's, would joyfully recall this story whenever I visited home in later years.

Paddy McGuiness wasn't the only villager who loved the Sunday game. Gaelic football was very popular in west Fermanagh, and the GAA tended to maintain the Catholic cultural traditions of the parish. The organisation had been banned by the British government in 1918 for its association with the nationalist cause, and the GAA had immediately reciprocated by expelling civil servants who had taken the oath of allegiance to the Queen of England. This had alienated some Protestants, who already viewed the organisation with suspicion. Still, the GAA was very popular, with every county in Ireland participating in intensely fought football and hurling competitions each year. This was part of the Irish psyche and, in the days before television became popular, many people spent their Sundays listening to these matches on the radio.

County Leitrim lay less than a mile from us, across the border, in the Republic. As technology improved and we became glued to colour televisions, a lot of homes in nearby Leitrim still owned old valve radios powered by four-volt glass batteries, which required weekly recharging. Every Saturday evening, these radio owners would leave our bicycle shop, cycling in small flotillas with the glass batteries attached to the spring carriers on the backs of their bikes. My father got good business from them, but as the demand for the service decreased, he relocated the chargers from the bicycle shop up to the garage, where my brothers and I worked, modifying all types of old demolition cars for rallycross competitions. In this sport, villages pitted their best drivers against each other on summer Sundays, churning up fields that had been made available by local farmers. It was a great way of disposing of the old Ford Anglias and Morris Marinas when stricter regulations forced them off the road.

One night, when I was using an arc welder to build a safety cage on a Mini, I accidentally ignited the hydrogen gas being emitted from the batteries, and they exploded, scattering shards of glass all around me. The next evening, the Leitrim football fans started arriving to collect their batteries in preparation for Sunday's match. By the time four or five hostile customers had arrived, we realised that Leitrim were playing in the Connaught provincial final and the spark had ignited more than the batteries. Eventually, Dad hit upon the idea of inviting them all down the following afternoon to watch the match on a colour television placed on a box in the garage. Some of the farmers pitched in and brought along a crate or two of Guinness, and my mother made tea and sandwiches. It was a great afternoon and everybody was happy – except me. I had to replace their batteries out of my pocket money.

★

At the end of the '60s, ideological differences in the IRA led to a schism and the formation of the Provisional IRA, known as 'the Provos'. The prime minister of Northern Ireland, Brian Faulkner, introduced a new law giving the authorities the power to detain Catholics suspected of republican activities indefinitely without trial. I remember everyone in the village being shocked when some of our neighbours were lifted. Many of those who were interned had no affiliation with any paramilitary organisation. The years 1970-72 were to prove the bloodiest period of the Troubles, and the conflict came closer to Garrison. Five bombs exploded in Enniskillen in the space of a fortnight. A permanent gloom slowly descended over the county, our trips downtown were reduced and we were told to report signs of anything out of the ordinary. As fifteen-year-old boys in St Michael's, we were no longer immune to what was happening in the larger world around us.

The state of Northern Ireland was descending into anarchy and the government responded to the worsening situation by opening a second internment camp, at Magilligan, overlooking Lough Foyle. As the conflict deepened, five armed men entered the youth hostel in Garrison and planted a bomb, which destroyed the building. The Melvin Hotel, which my father's friend Fonsie McGovern owned, was blown up some days later, during a Catholic wedding reception. The local IRA issued a statement saying that it was retaliation for allowing members of the security forces to stay on the premises.

The Troubles then spread like a forest fire along the Fermanagh border, with the nearby village of Belleek being the target for several bombs, including one at the Carlton Hotel and one at the Custom House. Things worsened when a twenty-minute gun battle between the British army and the IRA broke out in the main street of Belleek. No day passed without an incident and before long came the inevitable deaths, with fellow Fermanagh men RUC Constable Raymond Carroll, from Enniskillen, and RUC Sergeant Peter Gilgun, from Belcoo, dying in a rake of machine-gun fire. After a spate of further shootings, hijackings and explosions, the border roads around Garrison were closed, bringing desolation and economic misery to the little village where I grew up.

The West Fermanagh IRA responded to these closures by taking forestry worker Thomas Fletcher, who was a private in the UDR, from his home and shooting him in the shed where my father and I used to go to fix his tractor. They asked five of Fletcher's farmer friends, who were also members of the UDR, to leave their homes, which they did, fearing they would otherwise meet the same fate; these were my neighbours, people I met every day, customers in my father's garage. The British army then cratered all access roads from the Republic of Ireland into Garrison, allegedly in an attempt to stop cross-border activities and close off Provisional IRA escape routes. Still not content, they then brought in helicopters and blocked the roads with concrete boulders and massive iron barricades.

All this further polarised our community. Local Catholic farmers were separated from their farms in the nearby Republic, while Protestants would have been quite happy never to see the roads open again. Garrison became the knot in a rope as the security forces and the IRA played tug of war for the community's hearts. The British army had added an extra hour to the journey from Leitrim to Garrison. Sadly, it was almost impossible for some farmers to make the trip, and my father's business suffered more than most as he was dependent on the Leitrim trade. He had once worked as a creamery manager across the border in Rossinver, so he was well known and liked over there.

While all this was happening, I continued at St Michael's, listening to news reports of bombings or shootings, holding myself in a kind of suspended animation until I had heard who the victims were. I worried that my parents, or one of my siblings, might be in the wrong place one day, that a simple decision to walk into a particular shop or bar might end their lives and I would never see them again.

Like many others, I developed a conscience regarding the escalating conflict and one day joined a civil rights demonstration of about 1,500 people at the Gaol Square in Enniskillen. I listened intently as facts regarding the level of government discrimination in Fermanagh were read out to us by the speakers. Frank McManus, the chairman of the Fermanagh Civil Rights Association, told us that although the county had a Catholic majority, more than three hundred Protestants were employed in government offices, and only thirty Catholics. Many were incensed to learn that there were only three Catholic school-bus drivers in the county and that the minister of education in Stormont had said he saw no reason to believe that the seventy-five Protestant appointments were made other than on the grounds of merit.

The crowd were seething at such blatant discrimination, but they became even further infuriated when they learned that thirty-five Fermanagh county councillors were Protestant and only seventeen were Catholic. Everybody knew that this was due to the manipulation of electoral boundaries and the spoiling of electoral votes. Many listening wanted to go and storm the civic offices, as it was obvious that something had to be done. It was time to stand up and be counted. No doubt many there were inspired by the recent Nobel Prize winner, Martin Luther King, who died trying to end racial segregation and discrimination.

As the months passed, civil-rights marches were repeatedly attacked by Protestant loyalists and by the RUC. Some of my friends wanted me to attend a march planned for Derry on 30 January 1972. From the outset, my mother told me she would be unhappy about me attending it. So I stood and watched as the car loaded with friends stopped on our street – and then left without me. Although annoyed with her decision at the time, maybe it was providence, as that day will forever go down in the annals of history as Bloody Sunday. The British army opened fire on the civil rights protesters who were marching peacefully through the streets of Derry and twenty-six unarmed citizens were shot – five of them in the back, as they ran away. Seven of the fourteen who died were teenagers like me. Father Edward Daly, from Belleek, flashed across television screens around the world, waving a bloody white handkerchief as he tried to rescue the injured while dodging the bullets.

In the aftermath, the British government held an inquiry that exonerated the soldiers, who claimed they had been fired upon first. It was widely considered to be a whitewash, but subsequent inquiries held to the same view. The Provisional IRA gained hundreds of new recruits as a direct result of Bloody Sunday. It would take the British almost forty years to admit that the army had fired without provocation and that the deaths were 'unjustified' and 'unjustifiable'. There were protests in most Fermanagh villages and I joined the Garrison Civil Resistance, which led the way in efforts to reopen the Garrison-to-Rossinver border road. The situation worsened daily, and two Enniskillen detective constables were blown up in an explosion on the Belleek-Garrison road. Both sides suffered dreadfully and it seemed there would be no end to the impasse. The landscapes and sounds of my village became less and less familiar, as I settled down to study for my A-level examinations.

Despite the impending civil war, I passed all my exams. I decided to study for a degree in biochemistry at Queen's University in Belfast, considered one of the better third-level institutions in the British Isles. My choice of field was influenced by the award I had received in Dublin the year before. I was excited at the prospect of meeting new friends – especially some Protestants, from whom I had previously been educationally segregated. I knew that living in Belfast would require me to adapt to new circumstances, but I was optimistic and hopeful for my academic future. I had no intention of pursuing a career in medicine at this stage. My only exposures to the profession had been an examination for an outbreak of measles by Dr McCollum in his satellite clinic at Gilroy's pub, and the lingering smell of carbolic at the Erne Hospital in Enniskillen when I went there to get some stitches after being bitten by a pregnant laboratory rat.

I began at Queen's University in the autumn of 1974 and entered my fresher year with relish. When the various societies and clubs set out their stalls, trying to entice new members, I joined them all. There was the Motor Club, the Music Club, the Wine Club and the Debating Society. In my excitement, I even joined the Queens Gliding Club but left when I found out it was part of the Royal Air Force Officers' Training Corps. Although I loved the thought of flying planes, that association might have raised a few eyebrows back in Garrison. Queen's certainly held true to its policy of non-sectarianism, and there were no restrictions enforced anywhere on campus. However, policies are made with good intentions and, outside the auditorium, students naturally gravitated towards their own communities.

During my second year, I moved into the halls of residence, the Queen's Elms. Our building, Alanbrooke Hall, was mainly Catholic; others were mixed or mostly Protestant. Many students had political affiliations – and not always benign ones – and seemingly innocuous remarks made on campus could lead to repercussions outside of the university. Belfast itself was a city battle-scarred from the years of the Troubles, with twisted metal from bombed-out bars, clubs and cars littering its sidewalks. On nearby Lisburn Road, which was largely Protestant, the British flag flew from houses and lampposts, a reminder to all that the marching season surrounding Easter had just ended. Although the Catholic Falls Road was decorated in symbolism of a more Republican nature, openly displaying the Irish tricolour would have been a defiance of the Flags & Emblems (Display) Act of (Northern Ireland) 1954 and considered treasonous.

One day, my father decided to oblige a friend by taking him up to Belfast. I was delighted. I looked forward to seeing my father's new yellow-and-white Ford Consul 375, which he had recently bought from the father of Formula One driver John Watson. When he arrived, I was horrified to discover he had parked the car on the Protestant Sandy Row, with a picture of the Sacred Heart on the left side of the windscreen and a badge displaying his Pioneer pledge on the right. I pleaded with him to move the car or, at the very least, remove the holy picture, but he refused, believing that doing either would be a denial of his religion. Eventually I gave up and decided to let things take their course.

I took them to the Europa Hotel, and I was sipping a pint of beer when a bomb exploded outside. Both men jumped up, instinctively checking out their environment and wondering what on earth was going on. Later, my father would tell everyone that I hardly blinked – it was a regular occurrence in my world and I would adapted to it. That's not to say I didn't care, because I certainly did. In fact, I found the violence repulsive. Miraculously, the car was still intact when

Dad went to drive home, and I remember mentally crossing my fingers as he opened the door, praying that his faith had been justified.

During my time in Alanbrooke, I became involved in organising a music club in a concert hall shared by all the residences. We mostly employed bands from Belfast and the surrounding area. There were a number of good bands in Dublin, including the Boomtown Rats, but, try as I might, I couldn't encourage them to travel north of the border after a massacre involving a well-known Dublin-based group, the Miami Showband. The band had been travelling home from a gig in County Down, when they were stopped at a British army checkpoint for what they thought would be a routine search. The checkpoint was actually manned by members of the UVF, who placed an explosive device in the van, which was supposed to detonate later. The bomb exploded prematurely and the rogue soldiers opened fire on the members of the showband, killing three and wounding two.

★

In the summer of 1977, I applied for a J-1 student visa so I could go and work in New York. On the way, I stayed with my brother Sean, who was at that time living in London, and we went to see Bob Marley and the Wailers play at the Rainbow in Finsbury Park. While in New York, I stayed with my Garrison childhood pal, Thomas Maguire, in the Irish suburb of Woodside, in Queens. My J-1 visa entitled me to a temporary Social Security number and the ability to work in the United States for a year.

Within a few days, I got a job buffing floors in a new apartment complex called the Manhattan Plaza, on 8th Avenue and 43rd Street, just around the corner from Hell's Kitchen. The building provided accommodation for Equity actors who were out of work, and breakfast was sometimes shared by people like Woody Allen, who for a time lived in the building. That summer was filled with memorable musical events: I skipped work and watched Elton John and Kiki Dee sing their duet 'Don't Go Breaking My Heart' in Central Park and witnessed the agony on America's brow when she learned of the death of Elvis Presley. Later that summer, the citizens of New York were stalked by a serial killer nicknamed 'Son of Sam', and I was with some friends in the Hamptons when he was captured there.

Often, at the hour of day when New York's humidity would drive its citizens inside, behind air-conditioned walls, I would wander down to the little cafés and bistros off Broadway and chat to the playwrights and actors there. It was a smorgasbord of American life, a celebration of theatre culture, a place where one could observe the city through the differing lenses of history. One lazy afternoon, I was fortunate enough to meet Jackie Onassis, who was speaking at a protest meeting across the road against the closure of the Lion Theatre, and have a worthwhile conversation about Ireland with her.

Searching, sometimes wandering alone, wondering what I would do with my life, I befriended an old Jewish man in Broadway who remembered meeting George Gershwin when he was a child. He was a pleasant man, with lively eyes and greying hair, who discussed my career options with me with the wisdom of an elder. One day, while sharing an afternoon coffee, he held a silver *chai* necklace before my face and said, 'You should become a doctor. I feel inside me that you have great healing power.' Although I had considered the possibility before, this old man's conversation filled me with a sense of inner peace. It was as if medicine had always been my destiny and my search for fulfilment was now within my grasp – my days of wandering alone were over.

Surrounded by all this excitement, it was difficult to imagine leaving New York and returning to the hate-filled streets of Northern Ireland, especially to spend my life standing behind a laboratory desk somewhere in Belfast. But it was clear I had to go. Back in Belfast, I decided to bide my time and do an honours research year in biochemistry while looking at my options for studying medicine. I found student life in the capital tolerable, but that was about to change.

3.
THE ATTACK

In October 1977, the Troubles in Northern Ireland worsened, mainly due to the continuing protests against internment. British Prime Minister Edward Heath decided to send an additional 1,500 British army troops to the province. Tensions on campus matched those of the outside world, and Catholic students were incensed by a British Union Jack that had continued flying over the Protestant-dominated Sinnot Hall student residence for months after the summer marching season had ended.

One morning we awoke to find an Irish tricolour flying from the roof of Alanbrooke Hall. It remained there, fluttering defiantly in the wind, for a few days before it was taken down. The action was seen by many residents of the Queen's Elms as treasonous, because the flag symbolised a united Ireland. This open resistance to established authority soon became the talk of the university. The mood on campus became distrustful, as students tried to figure out who was brazen enough to have done such a thing. The RUC came and interviewed residents, to try to determine who had decided to redress the imbalance.

As a result of this provocation, hostilities developed in the halls of residence and, one morning, a fellow student committee member of Alanbrooke Hall came to me with an envelope he had received in the post. It contained a bullet. For a moment, I looked at him in silence. It was a warning, and we both knew it would be foolish not to take it seriously. As the Catholic president of our hall of residence

I might be first in the line of fire should someone decide to follow through on the threat.

The situation was not improved by the fact that the Fermanagh ex-Westminster MP Frank McManus had been sleeping on my floor in Alanbrooke Hall during his nights in Belfast. He had been chairman of the Fermanagh Civil Rights Association, and he intended to become a solicitor, so he was attending law lectures at the college. His provocative voice in defence of civil rights for Catholics was well known to his adversaries.

During 1978, the violence on the streets of Belfast reached a new level of intensity, with a series of tit-for-tat murders. Innocent young Catholics were chosen at random for torture and murder by a loyalist Protestant gang, known as the Shankill Butchers, in retaliation for the deaths of British army soldiers by the IRA. The Butchers had murdered at least twenty people, and residents of the streets from which they operated were protecting the killers' identities. Many Catholic students, like me, who were involved in university politics, suddenly became targets, and some were killed. I remembered Micky Mallon, a student from Toomebridge who had been horribly tortured in a Protestant paramilitary club before being shot four times in the head. One of my classmates told me that he had heard of a student who had been horribly tortured, his body hung over Shaw's Bridge with a large fish hook embedded in his neck. The Shankill Butchers' power base was in an area close to where I lived. I learned to be vigilant about my own safety, especially as I had a high profile and the flag incident had still to be addressed.

The attack, when it came, took me completely by surprise. Perhaps I had dropped my guard because the weeks since the bullet incident had passed so quickly. It was just past midnight when two or three men appeared from the darkness outside a disco in the Student's Union and tackled me, pinning my shoulders to the hard concrete. They kicked and punched me, their blows raining down with furious speed. Instinctively, I curled up into a tight ball and tried to protect my face. The blows continued, each more savage than the one before, as my pleas for mercy whipped the attackers into a frenzy. I heard the sickening crunch of the bones in my leg breaking, and felt the agony of something hard hitting my ankle. As the pain became unbearable I said a prayer, silently begging God to save me. Suddenly they stopped – somebody had interrupted them.

I lay there on the concrete, unable to move. The pain in my left ankle was excruciating, and I felt warm blood trickle onto my neck and down onto the ground from a wound at the back of my head. I was thankful to be alive. Eventually, some passing students found me and phoned an ambulance to bring me to the accident and emergency department of the nearby City Hospital on the Lisburn Road.

A doctor there stitched the open wounds on my head and told me that the attackers had broken bones in my left leg, and I would need an operation. The next morning, the orthopaedic surgeon arrived. 'Your left ankle is badly shattered and it'll require some reconstruction with the help of titanium plates, I'm afraid,' he told me. Belfast orthopaedic surgeons were considered to be amongst the best in the world, because of the vast experience they had gained in managing patients from bomb blasts, punishment beatings and kneecappings. I knew I couldn't be in a better place.

That evening, some friends and family arrived to see me. After eight years of war, the daily terrors of the Troubles had taught them how to put a brave face on things. I was later transferred to Musgrave Park Hospital to receive carbon-fibre implants to replace my ankle ligaments.

A few days after my ankle operation, I went back to Fermanagh to recover from my injuries. While there, I began considering the practicalities of going back to college and restarting a degree in medicine. It would mean sacrificing a lot, starting life again as a mature student with no money, having to fund six extra years at college. No one in our family had ever studied medicine before, and this made it more difficult to discuss my thoughts with my father, as he wanted me to take over the family business. My brother Sean was living in Lisburn, and Raymond was a construction engineer with Taylor Woodrow, building universities and airports for King Khalid in Riyadh, Saudi Arabia.

The opportunity to discuss my career plans with my father arose one evening when we were building a new outhouse beside the garage.

'I hear you're thinking of going back to Belfast to study medicine. What's the point in more book-learning when you could take over everything we've built up here together?' he asked, casting his eye around the place.

The last thing I wanted to do was insult my father by turning down his offer of inheritance. I knew how hard he had worked all his life and how proud he was of his achievements. But I had out-grown the desire to remain in the village that had nourished me.

'Who put the notion into your head?' he said. 'There's never been a doctor in our family.'

'Nobody did,' I said, thinking for a moment about the old Jewish man. 'I just want to do something worthwhile with my life.'

My father and I had always been very close. From a young age, he had always made me little presents shaped with his own hands. When I was seven, he made me a red spinning top and, later, a fish-ing rod with a carved wooden spool. Before I left for St Michael's he assembled a magical chain-driven merry-go-round, which he sculpted from the sprocket wheels of old broken bicycles.

For a moment, we looked deep into each other's eyes and a life-time passed between us in the silence. I hated seeing the sadness in his eyes. My father and I worked late into the evening, long after the sun had set. We never talked much about the subject of my inheri-tance after that.

★

Northern Ireland was in chaos, caught in a spiralling ethno-political conflict between unionists, who wanted it to remain part of the United Kingdom, and nationalists, who wanted it to unite with the Republic of Ireland. These antagonistic views were based on differ-ent cultural extractions and religions. The Protestants had genetic and traditional links to the border hills of Scotland and northern England, while we Catholics saw ourselves as the descendants of an ancient race that had inhabited Ireland's green patchwork hills for millennia. Fanning the flames of the ethnic conflict was institutionalised discrimination by the majority Protestants against the minority Catholics.

Everyone I spoke to was convinced that if I remained in Belfast, I would be subjected to more attacks, and that I might even be killed. And the daily reports on the radio of bombs and murders in Belfast made me less and less interested in living in a city where life seemed to have so little value. But I didn't want to spend my time working in a laboratory – I was determined to pursue a career in medicine. So, after my plaster cast came off, I went to Belfast for an interview with the medical department at Queen's. While waiting for their decision, I lived at home and earned some extra money teaching A-level physics to sixth-form convent girls in Mount Lourdes Grammar School in Enniskillen.

One Saturday morning in May 1979, I heard rapid gunfire and went out to Carty's shop near the main street in Garrison, where I found a few people gathered around something on the ground. When I got closer, I realised it was our bread-delivery man, Jack McClenaghan, lying on the footpath beside his van. I can still see his red blood running down the guttering. After others established that he was dead, his body was covered. I turned away from the hideous scene, engulfed in sadness. His only 'crime' was that he had been a member of the Ulster Defence Regiment – a reserve force of the British army, which became operational in 1970. During the '70s, few Catholics trusted the security forces, as some of their members were complicit in the ongoing sectarian murders, and there was a belief that countless innocent people had been murdered by agents of the state. Unfortunately, whatever the rights or wrongs of the situation, many of my own neighbours probably also saw Jack McClenaghan in this light.

Over the years, my mother, Sheila, had built up a friendly relationship with Jack when he delivered fresh bread to her shop. She often brought him into the house for a cup of tea and listened to news and gossip from the county town of Enniskillen. I went home to tell her the bad news and found her in the shop. She was visibly horrified.

'I've been meaning to talk to you for a while,' she said, 'and this only brings it all to a head.'

Our home was incorporated into the business, and the front room was always occupied. At any given time, there could be three of us wandering in and out to eat, answer the phones, listen to the radio or watch television. The 'good' room next door, where the family photos were displayed, was always tidy and kept for visitors, except at Christmas when we all sat together to enjoy our lunch. So I was a little surprised when my mother closed the shop early and asked me to join her there. She made herself comfortable, and told me to sit down.

'I don't think it's safe for you any more in Belfast,' she said, tears in her eyes. 'If you really want to do medicine, I think you'd be better off finding a college in the Free State.'

My mother had grown up in the south, in the Republic of Ireland, which had earlier been known as the Irish Free State. She was a supporter of Fianna Fáil, a political party there, and had made many connections over the years, including with members of the Irish Senate and university professors. Over the years, she had made most of the academic decisions in our household. It was through her persistence that all seven members of our family were educated; five of us went to university.

'I've had a chat with an old friend, Professor McKenna, in the Royal College of Surgeons in Dublin, and he said you can go there for an interview next week,' she said.

I hadn't even considered Dublin as an option. If I was fortunate enough to get another grant, I had presumed it would be for a British university. Consequently, I had only applied in Belfast and Edinburgh.

'I've also talked to some people in the Department of Education in Belfast and they said if you are accepted in Dublin, they'd be willing to give you a further grant for a degree in medicine, for another six years,' she said.

I looked into my mother's worried eyes and noticed how her hands clasped and unclasped in her lap while she talked about my future.

'You'll be safer there, P. J.,' she said, and that was that – she said no more on the subject.

★

That summer, I went with my brother Raymond and Marty Leonard, a friend from Garrison, to see the Who play in London. We stayed at my sister Anne's house in Chiswick. It was a great parting before I left to start a new life in Dublin.

The Who were supported by the Stranglers and AC/DC, with former Faces drummer Kenney Jones taking the place of the late Keith Moon. It was their first really big gig after Moon's death, and they drew a capacity crowd of 80,000 at Wembley Stadium.

During the concert, we sang along: 'Who are you? Who, who, who, who?' I thought about the old Jewish man I had met in New York, and thought to myself, *Soon I'll be a doctor.*

4.
STARTING MEDICINE

The Royal College of Surgeons was unusual in Ireland in that one-third of the student body was Irish, one-third was European and American and one-third was from the rest of the world. This meant that students there forged friendships with people from all over the world, which endured for decades. The college authorities found accommodation for me with a family near St Stephen's Green, but I spent many Saturday mornings dissecting rats and dogfish in the back garden of my classmate David Keane's house in Sandymount. His poor mother never knew what we were going to arrive home with next in those black plastic bags.

In the evenings, Owen Brady, Simon Donnelly and myself would often go down to Jervis Street Hospital and hang around in the accident and emergency department, hoping to get a chance to assist in sewing up patients' injuries. Owen's father worked as an orthopaedic surgeon in the hospital, and we gained a lot of valuable experience from the staff there. With their help and supervision, I quickly became proficient at suturing lacerations. Many of the senior staff there came to trust me, but they never let me do anything beyond my capabilities.

During my first year, I spent a lot of my time socialising in the Bailey Inn and Davy Byrne's, which became known as 'Lecture Theatre 3' and 'Lecture Theatre 4'. My friend Simon knew Robbie Fox, who ran the Pink Elephant Night Club, and I have fond memories of meeting Def Leppard, Paul Cleary and the Blades, and

Clannad and their friends U2 there in those memorable days of Dublin rock.

There was a derelict bit of land beside the college, called the Dandelion Market. The site, originally part of the Taylor-Keith bottling plant in St Stephen's Green, had become a cultural nirvana, bustling with stalls selling punk badges and Sex Pistols posters. Punk culture was in decline, but still had some diehard Dubliner fans who dressed in bin liners and exuded a sense of nihilism towards politics and economics. The Boomtown Rats and the Vipers were in their ascendency, while bands like Stiff Little Fingers and the Undertones could still be heard at the college parties.

One Saturday in the Dandelion Market, I watched U2 perform – it was the first time I had seen them. They played there at weekends, and we became friends. Later, I watched them on Saturday mornings on Dave Fanning's RTÉ television show and, even further on, I went drinking with the Edge in Strings Nightclub in Leeson Street. My friendship with the band continued long after the old market closed.

Before long, an academic year had passed and it was time to plan how I would spend my summer vacation. Some students joined the Overseas Electives Scheme (TOES) and went abroad to treat patients in the Third World. This required some experience in performing surgical procedures, especially caesarean sections and appendectomies. The rest of us, who were still much too inexperienced for this, thought about ways of earning enough money for the next year at college by working abroad.

★

Royal College of Surgeons students hung out together in Rice's pub near the college. Although it seemed that most of them had bottled gherkins and lived in camping sites near Munich, two students in the year above me convinced me that it was much more lucrative to work in Germany as a house painter. They wanted me to join them that summer, and assured me we would easily find jobs through some Dutch employment agency. One of the students, Damien, still

47

had contact details from working there the previous summer. The trick, he said, was to convince everyone that we were skilled workers worth hiring, and not just unskilled students looking for summer work.

During the early '80s, Germany was the destination of choice for British migrant workers, as it promised large hourly rates for those who could hold down jobs as bricklayers, joiners or painters. The migrant-labour scheme was largely run by Dutch agents from Nijmegen, who employed seasonal labourers who didn't pay union fees or public taxes. This system irritated ordinary German workers, who often earned lower rates of pay but still paid their dues. My friends wanted us to take advantage of this unconventional scheme and try to bluff our ways into lucrative jobs as painters or decorators.

In June 1980, over a few beers in Rice's pub, Damien and I decided to pool our meagre resources and travel to Germany. We crossed to Hamburg and, after contacting the Dutch agents, took the train south to Mannheim, where we were given comfortable lodgings at the Hotel zum Autohof in Landstrasse. It was quickly noticed that we had arrived without painters' overalls or brushes, and some painters from Liverpool cheekily asked whether we were students. That evening, we went out to a Herties store and spent the last of our savings on proper decorators' uniforms and equipment. The next morning, when the boss saw us in our brand-new uniforms, he realised we were probably students and exploded into a tirade of abuse.

'*Was is das?*' he said, pulling at the straps of my uniform.

My inability to speak German just compounded the problem, but I felt I had to say something before we lost our jobs.

'*Deutschland über alles,*' I replied, innocently meaning 'German overalls'.

The boss looked me up and down for a moment.

I then realised from the look on Damien's face that I had just uttered the opening stanza to the Nazi national anthem, '*Deutschland, Deutschland über alles, über alles in der Welt*'. When translated it meant, 'Germany, Germany above all, above everything in the world'. It was a nationalistic statement which had evidently struck the wrong note with the Yugoslavian boss. He turned back to the other workers and laughingly said, '*Ja . . .* fuck the Queen!'

Damien, who had acquired some German the previous summer, stutteringly explained that we had wanted new clothes to impress, and that we were actually Irish. The old Yugoslavian boss laughed heartily when he realised my innocent mistake. He patted me on the back and gave me some cans of paint to carry into the back of a small VW minibus.

'I like Ireland – IRA,' he said.

A couple of painters from Belfast who were waiting on us in the van overheard this. When the van started moving, one of them introduced himself as Billy.

'You know, none of that auld IRA stuff here, son – we still think you're both students from Dublin!' he said.

'But I'm from Northern Ireland,' I replied

'Leslie, your man says he's from Northern Ireland,' he said to his friend. 'Who did you work for then, back home in Northern Ireland?'

For a few moments, I hesitated with my answer. Once again, our careers as budding painters lay in the balance.

'I worked with Robert Dickie for a while in Enniskillen,' I replied, quoting the name of the wholesaler who supplied my mother with house paint in our shop.

It hit the right note, both politically and professionally.

'OK, fair enough, and where did you meet that other boy from Dublin?'

'Oh, he's a painter by trade and I met him on the last job we were at, in Hamburg.'

The minibus eventually pulled up outside a modern clothes boutique, which was due to open in a few days. The boss left the Belfast painters in charge of delegating the work.

'He wants a tortoiseshell effect on those panels at the front of the shop – you could do that,' Billy said, handing me some small cans of bronze and brown paint. 'A good tip here is to rub the acrylic with a bit of alcohol before lacquering it with polyurethane.'

I knew from the worried expression on Damien's face that we were now in deep and there was little he could do to help me.

'We'll see you in a few hours then, wee son,' he said, before disappearing with Leslie and Damien inside to paint the interior. 'Remember, this place has to be open by Monday.'

I knew that unless some miracle occurred there was no way that I could bluff this highly specialised technique. I decided to have a coffee and think through my options. Across the street was a statue to Karl Benz, who reputedly produced the world's first automobile in Mannheim in 1885. Behind the statue was an antique shop with a large collection of faux-tortoiseshell antique shelf clocks in the window. It was a long shot, but I thought that maybe the owner knew how to repair the paintwork on them and he could give me a quick lesson. I had nothing to lose, so I took off my overalls and put them into a plastic bag and went inside to chat to him.

'Can you repair the tortoiseshell paint on these clocks?' I asked in faltering English.

'*Ja*, of course, I am *repareering* one just now,' he replied.

'Is it very difficult? I have one at home in Dublin. Can you show me?'

'Well, first you need this *gelbe* paint to get a good reflection,' he answered.

'*Gelbe*?'

He lifted a large spray can of yellow enamel from the counter and waved his hand in front of his mouth in an effort to encourage the English word to come out.

'Yellow?' I guessed.

'Yes, yellow is best for this – that's the secret!'

He sprayed some of the yellow paint onto the old clock and allowed it to dry. Then he buffed it with fine sandpaper and a glaze mixture of an almost translucent darker acrylic paint. He proceeded to show me how to apply sienna, burnt umbers and mild blacks in swirling layers of differing translucencies and opaquenesses. It was a simple technique and the outcome appeared to depend on patience, and some final deft brushstrokes. The old man took pride in showing me his work and before long an hour had passed. I asked him if could I buy the paint spray can for twenty Deutschmarks but he just slowly smiled and gave it to me. We had become friends and, before I left, he also gave me some acrylic colours. I made my way back across the square to where the van had dropped us off.

Thankfully, nobody had come down to check my work while I'd been gone. I took out the spray can and, with free-form strokes, began turning the outside of the boutique into something that looked like a cross between a Jason Pollock action painting and the cover of the Beatles' *Yellow Submarine* album. Gaining confidence, I painted some brown and bronze around in little glazed circles. As people stopped to watch me, I was conscious that the building was beginning to look more and more ridiculous. With little to lose, I began to experiment with some of the other paints, adding 'scales' of different shapes and sizes and laughing quietly as I thought about the day my brother Raymond and I painted Johnny Keenan's car. There must be something I'm missing in my appreciation of these unplanned artistic creations, because when the owner arrived to inspect the work that afternoon, he appeared to be absolutely thrilled with the result.

I was even more amazed when he brought Billy and Leslie down to look at this new *modern* specialist effect, which he felt was totally in keeping with the look of his boutique. The other painters looked at me and gently nodded their approval, but I quietly wondered what they'd have thought if the owner hadn't liked it.

'Where the fuck did you learn to paint like that?' said Billy.

'Oh, an old farmer called Johnny Keenan from Garrison in County Fermanagh taught me a long time ago,' I said, smiling to myself, happy I'd survived the first day.

★

After a week, the Belfast painters left to work in Augsburg, and Damien and I started restoring the exterior of a large secondary school in Mannheim. In early August, we got tickets for the German Formula One Grand Prix in nearby Hockenheim, only a few miles up the road. We were saddened to learn that Patrick Depailler had been killed during practice sessions. The race was won that year by Jacque Laffite driving a Ligier, but my heart was quickened by the Ferrari drivers, Gilles Villeneuve and Jody Scheckter, when they passed me each time. And that's how my lifelong love for this Formula One team began – I later followed them to other racetracks around the world.

When work at the school in Mannheim finished, the agents transferred us to a new job in Heidelberg. This was a baroque tourist town with an old castle where Mario Lanza had filmed *The Student Prince*. It brought back memories of watching the film while I was a student at St Michael's in Enniskillen. In Heidelberg, we were joined by Bernie, an amicable young painter from Liverpool who had been working with the company for more than a year. Our first job together involved painting the interior of a private house in the old part of the city. The property was owned by a pleasant old woman who trustingly left the three of us working downstairs while she went out to do her shopping. The snug house was airtight and before long we were all getting 'high' on the vapours of the high-gloss paint we were using.

'Better open some windows, lads, before one of us passes out!' I said.

'It's a bit late for that,' said Bernie, pointing to a cage in the kitchen where a small canary lay upside down, dead.

'Damn! We'll definitely lose the job over that,' Damien said.

'No we won't!' said Bernie, opening the cage and deftly pulling the canary's head out through the bars in an effort to make it appear that the bird had accidentally choked itself.

'Now, everybody upstairs – we'll paint up there and just wait till she comes back.'

Eventually, we heard noises at the front door. Standing stock still, paintbrushes in hand and open-mouthed, we waited until we heard the old lady turning the key in the lock. After a few minutes we heard her emit a small shriek. The noise jarred us into action. We all started talking at the same time, each wondering how best to handle the situation. The general consensus was that Damien spoke the best German so he should go down and talk to her. He descended the stairs slowly, obviously dreading the task. After ten minutes of comforting the old lady, he returned to join us.

'Well, what's the story?' Bernie and I asked at the same time.

'You'll never believe this!' he replied.

'She got a shock when she saw the canary all right, but only because it was dead when she got up this morning and she'd gone out to get a box to bury it in! Now she thinks it had a revival for a while.'

Damien's concern for the old lady earned us cups of tea and biscuits and a glowing recommendation to the boss when he arrived later to inspect the work.

After Heidelberg, we travelled south to Munich, the capital of Bavaria. The city lay in the foothills of the German Alps and was home to the greatest beer festival in the world: Oktoberfest. The Dutch agents put us up in the Hotel Winhart, in the south end of the city. I loved it all, the *Weisswurst*, the *Weissbier* and the oom-pah-pah bands in the Hofbräuhaus. After the violent streets of Belfast and the economic problems of Dublin, it was great to be in a city that exuded a hearty feeling the Germans called *gemütlichkeit*.

At the end of summer we visited the Oktoberfest with another 5 million revellers. A long shadow was cast over the event when a bomb exploded and thirteen people were killed. The horror of it brought back fading memories of Belfast.

★

I returned to the Royal College of Surgeons to resume my medical studies for another year. My new courses included biochemistry, physiology and anatomy and, in that 1980-81 academic year, I won the Norman Rae Gold Medal, earning me a place in 'gold' script on one of the large wooden plaques that adorned the hallway of the college. It was my fifth medal in the college. My ambition to study medicine was beginning to pay dividends, and put some of my original fears about moving south to Dublin to rest. I often thought about the old Jewish man in New York, and whether he would know that I was fulfilling his prophecy.

When the year ended and the summer came around, I decided to return to Germany with another of my classmates. The Dutch agents found us work near the McGraw Kaserne US military base in Munich, where we shared basement lodgings with eight British painters. Within a short time, we had struck up a friendship with Kenny, a professional painter from Hartlepool, and Nicholas, a music engineer from Brighton. With his connections, Nicky was able to get us into the after-parties in the Sugar Shack nightclub, where he introduced us to a lot of visiting celebrities. That summer, we partied with Bob Dylan, Santana, Kraftwerk and The Cure.

Also that summer, US President Ronald Reagan escalated the Cold War by threatening to place Pershing II missiles in West Germany. He wanted to throw the outdated ideology of Marxism-Leninism onto the trash heap of history. Like Margaret Thatcher, he was impressed by the economic theories of Milton Friedman, who advocated reducing expenditure on social services such as education. Shortly after my return to the Royal College of Surgeons, I saw this policy in action when I received a letter informing me that the British government was going to take away my educational grant. I would have to pay my own way at one of the most expensive universities in the world. My future in medicine now hung in the balance, as it was being sacrificed on the official altar of Conservative politics.

5.
MAKING A LIVING

The next summer, 1982, I left for Munich with another classmate, who was also from Northern Ireland and was in an economic situation similar to mine. Germany was by now going through a severe economic recession and the tide was turning against the working practices of the Dutch agencies. As a result, all painting and decorating jobs in Munich had totally dried up for migrant workers.

We eventually found jobs painting a large gantry hoist crane at the Krauss-Maffei Wegmann (KMW) Panzer tank factory. The work had to be completed over a weekend and involved painting an iron structure suspended above an assembly line of Panzer tanks. With some ingenuity and the help of a spray gun, we finished the job in less than two hours. I wished my father could have been there to see the Panzers below us – with his love of engines, it would have been a real treat for him.

When I was in Germany, my mother sent me a letter posted to Ireland from the deputy dean of medical education at the University of Cape Town, offering me an elective in cardiac surgery that summer. It would have been wonderful to work in the same hospital with the team that had performed the first heart transplant in the world under Christiaan Barnard. Although I didn't accept this wonderful invitation, I remained determined to work in South Africa at some stage, preferably when apartheid had ended.

By mid-June, some Germans began refusing to work with casual British and Irish labourers unless they had proper papers, and many migrants found it difficult to find work anywhere in Germany. Some British labourers ended up living in squats, or even homeless on the streets, as things were also bad in England. As the recession deepened, tradesmen looked for other sources of income, and I was among those who rented out their bodies in clinical drug trials at the Iphar Institute for Clinical Pharmacology, just outside Munich. These trials paid handsomely, and a lot of the lads used the money to survive – and try to get back on their feet.

Around this time, things were looking bleak for me: I had little hope of saving the tens of thousands of pounds required to pay my college fees for the following year. But, just about then, I met a brickie called 'Geordie Ian' in an English pub named The Coach and Horses, where many of the newly unemployed labourers drank. He told me that a few of his workmates were delivering Mercedes sports cars from Munich to Istanbul. He said that the Pakistani businessmen involved were looking for British and Irish drivers with clean licences and they were paying five thousand Deutschmarks per trip. It would take many trips to secure the funds that I needed, but Ian said he intended to go on the next 'Turkey run' and told me I could join him if I wished. It sounded like a wonderful adventure to me. My college friend was more apprehensive, warning that the whole thing sounded too good to be true.

'Nothing is that easy in life,' he said. 'Let's see what they're up to before we commit ourselves to anything. I don't fancy spending the next few years in a Turkish prison.'

The opportunity to learn more about the operation came a few days later when we met the Pakistani businessmen who ran the car operation, at a Wendy's hamburger restaurant in Arnulfstrasse. It was an ideal location for a meeting as it was near the main railway station, where all the rail lines in the city converged. My college friend opted out, but I decided to see what it was all about. There were labourers from all over the UK – some from Glasgow and Sunderland, and others from Nottingham – all eager to go on an adventure to the East.

I spent some time talking to some of Ian's friends, who had

already made the trip. They said the only prerequisite for the job was a clean international driving licence and a British or Irish passport. They had been well looked after by the Pakistani businessmen, put up in a good hotel and paid well for their two weeks in the sun. They assured us that many German students drove Mercedes on export plates down to Turkey, where they were four or five times more valuable, but the Pakistanis who ran the operation preferred to work with fluent English speakers.

'How long does it take?' I asked one of the drivers.

'About three days, but if you're in a hurry, you can do it in thirty six hours,' he replied.

An immaculately dressed Pakistani man in a blue sheen suit came over to us. I was told he was Mohammed, the boss.

'Do you want a drive? We are going to Istanbul tomorrow and one of my drivers can't make it. I need someone to take a two-year-old Mercedes 500 SL there. I'll need a clean driving licence and your passport to get the export documents, and your visa – do you have these with you?'

I felt very uneasy about handing my passport over to a complete stranger, but the other drivers assured me that it was OK. When he returned with the documentation, about twenty minutes later, all doubts fled my mind, and I grew more excited about the trip. It was late August, and I didn't want to desert my classmate. I asked him to come with me, as a passenger, on my first Turkey run, and he agreed.

The following morning, we headed south to Turkey, birthplace of St Paul, the land of tall minarets and sweet baklava. Our journey would take us across Austria's snow-peaked Alps to Yugoslavia and Eastern Bloc Bulgaria.

On the second day, while we were having a meal in Belgrade, 'Nottingham Ray' offended some Serbian locals by getting up to dance on the restaurant table with the red, blue and white Yugoslavian flag draped on his shoulders. His claims that his grandfather had died trying to protect Yugoslavian Serbians during the Second World War went unheeded, and they rewarded his family's efforts by stealing the seventeen-inch light alloy rims off one of our Mercedes. The incident lost us a day's travel time, but my idea of buying some wheels from a local scrapyard put me well in line to be team leader.

We reached Istanbul on the afternoon of the fourth day, and parked the cars in the Sultanahmet neighbourhood. There we visited the infamous Pudding Shop, which had featured in Alan Parker's film *Midnight Express*, about an American student called Billy Hayes who was sent to prison in Turkey for trying to smuggle hashish out of the country. We were given lodgings in the dilapidated old part of the city, which had been the capital of two of the world's greatest empires: the Byzantine and the Ottoman.

The hotel was comfortable and, from my window, I could see the ruins of the former Hippodrome of Constantinople, where Roman chariots once raced in the afternoon sun. Below me, the street vendors cried 'Kebab! Kebab!' and mournful seagulls screeched and circled, looking for whatever scraps they could find before swooping down over the hooting ferryboats, labouring their ways upstream. The next day, we handed the Mercedes over to some Pakistani businessmen, who promised us lots of work if we wanted it. I could accumulate funds by smuggling cars, but I would have to take some time off from college to make enough trips to get together the amount I needed.

Meanwhile we stayed in Istanbul. It was my first encounter with an Islamic city, and I bathed in its wondrous sounds: the muezzins calling the faithful to prayer, and the rich tapestry of musical styles that celebrated the diversity of contemporary Turkish life. It is said that St Augustine once wrote, 'The world is a book and those who do not travel read only one page.' Well, Istanbul was my Bible, my Koran, my Torah, and I wanted to read it right through to the last chapter.

★

It was early September 1982, and the Pakistanis said that the next Turkey run from Munich would not be for another three weeks, so I decided to stay in Istanbul for a while and gather my thoughts. On those balmy sunny afternoons, I'd often sit reading in the elegant gardens of the Blue Mosque and learn some Turkish from the local children. We'd begin by counting the six minarets nearby: '*Bir, iki, üç, dört, beş, alti.*'

The building got its nickname from the magnificent blue haze created by the blue and white Iznik floral-motif tiles that decorated its interior. Other times, I'd go to the river bank and wait until the evening sun set and the towers melted into the rivulets of violet colours in the evening sky. Russian cargo ships would pass on their way upriver.

To save money, I moved to a cheaper hotel near my boss, Mohammed, and every Wednesday night we'd meet at the Sultan Bar at the Sheraton Hotel. I was interested in getting to know how he operated and toyed with the idea of exporting my own cars to gather the funds necessary to complete my degree. He wanted to do another Turkey run in October, before the weather in Germany started to deteriorate, so I went back to Munich and met two British drivers, Nicky and Richard, and drove some older BMWs to Istanbul.

When I arrived, I found a cheap hotel on the Asian side of the Bosporus strait, near some older wooden summer houses that lined the waterfront. This meant taking a twenty-minute ferry ride to Sultanahmet each morning to meet the other drivers. It was a nice journey, and the ferry moved along at a leisurely pace, as boys clanged little bells and served glasses of sweet tea to the seated passengers. On those mornings, I often leaned over the railings and thought about my family back home.

Ahead of me lay the great land mass of Anatolia, gateway to the East, the approach route to Iraq and Iran. Sometimes on that journey, when I looked eastwards, my mind played tricks with me and the very essence of the air appeared to change. Slowly, the people on the boat seemed to take on a drearier look. Maybe it was the prominence of their cheekbones or the shapes of their eyes that reminded me that they were descended from nomadic tribesmen of Central Asia. It could have been the styles of their cloth caps or collars, as

Turkey had only adopted a Western style of dress some fifty years before. It made me slightly fearful, but I knew that one day I would travel east into Anatolia. I wanted to experience the modern state of Turkey and its amalgam of differing traditions.

★

As the summer days shortened, I left Istanbul and returned to Munich. It was early in the winter of 1982, and I was horrified to see how many British tradesmen were without work, sleeping rough on trains parked in the Hauptbahnhof at night. Some were reduced to sharing free food with the homeless at the Klosterkirche centre in St Anna Platz. Others told stories of being attacked by employees of private-security firm Schwarze Sheriffs, who patrolled the U-Bahn stations at night in menacing black uniforms. What amazed me was that most of the labourers still preferred to live in Germany rather than return home to Britain. Maybe worse lives awaited them there, maybe they were all running or hiding from something, or maybe they were just like me – too embarrassed to go back home until they'd completed what they had come to achieve.

Snow had already started to fall in Munich, and I allowed some friends to sleep on the warm floor of my hotel for a few nights. I phoned home as often as I could, but it was very difficult for me, as my family – especially my father – missed me terribly. I always tried to keep his spirits up, but I'm not sure if I ever really succeeded. Hardest of all was the fact that I would have to tell my family that I was staying in Munich for Christmas. I missed my family, but hadn't enough money to travel back to Ireland, and was determined to finish what I had set out to do – to raise enough money for my medical fees. The icy winds came off the Bavarian mountains for most of December and chilled me to the core. The citizens of Munich prepared themselves for the cold days ahead by heating up a selection of hot beverages, including mulled wine, which they sold in little markets.

The weather remained freezing cold until February, when Mohammed contacted me and asked me to drive a new Mercedes 280 SL to Alanya, a coastal town in the south-west of Turkey. He gave me ten thousand Deutschmarks for the journey and told me to keep the car for a month and put as much mileage on it as possible so that the Turkish authorities would think it was second-hand. One afternoon, on my travels around the Gulf of Antalya, I met a beautiful blonde German girl called Monika lying on the beach. After a few days of friendship, I noted that her father drove an old blue Mercedes saloon with Hamburg plates and, every day, he parked it in the same place by the Mediterranean shoreline. One night, while drunk and leaving Monika back to her hotel, I accidentally ended up in the wrong bed – with Monika's mother, whose screams were enough to awaken the whole floor. I had to hide outside for over an hour until the furore had died down. I could have died when Monika introduced me to them some days later and her mother said, 'Haven't I met you somewhere before? Your face seems so familiar.'

Despite this disastrous introduction, we all ended up the best of friends, and I told them about the smuggling scam selling the Mercedes in Turkey. When Mohammed later arrived and offered her father three times the market value of his old car, her father suggested that Monika stay with me for a few more weeks in Turkey: we could make our way back up to Istanbul, and Mohammed would pay for the car whenever we arrived there. It was a wonderful idea and, for the next few weeks, we travelled together, taking the long route back to Istanbul, exploring the plains of central Anatolia and one of the famed underground cities of Cappadocia.

One morning we reached a small eastern village with the snowy peaks of Mount Erciyes just visible behind us on the distant western horizon. I knew we were now nearing the gateway to Iran and thought about the ancient wondrous cities of Isfahan and Tehran across the border. On that peaceful morning, I lay back on the grass, looking up at the cobalt blue sky, without a care in the world. Monika lay beside me; a gentle breeze fluttered her light cotton dress. In the stillness of the midday heat, the tinkling of nearby sheep bells created a soothing sound that convinced me that we should travel further east. I knew it would be dangerous, as Iraq had invaded Iran just a few months earlier and, by all accounts, the conflict was a bitter one.

'Why don't we travel over the mountains to Iran? We could still take a few more weeks together and it'd be a wonderful adventure. You'll probably have to wear a veil over your face,' I said, and laughed.

'Oh, I'd love to see Iran,' she replied.

★

Iran, in that period, was changing its destiny in the world. Ronald Reagan had just been inaugurated as the fortieth president of the United States, and the world had witnessed the release of the hostages who had been held in the US embassy in Tehran for over a year. The recent SAS assault on the Iranian embassy in London had created problems for British citizens, who had to wait more than six months just to get visas, and I considered asking Mohammed to obtain me some from his usual passport contacts at the embassies in Istanbul. When I chatted with him about it, he told me he could get one for my Irish passport and Monika's German one from his friends fairly easily.

Monika and I returned to Alanya and started to plan for the journey. We went into a store and bought some black burqas for her, as we were determined not to create any suspicion in Iran and to respect the Islamic tradition. I spent the next few weeks reading some books and informing myself better about the history behind the Islamic Revolution. I learned that the problems had begun about five years earlier, when the Shah's information minister published an article that slandered Ayatollah Khomeini as a tool of British neo-colonial interests and a 'man without faith'. The next day, theology students in the city of Qom had exploded in angry protests. The Shah's security forces put down the demonstrations, killing at least seventy students in just two days. Up to that moment, secular and religious protesters against the Shah had been evenly matched, but after the Qom massacre, the religious opposition became the leaders of the anti-Shah movement. The Shah was subsequently overthrown and replaced with an Islamic republic headed by Khomeini.

After a few days, Mohammed returned to Alanya with our passports, with our Iranian visas inside. When he left, he hugged me and warned us that the journey would be very dangerous, that there were many stories of tourists who went into Iran and never came out again. And then we set off to the east.

As we drove across Turkey, towards the border at Bazargan, I thought about our future and considered how religion appeared to be at the core of nearly all of the strife in this region. To the west were the ethno-religious memories of the Turkish-Greek wars, to the east, the Afghan *mujahedeen* were waging an Islamic *jihad* war against the Soviet Union, and to the south, Israeli Jews were in open conflict with nearly all of their Muslim Arab neighbours. Whenever eternal salvation is at stake, compromise is extremely difficult, as any threat to one's religious beliefs is perceived as a threat to one's very being. I remembered my father showing me the Mass rocks around Garrison, and wondered whether we were all any different.

The journey to the border was forbidding and became more so when I discovered that the English spelling on my Iranian visa was completely wrong. One stamp said 'acompiagned by Monika' instead of 'accompanied by Monika', and the blotched-out dates were equally worrisome. I didn't want to startle Monika, but my faith in Mohammed to get the job done had obviously been misplaced. I couldn't believe that I hadn't noticed the printing errors earlier. If the Farsi on the passport stamp was as bad as the English, we would soon be in serious trouble. A cursory look at Monika's German passport left me in no doubt that our visas were probably not official embassy documents. We crossed the border at Bazargan, where the guards searched our car boot but took only a cursory look at our passports before waving us through.

So this was Iran, a nation in the throes of a cultural revolution, one where centres of learning were being purged of Western influences and converted to the dogmas of Shia Islam. It was important that people didn't think we were from Britain or America, and we travelled carefully, mostly on smaller roads, away from the army roadblocks. Even though we were ultra-cautious, we were detained after a few hours, about three kilometres from Tabriz. In some ways it was my own fault, as I had dropped my guard and stopped to take photographs of a line of older people being shepherded onto a waiting bus. There had been recent reports in the media that older people were being sent to the frontline battlefields to attack the Iraqi soldiers in 'human waves', and I took a chance in snapping some interesting pictures for an article I intended to write for my local newspaper, the *Fermanagh Herald*. My curiosity aroused suspicion, and we were eventually taken in for questioning by the local police.

The police were not immediately hostile, and our story – that we just wanted to travel together on a romantic journey through an exotic land – seemed to have a ring of truth to it. After all, we both carried passports from neutral countries, and they could see we had already been living in Turkey for a few months. In earlier times, it was not unusual for busloads of Western travellers to pass this way to see the mosques of Abyaneh, the Chehel Sotoun and the Alamoot castle.

They took us to the police station and we waited while they developed our photographs. Surprisingly, they never mentioned the entry stamps, and I wondered again whether Mohammed had actually put us in this dangerous situation. They held us overnight, during which time they asked me about the photographs that I had of the bus, which could just have been a day trip for older people down to the coast. But they focused more on Monika's father's car, saying that we had no import papers to bring it into Iran. I shrugged and told them that the customs officials at the border had let us through so I hadn't realised it was a problem. Although it was an unnerving time, I never really felt threatened by the Iranian police.

Eventually we were brought before a judge, who fined us. We didn't have enough money to pay for our release, and Monika didn't want her parents to know that we had been arrested in Iran, so we decided we should try to sell the car to pay for our fine. We sold the car to secure our freedom and exchanged the remaining Iranian money we got for it for some gold rings that we would try to sell later. We then caught a bus back towards the border.

From Sero, on the Iran side, we took a dolmuş shared taxi to the Turkish town of Yuksekova, where we stayed overnight. The next morning, Monika just wanted to feel Western again, having worn shawls and long dresses for so long, so she was wearing a type of hot pants. A crinkled old matriarch took exception to the way she was dressed and beat her soundly around the legs with a small stick, much to the amusement of onlookers. 'She's an agent from the Ansar-e-Hezbollah!' I joked, in reference to Iran's religious police.

We exchanged the rest of our Iranian money and travelled by bus back to Istanbul, where we finally parted at the airport. I gave Monika some Deutschmarks to give to her father. I cried as we hugged each other closely, thinking about how different it all could have been. For us, the adventure of travelling to Iran was over and in many ways we were lucky to have survived it.

★

In late March 1983, I decided to take a break from Turkey and went to live in Athens. On the way there, I met an Australian backpacker who gave me an address for cheap lodgings at the Athens Connection Hostel in Ioulianou Street. The price per room was 450 drachma a night or one could share a spot on the open roof for 150. Better still, one could work at the hostel, meeting the trains and handing out advertising leaflets to passengers, in exchange for free accommodation and drink. The roof was fine and it was there that I met a Swedish dental student called Pia. We shared an interest in travelling and, after a brief courtship, we decided to join forces and venture into some of the nearby towns of the northern Peloponnese region, where, rumour had it, one could find work picking fruit on the apricot farms.

Pia really wanted to travel to the Greek islands but it was too early, as the tourist season didn't start for another few months. We found work picking apricots in Kiato, a small coastal town set amongst the olive groves north-west of the Isthmus of Corinth. The farm was owned by a middle-aged widow called Maria, whose husband had recently been killed in a car crash. She needed whatever

65

assistance we could give her. Every morning, Pia and I helped her prune the apricot trees and collect the fallen branches and, for the equivalent of two pounds a day plus free accommodation, we spent some of the happiest days of our lives there.

My most abiding memory of that little village was sitting in the saffron sunsets with the old men in the coffee shop, sipping espresso. Their village leader, Spiro, was a devious person with a deep voice and very searching eyes. I suspected he didn't like us, probably because we knew he couldn't speak English, despite having lived for more than twenty years in New York. Whenever he engaged us with his senseless mixture of Brooklyn, Times Square and other Anglo-sounding names, we thought it best to keep his secret intact and just nod along with the others and laugh at his jokes.

One morning, Maria banged excitedly on the door of our room, waking us up. There had been an earthquake in the early hours of the morning and some villagers were injured. I got into Maria's Suzuki pickup and brought some of the injured a few kilometres down the road to the doctor's house. It was surreal passing houses where men were chalk-marking the buildings with large 'alpha', 'beta' or 'delta' symbols, depending on whether they were still habitable or would have to be torn down. News spread that thieves had taken advantage of the catastrophe and stolen antiquities from the local museum.

There were a lot of casualties, and I spent most of the morning helping the doctor to splint limbs, clean wounds and suture injuries. The stitching experience that I'd obtained in Jervis Street Hospital proved invaluable. That evening, I had to sew a girl whose beautiful face had been torn apart – two great lacerations ran all the way from the corner of her mouth and nose to the bottom of her chin. By the time the sun had melted back into the waters of the Aegean, I had placed more than forty sutures in her face with a threaded needle. When I'd finished, her mother broke into tears, and cried a dozen thankful 'efharistos'. The old doctor heard the commotion and entered the room. There, between the pride in his eyes and the smile on the young girl's face, I reconfirmed my destiny in life: I wanted to return to medical school as soon as possible.

A few weeks later, Pia and I left Kiato to return to Athens. When we parted, she wrote in my travel book, '*Nar du kommen till Goteborg* – your private dentist from now on.'

6.
THE LAST TURKEY RUN

In April, I returned to Munich. Mohammed was again looking for drivers, this time to take some cars to Van, a town in eastern Turkey. We had a long chat, and he told me he was willing to give me six thousand dollars because of what had happened in Iran. He seemed genuinely embarrassed and tried to assure me that the visa was real. I had to admit that, when we'd been detained in Iran and questioned, the validity of the visa was never called into question. I wanted to believe him. With the money from the next few runs, coupled with a donation my mother had promised, I would have enough to complete my education. Perhaps, as he said, English spelling just wasn't a strong suit with officials in the Iranian embassy in Istanbul. My sixth sense was furiously sending up flares, but I chose to ignore them. In the end, we shook hands when he agreed to give me the opportunity to sell some cars myself.

The drivers had a small send-off in The Coach and Horses before we left. We were joined by Pat, a lad from Dublin who was trying to make some money to go and meet his wife and young son, who were living in New Zealand. I'd met Pat at a Van Morrison concert in Athens and told him about the Turkey run. Then there was Scottish Alan, a miscreant who had a tendency to sleepwalk at night – often with other people's wallets. After five days, we arrived at the Hotel Emrah near Aksaray Junction in Istanbul, and Alan was given the choice of either staying in another hotel or returning to Munich. Thankfully, he decided to return.

The next morning, Mohammed came to the hotel and collected our passports to bring to customs. Because of my discomfort at what had happened in Iran, I decided not to trust him, and I follow him to see where he was going. He drove his BMW from the hotel to somewhere near Sultanahmet, where he parked. I followed in a taxi and watched as he ducked down a dimly lit laneway. I paid the driver and then followed Mohammed at a discreet distance. There were no obvious hotels in the area, but I presumed he might have friends there and had decided to pay them a visit. He knocked on a door and an old Turkish man answered, adding to my belief that this was a social call and I had wasted my time. However, I waited for a moment or two and then peered through a small window at the front of the house.

I watched as Mohammed handed the old man a small bundle of our blue and green passports. The old man chose one of them and slowly selected a page, working under the light of a flickering bulb, which threw wandering shadows across the room. The Turkish leader, Mustafa Kemal Atatürk, stared authoritatively down from the far wall. My heart sank. Some voices in the alleyway startled me, and I pressed my body into the doorway to avoid detection. It suddenly occurred to me that I might not be in the best of neighbourhoods. My heart raced. After a while, the voices disappeared and I went back to the window again and watched while the old man placed a heavily inked entry stamp on a green-covered passport. He blew on the ink and held it for a few minutes under the warm yellow bulb. Within minutes, the forger was finished. Mohammed examined the stamps before handing him some money.

I was unsure of what to do next. There was little point in confronting them, as it might terminate my relationship with Mohammed and jeopardise the six thousand dollars he owed me. I wandered slowly back to the hotel, deep in thought. This world of nods, smiles and friendly handshakes was new to me and, entrenched in the arrogance of youth, I had been foolish enough to think I knew what was going on and could handle it. Even in Queen's University, where a gloss had been deftly painted across the political divide, you knew who the 'enemy' was. You knew that if you scratched the surface of any given student, you would eventually see the green or orange shine through. This was a lesson I would never forget. Back at the hotel, I told Pat what I had seen. We sat up most of the night talking, and decided it was best to wait until we had been paid before confronting Mohammed.

Faced with the evidence, there was little he could do. Mohammed shrugged and stutteringly explained that the German export cars required an entry stamp on arrival in Turkey, which they all acquired at the Edirne border. He told the authorities that they were en route to Damascus and Saudi Arabia. It was illegal to sell them in Turkey, but Mohammed had a 'friend' in customs who had given him his exit stamp, and the passports were modified to say they had exited on the Syrian border.

'You see, it's really no big deal. The border guard is paid, the drivers are paid, the new owners are delighted, and the Turks are happy that no illegal cars remain on their soil,' he said. He shrugged and laughed. His flippant attitude infuriated Pat, who lunged before I could stop him. He caught Mohammed by the lapels of his very expensive suit and slammed him against the wall, cursing and threatening to kill him for putting our freedom at risk.

When everyone calmed down, a new deal was negotiated. It was decided that I would get another ten thousand dollars to leave my car in Van. In reality, Mohammed knew he had little choice, as the Mercedes was in my name and I could leave with it to Syria at any time. Pat said we should split the money fifty-fifty, and he would take the risk by driving the car there. It suited everybody. Mohammed would get his car delivered and knew that it was in my name, so the driver could not abscond with it. All I had to do was sit tight until Pat returned, and I would get paid for doing nothing.

A long week passed until Pat returned. He and I both continued to stay at the Hotel Emrah, where I met Jackie from Alberta, Canada. From an upper-middle-class background, she had refined manners and often used to dress up in expensive jewellery just to accompany me for a kebab dinner at a local restaurant. I enjoyed our rambling conversations, basking in the fact that she seemed to take our rather bohemian lifestyle in Turkey as a type of colonial adventure from another time period. We spent many afternoons chatting about politics with university students in the little cafés around Topkapi. Many felt that their new constitution was to protect the state from the actions of its citizens, rather than to protect individual liberties. I loved the way Jackie could intelligently engage in any conversation, the way she delicately held my hand while we were walking, her ability to see the history in the buildings around us, and the little notes and poems she left for me on my pillow before we went to sleep.

> I ebb, I sway, I dance, I kick
> I drag, am slug like
> But up again, on again, I'm high
> I'm swept away by it all.

We were still hanging out in Istanbul when Mohammed arrived in early June with a convoy of ten cars. He had mentioned to me that he wanted to do one last big run before leaving to live in America. The drivers were accommodated in hotels in Sultanahmet, and soon everyone was aware of their presence, due to their rather boisterous behaviour. It was good to hear English voices again, especially the conversations about Munich and David Bowie's Serious Moonlight Tour concert in the Olympiahalle. It reminded me of the old Munich, the after-parties in the Sugar Shack and Mad Max's and how my life had become such a roller coaster: one day, I was dating Nena from '99 Red Balloons', and the next I was living with some unemployed labourers in a squat.

Over the next few days, the drivers became increasingly concerned. They said that Mohammed had been edgy for days and they had not received their passports back from him. Others heard he was having difficulty selling the cars they had brought into Istanbul. He had even berated one of them, 'Lazy John', for being too loose with his tongue and telling the locals he was importing used

Mercedes for sale. They were also concerned that they might not be paid and would run out of money and not be able to stay in the city.

I didn't have much sympathy for Mohammed, as these English lads thought that what they were doing was legitimate, so why wouldn't they discuss their work with the locals? My advice was to stay away from local pubs, wait until they got their passports back and were paid, and then forget about the Turkish car-export business. I told them how I thought the business operated and left it up to them to decide whether or not they wanted to be involved with Mohammed any more. However, the drivers' paths and mine were now entwined and destiny was soon going to play an even bigger role in all our lives.

★

Recently, there had been a lot of terrorist activity in Turkey. A group called the Armenian Secret Army for the Liberation of Armenia (ASALA) had killed some Turkish diplomats in an attempt to draw global attention to the Armenian Genocide of 1915. The incident had occurred during the First World War, when the Turks expelled Armenians to Syria, but didn't provide food or water for the journey, resulting in the deaths of as many as 1.5 million Armenians. One sunny afternoon, the drivers and I were down in the Grand Bazaar having a meal in a small café. It was one of those balmy days when you would expect little to happen. We were chatting about Mohammed when there was an explosion and a lone gunman appeared out of nowhere amidst the confusion and fired randomly into the crowd. The bazaar was soon in complete turmoil, with smoke and people screaming and running for the exits. A young German girl ran towards us, covered in blood, and we lay her down in the alleyway. Watching her dying on the ground, I was horrified at how close I had come, again, to being killed. We later discovered that the gunman had killed two people and wounded twenty-one. I decided to leave Turkey as soon as possible.

I agreed to meet Mohammed to find out what was happening to the cars. We met at his hotel and he told me he was having major problems with the Turkish custom officials, as his Syrian friend had died suddenly from a heart attack some months before. Apparently the Turkish customs had been suspicious of him for some time and had waited until British passports stamped with his dead friend's name appeared. They had already seen the stamp on Lazy John's passport, and the word had gone around Istanbul, ensuring that none of the normal buyers would touch the cars.

'You also need to be careful Patrick – that stamp shouldn't have been used since last February or March. You have to make plans to get out of Turkey immediately,' Mohammed told me.

Customs moved quickly to put a stop to the illegal importations. Good fortune dictated that I was dining with Jackie in a nearby restaurant when police cars with blue flashing lights arrived at the drivers' hotel. I had already told her of the danger and she clasped my hand tightly as the colour drained from her cheeks. We just looked at one another for a moment, knowing that this could mean the end of our relationship, or even prison for me. We watched as four of the British drivers, including Lazy John, were taken away by police. Erkan, our waiter, stood by the door, shook his head and said, 'They make too much noise.'

I had to think fast. Customs were probably looking for me too, as, in all likelihood, they had seen me associating with Mohammed and the other drivers. My money, clothes and passport were still at the Emrah Hotel, and I didn't know if police were going to raid it as well. We would have to make our way back there and warn Pat about what was happening. Jackie gathered up my belongings and we joined Pat at the hotel.

'Mohammed's on the Asian side of the city, and he doesn't know what's happening to his cars and the drivers. I think we should let him know,' I said.

'Let him hang,' Pat replied. 'That bastard wouldn't do it for you.'

I remembered how desperate I had been when Mohammed first gave me a job, and how he had been good to me when the chips were down. We had become friends, often socialising together, and I felt that he had been more than generous in his financial dealings with me. I knew that Pat and Jackie wouldn't understand, but I felt a peculiar sense of loyalty towards him. Thankfully for Mohammed, the other drivers didn't know where he lived – but it wouldn't take the authorities long to discover his whereabouts.

I said goodbye to Pat and Jackie, and took the ferry across to the Asian side. It was a short trip, twenty minutes or less, but it seemed to take an eternity. As the boat churned its way through the dark waters of the Bosporus, my heart quickened as I thought about what might happen to me. I held on, white-knuckled, to the deck rails, imagining my mother's face as she was told that her son, the potential doctor, was in a Turkish jail.

I met Mohammed at his hotel and related what had happened. For the first time in our acquaintance, he seemed afraid. He looked crumpled, worn out, as if he hadn't slept for days. He thanked me for the update and advised me not to leave by the Edirne border crossing but, instead, to take the bus to Izmir, where I could get a ferry to Greece. Embarrassed, he asked if I could give him something to help him leave the country. I fumbled through my knapsack, extracted five hundred Deutschmarks and handed them to him. He hugged me for a few moments, then his eyes caught mine in shared recognition of the wonderful adventures we had had together. 'Goodbye Patrick, you are a special, brave person,' he said. 'Good luck when you get back to medical school – and become a great doctor!' he said.

I left Mohammed and caught the next ferry back to meet Jackie. My heart was beating wildly. I knew how difficult it was going to be to say goodbye to her. I stood on deck by the rail and watched how the evening sun made the needle-like minarets of the Blue Mosque melt into the waters of the Golden Horn. My fellow passengers were mostly urban Turks, and they gathered around in respectful silence to watch the balconied minarets descend into the waters as the skyline of the old city receded into the far horizon. It was almost like nature was providing a requiem for my adventures in Turkey. It had been on the same waters, which Jason was fabled to have negotiated with the Argonauts, that I had first fallen in love with the country.

From the port, I caught a taxi back to the restaurant to find

Jackie. Together, we went to Büyük Otogar bus station, so I could start the ten-hour journey to Izmir. There were tears in both our eyes as I boarded. As we said our goodbyes, she handed me a small scribbled note, which I read as we passed the city of Bursa.

> P.J., Just one great adventure after another! If you ever make it back to Istanbul there will be a note there for you in the Pudding Shop. I'll meet you in Dublin at any time if you want. Remember this. My destiny is not to serve, it is to create. I am a woman. Jackie xxx

The next day, I caught the ferry from Izmir to Chios in Greece. Hostilities between Turkey and Greece ran very deep, and I watched the disembarking Greeks shake the dust from their shoes before leaving the end of the gangway; even minute particles of Turkish soil were viewed as contaminants. Since Greece had won its independence from the Ottoman Empire in 1832, it had faced Turkey in four major wars.

I went to Athens and, from there, caught a ferry to the island of Ios, where I lived for the next two months, mostly chilling out with my memories and meeting girls – lots of girls. It was a hedonistic lifestyle, mostly dedicated to the pursuit of sexual pleasure. During that period Dublin seemed very far away. As one friend wrote in my travel diary:

> Hot sun, hot sand and you
> For a while we all become one
> The sand and sun and then us
> I look out on sea and sky
> Blue on blue and again you
> And wish this would last forever . . . forever . . . forever . . .
> — Diamond Debbie Vancouver

I stayed at Papa Antonia's hostel, at the top of the village on Ios. I shared my room with some Swedish and Danish backpackers, and we formed a band that practised on a small beach near Scorpion's disco. Before long, I started dating Trine, who came from

Skanderborg in Denmark and, when the band split up, we returned to the Athens Connection Hostel to try to find work. However, we were both bitten by the free life of the islands, and working the dusty old streets of the capital for a few dollars a day didn't appeal to us. So, one night, we decided we had had enough and took the advice of some American tourists we'd been serving. We said goodbye to the owner, Thasos, and caught the ferry across the darkening waters of the Aegean to the volcanic isle of Santorini. It was early morning when we arrived.

Lonely seagulls swooped and cried around us as we slowly ascended the 587 cobbled steps up the face of the red hill. Somehow, we felt at home again. Maybe it was seeing the sparkling blue waters of the Aegean or smelling myrtle and eucalyptus in the air – whatever the reason, we were both alive again. Trine and I went further up the hill, passing along rows of whitewashed houses where old men gathered to gossip away the morning. We eventually found a small hostel on a back road that snaked its way towards the village of Firostefani.

In the afternoon, we hired scooters and found a quiet black-pebble beach on the east side of the island, shaded by a bank of tamarisk trees. We lay back on the beach. I watched as Trine pulled her blonde hair up into a ponytail and started reading John Irving's *The World According to Garp*, which I had carried with me from Turkey. I realised that I was falling in love with her – we were similar spirits, and I wanted to travel further with her.

That evening we sat together on the steps in Oia, on Santorini, as the last church bell pealed and the orange-and-red sun tried to set the surface of the sea alight. If ever there was a place on earth to be in love, it was there. As the sun descended further into the sea, it seemed like the volcanic caldera was still alive, turning the sky into a mixture of violet, mauve and pink. I reached out, pulled Trine into my arms and hugged her tightly. There were many things about our developing relationship that I wanted to say to her. She knew. As I looked deep into her eyes, she said, 'Patrick, what are you thinking?'

I wanted to say that I was falling in love with her, that I wanted to take her to another place, a gentler one, far from the violence of Northern Ireland, the bombs of Munich and the gunmen of Istanbul. There are times in life when things are said that can change a person's destiny forever. I had gone through a lot to fulfil my dream of becoming a doctor and I couldn't let that go. I looked out across the magnificent palette of colours reflected on the Aegean waters, unsure if our relationship could survive everyday life in Dublin. Resting my head in the hollow of her shoulder I said, 'Oh, I don't know – just thinking about food tonight. Why don't we find a little courtyard restaurant that only Greeks go to.'

She looked at me sadly. Something was lost in the moment and we both recognised it. Her eyes softened as she sensed that I was on another journey through life – one that didn't include her. We hugged each other tightly for a long time before getting up and making our way back to the scooters.

'OK, let find a little restaurant and we'll get drunk,' she said.

'Let's spend all of those traveller's cheques I have from Munich,' I said.

We laughed, but I also knew my inability to deal with my emotions had weakened the bond that had developed between us.

We travelled south on Santorini until we reached a remote village called Akrotiri. There, we found a little courtyard restaurant with green creepers on flaking white walls, and farm animals wandering near the entrance. The locals stopped dining when we arrived and they watched us intently as we waited by the doorway. An old woman came by, but left us standing where we were, seemingly unwilling to give us a table. The smell of *magiritsa* soup cooking wafted on the night air. After some time, we nodded across at the old woman, even smiled politely, but she muttered under her breath and stayed away.

Eventually, we took our own seats at a long wooden table under a pomegranate tree. A squeaking metal fan with three and a half blades provided the only sound. Despite our best efforts to get some attention, we couldn't get served, and I became increasingly annoyed as the other diners began to giggle amongst themselves.

Eventually, an old man approached us from one of the other tables and said, '*Ti na kanoume?*' What can we do?

'*Retsina!*' I declared, demanding wine, striking the wooden table in defiance.

An instant hush descended on the gathering, and many mouths opened in anticipation of what was going to happen next.

'And *magiritsa!*' I continued.

I glanced across at Trine, all the time wondering why the old woman was so unwilling to serve us. Another customer got up from his chair and talked to the old woman. He spoke gently, all the time retaining eye contact with her, as if he was eager to see her response. The old woman slowly smiled, cackled something aloud and then went back inside to the kitchen. She returned a few moments later with a bottle of *retsina* and a large platter of food. A young girl appeared with a jug of water and glasses and placed them on the table.

There was something likeable about the old gentleman, and I thanked him for his help. I smiled at the other customers, hoping they would forgive my previous rudeness to the woman. The old man was eager to know if we came from Australia, and the other guests wished us '*Kali orexi*', Greek for 'Enjoy your meal'.

The girl brought us more food, and we feasted until every plate on the table was empty. She then went upstairs and returned with a small candle, which she lit and placed on our table. I watched its flickering flame and noticed how its golden glow fell upon the edges of Trine's face; its light raised our spirits, giving us a thirst for more *retsina*. I'm sure the fact that we were in love played a role in our desire to remain there as long as possible. I told her that I would be going back to medical school in a few months and it was probably better for both of us to start facing that fact. 'I know that, Patrick,' she replied.

We stared into each other's eyes for a long time before asking the old gentleman if he would get the owner to fetch us another bottle. The old woman reappeared, small beads of sweat gathered on her forehead, and placed another bottle of *retsina* on the table. Soon it was past midnight and time for us to make our way silently back to our hostel near the village of Thera. A thousand stars glinted in the night sky as I reached for some traveller's cheques to pay for our meal. The old woman took one and studied the writing under the glimmer of an Aegean moon. She examined it for a long while before handing it to one of the guests at the table. He passed it around from person to person in the dusky light, each one reading aloud my name and the value in dollars. Then, a younger man started laughing, and the others joined him. He turned to me and said. 'Mister Patrick Treacy, this place is not a restaurant – you have been eating and drinking with my family in our private house!'

★

Trine and I eventually parted in August 1983. I continued my travels without her. In Cyprus, I met John, a Buddhist from Dunfermline, who wrote these memories in my diary:

> Here we all are in Limassol, Cyprus en route to Israel, as Eddie Grant would say, living on the front line. However, Bob Dylan would probably have explained it better, The Exodus from Genesis has begun. I'm glad I met someone at last who both understands the system and reads the *Guardian*.

After Cyprus, I travelled to Israel and stayed with a tantric Buddhist sect in Haifa for a few days. It was a convivial atmosphere, not at all what I had expected in Israel. I parted company with John and went to visit some *kibbutzim* in the Judean Hills, before making my way to Jerusalem. I took accommodation at the Hotel Zefania, where I met Wolfgang, a student from Dortmund who wanted to travel south to Egypt. Everywhere we went, the Israelis were zealous in their attempts to educate us on the moral war that was raging over the Palestine question.

Politics aside, the ideology of the kibbutz impressed me, and Jerusalem was a wondrous city with many sights from ancient Christianity. These included the Church of the Holy Sepulchre, where Jesus was buried, and the Chapel of the Ascension, where he later ascended into Heaven. As I walked along Via Dolorosa, the route that Jesus walked to his crucifixion, I thought of how my parents would have loved to visit these places, and I was determined to bring them when my education was complete.

As the days passed, I started making plans to go back to college, but first I wanted to visit Bethlehem, where Jesus was born. Wolfgang and I took a bus there and got off in the dusty square outside the Church of the Nativity. An elderly Arab man approached us, his mottled teeth stained in the differing hues of the olive-wood rosaries he carried.

'*Salam!*' he said, as his teabag eyes beseeched us to buy his wares.

He followed us along the square, gaining the attention of the Israeli police, who rather forcibly moved him along, instructing him to stop annoying the tourists. I had seen enough of this type of behaviour in my childhood and, in mild defiance of their actions, I called him back and deliberately bought some rosaries from him. I felt that whatever we thought about our fellow man, there, outside the birthplace of Jesus, there should have been some sense of human compassion – or his time on earth was wasted.

A guide brought us through a small entrance into the church, which tradition held to be the birthplace of Jesus of Nazareth. We made our way through a small basilica lined with Corinthian columns, which had been donated by King Edward IV of England to hold up the roof. The guide told us that the original roof had been stolen by the Ottoman Turks and melted down to make ammunition for a war against Venice. We reached an underground cave where a fourteen-pointed silver star set into the marble floor enshrined the site where Jesus was born. This was the cradle of Christianity and the birthplace of the person who shaped my beliefs and conscience. There are few moments in life when one feels really humbled and this was one of them. I stayed there a while trying to absorb the spiritual presence of the place, and whispered a small prayer asking Jesus to help me in my studies when I returned to college. It was an overwhelming experience, and I carried it with me for many days as I travelled overland across the sands of the Sinai desert to Egypt.

The winds of change were turning in favour of Egypt, as Israel was pulling out of these lands and dismantling Israeli settlements. We arrived first in Alexandria and then went on to the cockroach-ridden Oxford Pension in Talaat Harb Street, in Cairo. It was there that I parted company with Wolfgang, as he was heading further south through Africa. He wrote a few words of wisdom in my travelogue.

> P.J., I have come to the conclusion after many years of travelling that life is basically about finding something to eat. Be sure to make it back to college, man, and do Africa at another time.

It was with these rather profound words that I returned to the Royal College of Surgeons in Dublin late in the fall of 1983 to try to continue my studies in medicine. It took some time to sort out my absence from studies with the college, but they were tolerant when they realised the circumstances surrounding my decision.

7.
THE DEATH OF MY FATHER

It was the early hours of the morning when I opened the door to my rented house in Dublin and saw them standing there in the darkness. The two policemen faced me, composed, hands behind their backs. I looked beyond them to the street outside for a moment, but all was quiet.

I was renting a house in Harold's Cross with a fellow student, Greg Murphy, and a young doctor from what once had been Rhodesia, whose father had fled the Mugabe regime when that country had become Zimbabwe. We couldn't afford a house phone and, in such cases, bad news was always delivered by the police. So I knew why they were there.

The younger of the two, probably new to the role, bit his top lip every now and then. Both faces communicated that they hated this part of their job. Asking them inside might delay the inevitable, I thought, as if not hearing someone speak the words would mean that my father was alive and well and safe at home in Garrison. Maybe he had just been hospitalised.

At that time I travelled home most weekends to see my parents, who were living alone in the family home. My brother Brian was helping to run the business, but the rest of the family had scattered throughout Northern Ireland and abroad. I had only left them that morning, grabbing a lift to Dublin with a friend. My father had an irregular heartbeat and was taking Digoxin for the condition.

That morning, he had complained of feeling unwell: he was dizzy and his pulse was very slow. He had a small amount of fluid in his chest, but he was taking water tablets for that. There was a little fluid in the back of his hands, which he used to show me from time to time whenever it became a problem, and we would just increase his diuretics.

When he had complained, I had considered calling an ambulance, but he recovered somewhat; he was speaking normally and was fit to drive. We had agreed that he should see his doctor that day, so I had told him not to take his tablets until he did, just in case they were contributing to the problem. I wrote him a note to give his doctor, stating that I was worried he might have a heart blockage.

Sometime later, on the drive back to Dublin, he was still on my mind, so I decided to stop at a call box in Navan and ring home. I was surprised that I was able to speak to my father – I thought he would have been sent to the hospital.

'What did the doctor say to you?'

'Nothing – just put me back on the tablets.'

'Did you show him the note?'

'He didn't look at it – he just examined me.'

I hung up and made another phone call, this time to the doctor. I asked what was going on.

'My father's pulse is very slow, he's experiencing dizziness and, given his history, I'm worried that he may have heart block,' I said.

'Your father is my patient and he's fine,' the doctor replied. 'I don't think he's in heart block.'

I felt guilty that I hadn't taken my father to a hospital myself. Up to that point, like most people, I had believed in going through the normal referral system. But now something was tugging at me, and I felt I should go back up home or perhaps even have him seen by a consultant cardiologist in Dublin as quickly as possible.

Instead, I ended up going back to Garrison to attend his funeral.

The family gathered downstairs in the living room. My brother Brian was crying inconsolably. We shared the same pain, the same grief, the same devastation. I went upstairs and met my grieving sisters in the new extension, where the undertaker had placed my father's coffin on the bed. The room was full of neighbours, each relating stories about my father's great kindness to them during his life. Some tried to console me by saying that death was 'no more than passing from one room into another', but I was wiser than that and would have preferred to pass into the other room along with him. At least he had died in my mother's arms, but none of his children had been there.

The funeral was two days later in Garrison Chapel, a place that held many childhood memories for me. Even though I knew he was well respected in the locale, it was surprising, and somehow comforting, to see how many thousands of villagers came to his burial, and that many of them were genuinely upset at his death. The ceremony passed in a hazy blur of handshakes, condolences and soft rubs on my shoulders. My father was buried in the nearby cemetery, and I remember thinking how strange it was to be born, live and die within a radius of only a few miles. I wanted him back so that I could show him the world that I now knew. He might not have come with me of course – emotionally we were close, but my experiences meant that we had very different outlooks.

That evening, my mother went back up to the new extension, where my father's body had lain for the previous few days. When she returned, she told me she wanted me to stay in that room and had switched on the electric blanket on the bed so that I would be comfortable. I wasn't sure about how I felt sleeping in a bed where my dead father had lain only a few hours previously. Not wanting to create a fuss, though, I'd agreed. As it happened, fate intervened and I would never sleep in that bed again.

When the undertaker had put the coffin onto my bed, it appeared that he had neglected to remove the electric blanket folded beneath. This had absorbed the weight of my father for a couple of days, crushing the wiring. It never occurred to my mother, or indeed to any of us, that this might cause a problem. We were sitting downstairs, reminiscing about our childhoods, when Brian spotted puffs of smoke emanating from the electrical sockets. Further examination revealed that the room in which I was later supposed to sleep was completely engulfed in flames. The fire brigade was immediately called and everyone went outside to wait while they made their way over from Belleek.

Smoke billowed from the top of the house as we stood and watched. I felt so sorry for my mother. Within a few hours, her life had changed so much. First came the death of my father, her partner in life, and then came the destruction of the house where she had raised her family. But worse news was to come: she told me the property may not have been insured, and that my father had kept a lot of money under a floorboard in the new extension. 'I suppose that will all go up in smoke too,' she said, as she cried in my arms.

I asked her where exactly the money was, and immediately decided to make a run for it and try to get back inside. Perhaps I felt that it was the last thing I could do for my father, and that it would make my mother's future a little more secure. People shouted at me not to do it, but I ignored them. My Uncle Charlie grabbed me and tried to prevent me from entering the burning building, but I pushed him away.

My brother Brian joined me, and we tied a blue nylon rope between our bodies. We made our way up the smouldering stairs. Acrid smoke filled our lungs, and I pulled my jumper up over my nose, making a dash for where the money was located. I could feel myself growing weaker by the moment, and the floor of the room had partially collapsed. In the dimness of the room, I retrieved what I had come for and stumbled back out into the corridor, where Brian was waiting. We made our way back into the cold night air, coughing and choking. The fire brigade had arrived and one of them came over to me. It was Elwyn Chivers, with whom I'd been at St Michael's. 'That was a mighty stupid thing you did,' he said, 'but a very brave thing to do also.'

After about an hour, the fire was extinguished, but the whole top of the house was gutted by then. The Maguire family, our neighbours, kindly took me into their house that night, and I spent the next day coughing painfully and recovering from having inhaled so much smoke. Mrs McGuire consoled me, joking that it was the most fuss my father had ever created in his entire lifetime.

With my father's passing, my life took on a different meaning. He would not be there any more to see me qualify in medicine, to meet my future girlfriends or even to attend my wedding. The rest of the family, I'm sure, felt the same sense of loss, but there was nothing any of us could do to change what had happened. Over the years, I've heard countless heartbroken relatives say that, if they had done more, their loved ones would still be alive. I was no different – I felt responsible. However, I was determined that when I became a doctor I would treat people with more dignity and respect their concerns, founded or unfounded.

★

By June 1984, I had secured enough financing to allow me to spread my wings and join the visiting medical student clerkship programme in the Mayo Clinic, in Rochester, Minnesota. This facility was considered one of the top hospitals in the world, and I was lucky enough to be involved in phase-four drug trials in malignant melanoma skin cancers there. My time there also gave me the opportunity to write a seminal paper on the subject, describing an alarming incidence in the rate of this skin cancer in Rochester between 1950 and 1984.

After a very productive summer at the Mayo Clinic, I went back to resume my studies in Dublin. I presented my experiences at the Mayo Clinic to the fifty-sixth inaugural meeting of the Royal College of Surgeons in Ireland (RCSI) Biological Society, earning me a merit award for a senior paper.

The 1984-85 academic year passed quickly for me. I spent it mostly in Jervis Street Hospital. We had a lot of excellent teachers, and I really enjoyed the clinical training I was receiving as a young doctor. That year I had to do forensic medicine as part of my course. It was particularly difficult to treat a sick patient one night and then attend their post-mortem the following morning. You got to know their hopes, their dreams, their family and then their cruel death; but such was the life of a doctor.

As the months passed, my grief about my father's death lessened.

I started studying psychiatry at St Brendan's Hospital in Grangegorman, and a few of the young doctors from there decided to attend U2's The Unforgettable Fire concert in Croke Park, in June 1985. We found a place up front and listened as Bono faced the audience and spoke about the Bloody Sunday incident, which had occurred on the streets of Derry thirteen years earlier: 'This is a song I wish we didn't have to write, but we had to write it, and we want to play it.' The lyrics of 'Sunday Bloody Sunday' were even more poignant because we were standing on the same ground where British soldiers had gunned down fourteen civilians at a Gaelic football match in 1920.

Bono plucked an Irish tricolour from the audience and interwove the chorus of 'Give Peace a Chance' into to the lyrics of the song 'Electric Co', a song about a patient who had received electroconvulsive therapy at the hospital where I was studying as a medical student. A silence gradually descended on the crowd, and, as he sang John Lennon's words, we all looked deep within our hearts, listening to his words of pacifism. For the first time in all those years, the flames of Irish rebellion slowly mellowed into the embers of pragmatism.

The band was opening my eyes to the folly of the ongoing conflict in Northern Ireland. I had been living in Dublin for six years, and my attitude was slowly moving away from the political passion that would have brought me that day from my home in Garrison to the civil rights march in Derry. The sun started to set over the stadium, and, somewhere in that broad collective, as the stars appeared in the darkening sky of that late June evening, the band caught my mood, and perhaps that of others in the stadium, liberating us from the older links with nationalism, pastoralism and even Catholicism. One by one, Bono peeled off the protective skins of our forefathers and offered us a place in a larger world.

★

I qualified in June 1986 and, as I stood there taking the medical-degree scroll from the registrar of the college, I reflected on the many life experiences that had brought me to that point in my life.

I thought about the death of my father, how I had been denied the opportunity to say goodbye to him, and how he would have loved to see me standing there that day. I also thought about my mother, who had put me on the journey that had brought me to that point, and about my RCSI Class of 1986 yearbook entry, which read:

Suffering from heavy metal toxicity due to the habit of accumulating medals, Patrick took an eighteen-month break from college. Starting with the beer halls and opera houses of Bavaria (often not knowing the difference in both), he travelled east to Turkey and engaged in the profitable trade of selling Mercedes. A notable artist and a keen guitarist, his songs have been heard from the hillsides of the Afghan rebels to the yacht parties of Monte Carlo. His main interests are Danish women, German beer, Italian cars, French art, Turkish food, British music, Greek holidays and American money. His wide knowledge is based on sound personal experience and his deep love of medicine will surely see him through a highly successful and outstanding career in medicine.

8.
NOW A DOCTOR

My medical career began in James Connolly Memorial Hospital in Blanchardstown in the autumn of 1987. The hospital was initially built to treat tuberculosis, which plagued Ireland in the period after the Second World War. During the 1950s, the village of Blanchardstown was considered far enough outside the city limits to construct 'open-air' wards in which to treat this communicable disease. After the discovery of Isoniazid in the late 1950s, the rate of tuberculosis started to fall and the hospital lost its specialised role. By the early 1980s, the burgeoning population of Dublin meant that the hospital was upgraded and integrated into the accident and emergency service for north Dublin.

That autumn, the new Fianna Fáil government introduced severe budgetary cuts across all departments, including health. This meant all accident-and-emergency cases in one side of the city were taken to just one designated on-call hospital. This arrangement, known as 'supercall', put enormous strains on the system as staff had no previous knowledge of a patient's medical condition and no access to their records. These were the circumstances when I worked as a casualty senior house officer at the hospital.

The medical staff struggled to keep up with the workload. Sometimes we admitted more than sixty medical patients and the same number of surgical patients in one night. We often worked through the weekend without any sleep – that was just the way it was, and we accepted it. Junior doctors worked long hours, often in the absence of senior consultants, and provided a service to the best of their abilities.

Late one night, amidst this mayhem, I was called to see a new, wheezing patient, who had been brought in by ambulance. He was a young man of seventeen, about five and a half feet tall, emaciated, with unkempt brown hair and sunken eyes that stared vacantly, when they focused at all. I suspected he was a heroin addict even before I saw the tracks on his limbs, where the veins he used to inject himself had hardened. This was the ugly face, the *other* face of Dublin in the '80s – the high unemployment, grey rainy streets, and mass emigration; it was the Dublin portrayed in U2's song 'Bad'.

'He's an asthmatic on Ventolin inhalers and he's recently been given steroids from his GP. He wasn't bad earlier – called us himself,' said one of the ambulance men, who had stayed until the medical staff arrived. That was the extent of the medical history I would receive, but the patient's blue facial hue told me he was going downhill rapidly.

I put on a pair of gloves; he needed an intravenous line inserted straight away so that I could draw blood for analysis. The fibrotic nature of his main vessels caused some concern, but I gained access in a vein near his right ankle. I drew off about ten millilitres of dark bluish-red blood into a large syringe in order to distribute it into the relevant haematology and biochemistry containers and put it on the bed beside the patient.

Blood would also have to be drawn from one of his arteries: an immediate oxygen analysis was needed to get a base level before hooking him up to our piped supply. The test is very painful, but necessary; it would determine the oxygen levels in the blood coming from his lungs and their ability to function. In preparation, I began to examine the radial artery in his wrist.

One of the student nurses tried to get a temperature reading from the patient, who was becoming distressed. I searched his wrist again, hoping to find a bounding pulse, which would alert me to where his artery was. Unfortunately, my patient thought I was look-ing for a vein and, in an attempt to be helpful, rolled over to show me his other leg.

'I have one here,' he said, pointing to the last open vessel through which he could inject heroin.

As he rolled, the bedding caught on the syringes, tossing them onto the floor. I felt a sharp stabbing pain as the syringe full of blood embedded itself in the side of my right leg. I grunted from the pain, and the patient looked down and saw what had happened. He turned even paler than he had been already.

'Doc,' he said. 'I'm HIV-positive.'

There have been few occasions in my life when I have known that four words could change my very existence. This was a disease which had only been discovered a few years before. Everyone who contracted it died – there was no known cure.

I saw the look of shock on the face of the nurse standing beside me. I knew her. She was in the same year as my girlfriend, Trish.

My body stiffened. I hesitated for a moment before pulling out the syringe. Although I knew I should act quickly, there were no procedures in place to tell me what I should do. I grabbed some Betadine – an iodine-based antiseptic liquid – and applied it to the wound.

I went upstairs to the operating theatre, where an old classmate was preparing to assist with surgery on an elderly patient with a neck-of-femur fracture. I took him to one side.

'I need you to do something very important for me,' I said. 'I want you to excise part of the skin and muscle of my right leg just below the knee.'

My friend looked at me in some confusion, but trusted me enough to agree to my request without question.

'I just got a needle-stick injury from an HIV-positive patient. I want you to cut out the area around it like you are removing a malignant melanoma, OK?'

'Oh God!' he said, his face full of compassion.

'It had to happen to one of us sooner or later.'

'I'll put on another pair of gloves,' he said, and immediately set about excising a large lump of skin and underlying muscle from my leg. As he worked, a slow, circling wave of fear began in my stomach, making me feel nauseous.

'What's going on out here?' shouted the theatre sister, who had come out to see what was holding up her surgeon.

'Patrick got an HIV needle-stick injury.'

'What? And why did you bring that in here?' she bellowed.

'Cancel the hip operation and open up Theatre Two!' she called to the other scrub nurses, giving a major eye-roll in my direction.

I was left in no doubt that the theatre sister thought I had brought damnation on her theatre. For the first time, I realised that I was now the patient.

When my friend had finished with the operation, he sat me down for a chat. 'What are you going to do now?' he asked. 'And who'll take out the stitches?'

'I don't know yet, maybe I'll do it myself, but it's fairly obvious I'll not get much sympathy around here,' I said, nodding in the direction of the angry theatre nurse.

I knew it could be arranged through the emergency department, but that would mean opening a medical chart, and my HIV blood tests would then be available to my colleagues. I slowly made my way back downstairs. All heads turned towards me, and I realised that by the next day, every other person in the hospital would know what had happened.

I wandered over to see how my patient was doing. In a way, I felt cheated, as he had completely recovered from his attack and was sitting there using a nebuliser and chatting to the student nurse beside his bed. He apologised again as soon as he saw me, and I assured him that it wasn't his fault. Medicine was the choice I had made in life. I was a doctor, trained to treat illness and, unfortunately, these things happened.

I stayed in the department, treating patients until my shift was over. There was no risk to anyone I treated, though, as the virus, even if it had entered my blood, still hadn't had time to replicate. That could take another three to six months. During the night, I saw chest pains, kidneys stones, gall-bladder pains and whatever else the medical river of life washed up.

When my shift was over, I walked outside to the car park and stared at the Dublin skyline for a long time. It was November and the morning air was damp and cold. Slowly the implications of what had happened dawned on me – for the next few years, I was going to have to play a waiting game to see whether I'd seroconvert and develop the illness.

This was a time before the creation of the Internet, when information about diseases had to be gained by reading papers published in medical journals. Rumours and myths about HIV abounded – many physicians openly stated that the infection could spread through saliva, tears, sweat, mosquitoes and casual contact. Others said that if you kissed someone with the disease, you could die from it. James Connolly Memorial Hospital had just discarded a new gastroscope, worth tens of thousands of pounds, when it was discovered that one of the patients who had used it had been HIV-positive. In that respect, as physicians, we were just as ignorant of the facts concerning this virus as the general public.

I drove across the city to the cosy apartment I was renting on Serpentine Avenue in Ballsbridge. Exhausted, I climbed into bed but, despite the fact that it was nearly 9.30 AM and I had worked all night, I couldn't sleep. I just lay there wondering how I would break the news to Trish.

Even though we hadn't moved in together, she spent most of her spare time with me at my apartment. I had met her soon after I started work in James Connolly Memorial. She hadn't been particularly impressed by my advances, but eventually my persistence had won out. We'd been dating for nearly eighteen months; we had already met each other's parents. Trish's father, like mine, was a mechanic, and had passed away. Her mother was a matron at the hospice, so we had medicine in common. When I took Trish to visit my mother for the first time, she brought a wreath for my father's grave, which won her instant approval.

Sometimes Trish and I would sit for hours, listening to Pavarotti, planning our future – the places we would see together and even how many kids we would have. There were plenty of nursing jobs available in Australia, and we had given some consideration to emigrating there after she qualified. Many of our friends had already taken up the opportunity, and that added to the appeal. The prospect of losing her terrified me. It wasn't that I didn't trust Trish to stand by me – I knew she would – but should I ask that of her?

I stayed at home most of the day, trying to catch some sleep. I would close my eyes and the enormity of the event would wash over me. I prowled my apartment, waiting for some sense of peace, but it never came. The needle stick didn't necessarily mean I would seroconvert and, logically, I knew that, but my mind continued to flick through the pages of a future riddled with AIDS.

I thought about the actor Rock Hudson, who had recently announced to the world that he was dying of AIDS. His gaunt appearance and nearly incoherent speech were so shocking that his announcement was broadcast all over the world for weeks. He had originally told everybody that he had inoperable liver cancer, as HIV was considered the modern-day leprosy. People with the disease were stigmatised, not only in the employment arena, but socially. The spectre of his illness loomed large in my mind's eye and made me realise that if I ever seroconverted there would be no place to hide: the ravages of the disease would eventually show on my face and its incumbent prejudices would be mine to deal with.

As evening fell, I considered the possibility of just keeping what had happened to me private. I didn't actually *have* the disease, so why should I broadcast the fact that I might? Why should I worry those who loved me? These were just fleeting thoughts as the darkness enveloped the night sky – I knew I would have to tell my girlfriend and my family, especially my mother. I tried to plan how best to break the news without causing too much upset, but it was futile – Trish was a nurse and was every bit as aware of the danger as I was. She also had probably already heard about what had happened to me from friends at the hospital.

It was late in the afternoon when Trish arrived at the apartment. Smiling, she handed me a small container of potpourri to place on the kitchen table. She said she had bought it in the supermarket on her way.

I just looked at her, noticing how her blonde hair fell loosely over her pretty face, partially hiding the blue eyes that always held such love when they looked into mine. We had taken many journeys together, but this one would be different. I was unsure of what exactly to say and my silence caused her to speak.

'It's not like you to be so quiet. What's the matter? Has something happened?'

'Yes, I had a needle-stick injury at the hospital and the patient has HIV,' I said, the words tumbling over themselves in their rush to leave my mouth.

'No,' she said quietly. 'No!'

She lifted her hands and held them against her cheeks, eyes widening in disbelief.

'What does it mean?' she asked, the tears already welling up in her eyes because she knew exactly what it might mean.

She moved towards me and wrapped her arms around my neck. We stood like that for a long time, as if our lack of movement could shield us from any calamity. Tears ran down my face as I told her how it had happened and about the staff's reaction. I told her how nervous I felt about the wait for the results.

My emotional reaction took me by surprise. There had been no tears at the hospital, and I hadn't had time since then to think the situation through. Perhaps it was her closeness, the fact that she loved me, and would love me no matter what, that was the impetus for my suppressed emotions to surge to the surface.

We sat on the sofa holding hands. She reassured me that I might never catch the disease. Suddenly I was tired, emotionally drained. Trish held me tightly, stroking my hair and telling me all the things I wanted to hear. Through her own tears she said she would never leave me – if anything, she wanted to cement our relationship more firmly and talked of getting engaged, perhaps starting a family immediately, just in case I became ill later.

'You know, I got a surgeon to cut a big lump out of my leg,' I said, pulling off the dressing and showing her the stitches winding down the inside of my right leg. 'I did that immediately after it happened. I cleaned it with Betadine and went straight up to theatre.'

Perhaps I wanted her to tell me I had done exactly the right thing, had saved the day – and myself in the process.

Trish tried to comfort me by telling me that they were making progress on the treatment for HIV every day and, even if I seroconverted, it could be many years before I became seriously ill. Who knew what might be available by then? Someone might even find a cure. Realistically, we both knew there wasn't too much hope of that, but we managed to convince ourselves.

I was very appreciative of all Trish's assurances and grateful that I had someone who loved me unconditionally the way she did. It certainly helped me through that time, when I was trying to come to terms with what my future might hold.

★

The hospital authorities, conscious of their responsibility to me as an employee, made an appointment for me to see a doctor at the Royal College of Surgeons, a specialist in virology. I was happy to go along with this and felt it more appropriate to start investigations away from the hospital, somewhere my colleagues would not have access to the results.

On the way to my appointment, I noticed an article in one of the morning papers that said a global HIV crisis was developing. It said there were already 150,000 cases of HIV diagnosed worldwide, and worse – each one of these people was expected to die. The article was critical of President Reagan's inability to focus attention on the need for AIDS research, education and treatment. It filled me with dread.

When I got to the appointment, I sat down across from the doctor.

'When did this happen to you?' she asked, writing some notes.

'It happened just three days ago.'

'Well, let's do the tests and see how things are with you,' she said, pulling on her surgical gloves. 'At least you have the benefit of knowing that the medical people who have contracted AIDS or died of the illness are very few – only four, in fact, to date – and each one had a distinct history of blood being directly injected. It seems IM-IM transmission of the illness is not as serious as we are led to believe.'

She was alluding to the fact that most needle-stick accidents are caused by a medical professional receiving a prick injury to the finger muscle from an HIV patient who had just received an intramuscular injection. However, this was certainly not the situation with me. I had been injected directly with a 10-millilitre syringe full of HIV venous blood, putting me into the IV-IM classification.

'And what about IV-IM transmission?' I asked, almost not wanting to hear the answer.

'Oh, that's a different situation, and everyone to date with IV-IM transmission has died. In fact, the last one happened in London I think – a nurse accidentally got some blood injected into the back of her hand from a syringe full of blood lying on a worktop,' she said, unaware of the nature of my own needle-stick case.

I turned towards her, my anger rising.

'I got HIV blood injected from a full syringe directly into my leg,' I said. 'The blood was from a vein and still in the syringe when it fell from a height and stabbed me.'

I watched as a deep red blush of embarrassment made its way slowly up her face. The doctor may have been many things – academic, kindly, brilliant in her own way – but she had no experience as an HIV counsellor.

'Oh, I'm sorry – no one told me that,' she said, refusing to hold my gaze.

I was sitting with a scared academic, a research doctor who was probably unused to taking a proper medical history, and who had said completely the wrong thing.

'I could've told you, if you'd asked,' I said, unable to keep the sarcasm from my voice.

I left the consultation feeling disgusted that a doctor could actually heighten my fear and increase my sense of isolation. There had been many times up to that point in my life when I had had to tell patients' relatives that their loved ones wouldn't make it through the night. It took a special discretion to impart this terrible news.

In my view, the professor entirely lacked this skill. In fact, I felt that medicine had completely let me down. The environment in which I practised my profession caused the accident, yet my own colleagues would probably stigmatise me. Now, one of its experts had coldly told me that I was going to die.

I felt that I had to get out of Ireland until I could come to grips with what was happening. At first it was a passing thought, but, as I made my way home, the idea took root.

My thoughts over the next few days were distracted from my own predicament by the news that the IRA had detonated a bomb at Enniskillen's war memorial during a Remembrance Sunday ceremony – killing eleven people and injuring sixty-three more. The 'Poppy Day massacre' cast a dark shadow over the whole of Northern Ireland, and particularly rural Fermanagh. It was hard not to feel repugnance at what had occurred.

★

When my bloods came back later in the week, I got the good news that I didn't have the virus. I was elated, but I knew that the virus often didn't show up for years and that this was only the first test – I would have to be screened every three months for the next three or four years.

Trish joined me, to provide moral support, when I went home to tell my mother and the rest of my family about what had happened. The drive seemed endless, and yet Garrison was only a couple of hours from Dublin. On the journey, Trish talked about having a child just in case I caught the disease. It was an incredibly selfless gesture, borne out of love, but bringing a child into the world with the possibility that it might grow up fatherless didn't sit well with me. I was unsure if I would have been able to do the same thing for her if our circumstances had been reversed – watch someone I loved ebb away, getting closer to death each day.

I needed to get away and face this thing on my own.

My family's house lay nestled beside a small copse of trees. The petrol pumps stood out front and the large garage and a number of outhouses lay to the rear. This was where I had been hugged, praised and chastised in equal measure throughout my childhood, and its familiarity wrapped itself around me like a blanket. When I got my mother alone, I sat down with her at the kitchen table.

'I've something to tell you . . . ' I began.

'Don't tell me you and Trish are getting married!' she said, smiling.

I wished I had been visiting with such joyous news, something for her to look forward to, rather than to dread. There was nothing I could do about that, so I told her, hesitantly at first, what had happened, and the implications.

'Oh no! What does Trish think about it?'

'She's been brilliant, but I've applied for a job in New Zealand.'

'In New Zealand? God, you couldn't have chosen a place any further away!'

My mother was a stoical woman who usually gave good advice, and I wanted to hear what she had to say on the whole subject. Her advice was not to rush into anything. She adopted a 'what will be, will be' policy and thought I should take my time. In taking this approach, she was thinking of Trish. I explained to my mother that, rightly or wrongly, I needed to spend some time alone.

My contract in James Connolly Memorial finished in December and I got many job offers, all of which I rejected, aiming for New Zealand instead. I knew Trish wouldn't be happy, because she still had six months to go on her nursing contract in Dublin, but I thought I could take the time I needed, and she could join me later.

★

I took a trip back to Queen's University in Belfast to do more research about the virus. I hoped to chat to Professor Max Lewis at the Medical Research Centre (MRC) on the Lisburn Road, whose opinion I felt I could trust. But, before I went to see him, I wanted to go to the university's library and do some reading. I still had access to the computers, and I checked PubMed, an extensive database of articles on biomedical topics.

From what I read, it seemed that Luc Montagnier in France and Robert Gallo in the United States had both discovered the same virus in patients with AIDS, and the most promising hope for treatment came from a team with expertise in viral diseases working at Burrough-Wellcome & Company. Preliminary trials showed some therapeutic effects in humans, and a new drug called Zidovudine or azidothymidine (AZT) was receiving accelerated approval status.

The window in the library looked down upon the city streets of Belfast, where I had almost lost my life years before. It was late evening and, as I sat there alone, I took a letter from Professor G. D. Barbezet at the Department of Medicine at the University of Otago out of my pocket and read it again:

Dear Dr Treacy,

It was a pleasure to speak to you on the phone last evening. I am sorry to have awoken you but at least it is good news. We are setting things in motion to have your letter of appointment sent to you through official channels and also to have these processed through New Zealand House in London. We look forward to meeting you and welcoming you to New Zealand.

★

I met Max Lewis the next day and he consoled me and said there was little he could add to what I already knew. After that, I returned to Dublin and told Trish I was moving to New Zealand – indefinitely.

Trish wasn't happy and didn't understand why I wanted to go so far away, but she acquiesced to my decision, asking if I would buy her a friendship ring to wear until we met again. She just wanted to solidify our relationship in some way before I left, but I felt she was hinting at our engagement, and didn't agree to it, convincing her that we didn't need a ring. I truly believed it at the time.

9.
THE PLACE OF THE LONG WHITE CLOUD

From the window, I could see the snow-capped mountains of New Zealand's Southern Alps, stretching like the backbone of a fossilised animal below the plane as it carried me closer to Dunedin. We passed near Mount Cook, a snow-capped monolith of rock, known to the Maori as Aorangi, 'the cloud piercer'. They called the surrounding land Aotearoa – the 'place of the long white cloud', and I could see why.

One hundred miles to the south lay Dunedin – the capital city of the Otago region, and almost the last stop before Antarctica. I lay back in my seat, closed my eyes and thought about my new job as a respiratory registrar in Dunedin Hospital. It would be challenging: New Zealand had the world's highest incidence of asthma deaths among young people. The situation was causing international concern and special protocols had been put in place in Dunedin to ensure patient survival. Some doctors said the cause of the spike in asthma mortalities was related to the New Zealand flora, but most were sceptical about that theory, as the incidence had soared overnight, and the plants had been there for a long time.

The woman in the next seat noticed the copy of the *Irish Medical Times* that I was reading and started a conversation.

'Do you come from Ireland?' she asked. 'Are you going to work in Dunedin?'

I nodded that I was.

'Ah, I was at Ireland's Rugby World Cup game against Canada

and afterwards we went to a new, wee Irish pub beside the hospital,' she said. 'You'll like it there – it's called The Dubliner, and they even have Guinness on tap! It's run by Bob and Judy Walsh, and they're both from Dublin. I'm sure they'd love to see you. They probably don't get too many Irish in these parts.'

Dunedin had just hosted some of the matches for the first Rugby World Cup, which New Zealand had won. Indeed, the sport had evolved into a national pastime in this country, where – in contrast to South Africa – a Maori player could proudly stand side by side with the grandson of a former British soldier and they could chant the famous Haka together. I was looking forward to visiting the grounds and even possibly catching a match or two there.

When the plane landed, I loaded my cases into a taxi, which carried me through the rainy streets of Dunedin, towards the hospital quarters. The city was amongst the best-preserved Victorian and Edwardian cities in the Southern Hemisphere, and it was charming. Most of the streets were named after familiar avenues in the Scottish capital, and many people referred to it as 'the Edinburgh of the south'. My mind drifted. In Dublin, I had been happy, surrounded by friends, in the company of someone who really loved me and who I loved. And yet I had left it all behind to live in a new country, surrounded by strangers. When I reached the hospital, I was given some keys to my room, where I stayed alone for many hours, quietly unpacking and thinking about Trish's parting words, promising to stand by me no matter what happened.

As evening fell, I decided to take a stroll around the city I had adopted as my new home. Near the main gate of the hospital was a hotel called the Captain Cook, which had a lively bar. Three hours and four Steinlagers later, my memories of home had slightly faded. Sitting beside me was a sheep drover, whose eyes simmered in an alcohol-induced red haze.

'You know, Irish,' he said, 'when you take everything into account, New Zealanders are a bloody great race of people! We have the best rugby team in the world, we had the first welfare state and we discovered the atom. What the fuck have the Irish ever done?'

I didn't think it appropriate, considering his state of inebriation, to tell him that although New Zealand-born Ernest Rutherford is credited by some with splitting the atom in 1917, the man who got the official credit was Ernest Walton, who was born in County Waterford and studied physics at Trinity College Dublin. In a way, my new Kiwi 'friend' had lifted my spirits by giving me something to think about other than Trish and my family. After that conversation, I found myself chatting to quite a few of the locals and thinking that life in New Zealand wouldn't be so bad after all.

★

My first morning at the hospital passed pleasantly, if a little frenetically at times. There were two consultants in charge of the respiratory unit. Professor Malcolm Sears, an expert in the epidemiology of respiratory medicine, was known internationally as one of the first to use inhaled steroids in the management of asthma. He was a friendly, open man and I felt lucky to be working with him. Dr Robin Taylor had recently migrated from Belfast and seemed a little more reticent.

My intern was a New Zealander called Graham, who proved to be competent and efficient. It was gratifying to be working as a registrar and to have an intern who could keep me informed about which patients required admission and which were waiting to be seen in Casualty. Up to that point I'd been the one doing all the running around.

On that first morning, I had just started exchanging pleasantries about life in Ireland with Professor Sears when Graham entered the room and told me I was needed in Casualty.

'It's a pneumothorax! And Mike Ozimek, the registrar from Cardiothoracic, wants to watch you put in the chest drain, if that's OK.'

'How's the patient?' I inquired.

'She's a tall, thin girl, so it's probably a primary spontaneous pneumothorax and she's breathing OK at the moment.'

This meant that the gas leak that had collapsed her lung had occurred of its own accord, and wasn't secondary to another lung condition. When the leak is small, it usually resolves itself and needs no further treatment, but when it is large, it quickly leads to chest pain and shortness of breath and requires the insertion of a chest drain into the lung to allow the air to escape. I followed Graham to Casualty and placed the chest drain.

That afternoon, I attended Dr Taylor's outpatient clinic, where I saw mostly tuberculosis patients who were Vietnamese boat people who had been accepted for residency by the New Zealand government. Graham and I entered the room where Dr Taylor was discussing an X-ray with a patient and her interpreter. Dr Taylor smiled as I walked in.

'Ah Patrick – am I on call today? I can't remember!' he said.

'Yes, it's fairly quiet. I admitted a pneumothorax up on the ward.'

'Good man – drain in, that's what I like to hear!'

He turned and resumed his conversation with the interpreter for the boat people.

'Do you recognise this?' he asked, handing me a copy of the X-ray.

I could see a cavity in the upper lung and knew that it was active TB.

'Yes, that's tuberculosis.'

'Correct, but a wee bit quieter next time – I actually haven't told her yet,' he replied. 'Well done. Where were you working before you came here?'

'James Connolly Memorial in Dublin.'

'Ah, that was actually an old TB hospital in the past,' he said, and smiled.

When the clinic was finished, I chatted to the interpreter for a while, trying to find out more about my new patients. I learned that the Vietnamese boat people had begun taking to the open seas after the US-Vietnam war, and that over the twenty-five years that followed, more than 1 million of them had fled the communist regime and become refugees.

I felt privileged to be able treat these desperate people who had faced such hardship on the open seas. Although most couldn't speak English, I could imagine the horror they'd seen, and was impressed by how they seemed to accept their fate with dignity.

Over the next few weeks, I had a number of interesting patients under my care, including a Southlander called Ann Crawford, from the mining town of Invercargill. At fourteen, she had been struck down with a respiratory illness, which resulted in her spending much of the following eight years in hospitals. In March 1984, she had travelled to Harefield Hospital in England for treatment, and had become New Zealand's first heart/lung transplant recipient. When I saw her, she was suffering from continual infections in the bases of her lungs, most likely a result of a packing deformity that left the new lungs effectively too large for her thoracic cage. She had recently written a book about her experiences, called *Pumps & Bellows*. We remained good friends throughout those difficult times, and I was always there when she returned to us for treatment. She bore her illness well and without complaint. She died a year later, but her bravery and good humour remained until the very end.

One day, I was approached on the ward by a naval officer, who asked if I would be willing to screen some young recruits for asthma. He came from the Toroa base of the Royal New Zealand Naval Volunteer Reserve, which was located in nearby Andrew Street. There had been naval reserves in New Zealand since 1860, when local citizens volunteered to train as part-time sailors to help the regulars defend the country and her interests if required. The ward sister said that the two previous respiratory registrars had done the check-ups on the young cadets, and it was up to me. I thought it would be an interesting diversion, one that would get me out of the apartment for a while each week, so I said I would do it.

The officer invited me down to the naval base to meet some of his colleagues and to see their maritime museum. After a few weeks, I agreed to attend the main naval base in Davenport, Auckland, to undergo formal training and get my stripes as a surgical lieutenant commander. Initial difficulties with my Irish passport were overcome by granting me a New Zealand permanent residency with the proviso that I return at least once every four years to renew it. My life was settling into a routine, and the Naval Reserve was a nice pastime outside the hospital. There was a social aspect to it and a sense of pride and belonging.

★

While in Dunedin, I looked up one of my father's best friends, Bartley O'Reilly, who had travelled from Garrison and settled in Dunedin many years before. I vaguely remembered him as one of the men who had gathered round the fire in the bicycle shop, but he had left while I was still young. Bartley's emigration to New Zealand had come as a shock to my father, and I knew he had missed him terribly. I would spend time with Bartley and his wife Vicky whenever I could, visiting their home and listening to stories about the scrapes he and my father had got into as kids.

Once, Bartley told me a story about my father when he was only ten or eleven years old. It was back before the Second World War, when Irish villagers used to come together to *céilí* and play music in a neighbour's house. One night they had gathered at Paddy the Yank's to listen to jazz music being played on a portable wind-up gramophone. Paddy had become very Americanised after living in New York for a few years, and he was so proud of his jazz collection that he had even devoted a bedroom in the house to it, hanging his Louis Armstrong records on little nails around the bed. That evening, my father and Bartley cheekily changed all the records for Irish traditional music. It was very embarrassing for the poor man, as he had advertised the jazz night, and the two boys got in trouble with their parents. My grandfather had apparently laughed all night at what had happened to Paddy, which only added to the night's enjoyment.

I remember Bartley sitting back in his chair, smiling at the memory. I smiled too. It was special for me to hear stories about my father from another time and place – I still felt his loss and missed him dreadfully at times.

Vicky worked for the New Zealand Postal Service, which was going through a major restructuring at the time.

'Oh, you should have been here in the '50s,' she would say. 'You know, we had the highest standard of living in the world back then.'

It was true that there was a period during the 1950s when New

Zealand was at its peak as an agricultural economy, and had the highest living standard in the world. In the 1970s, though, life began to change. The social order became frayed, and violent crime was reported on an almost daily basis.

'I lay all New Zealand's problems squarely on the fact that Great Britain went into the European Community and closed down the market for our commodities,' Vicky said.

She wasn't alone in expressing this sentiment. New Zealanders felt very bitter about Britain abandoning them, and they hated the French for taking advantage of the British market.

After a few weeks, I realised that there were other unresolved social problems causing resentment in New Zealand, when a police station in Dunedin was bombed by a motorcycle gang called the Mongrel Mob. Apparently their name originated from comments made by a district court judge, who had called them 'nothing but a pack of mongrels'. They had a network of more than fifty chapters throughout New Zealand, each likely to bomb police stations or shoot at those in uniform. Most of these gangs inhabited the North Island, but there was an increasing rise in incidents – such as drive-by shootings – on the South Island.

One evening in early summer I was rambling through an area of town that was unfamiliar to me. I spotted a small bar at the top of Princes Street and decided to go in for a drink. The place was dark and nearly empty except for a few Maoris seated by the counter. A jukebox was playing in the corner as I asked the bartender for a bottle of Steinlager. One of the Maoris greeted me with an instinctive nod as the heavy, opening bass beat of Midnight Oil's latest hit, 'Beds Are Burning' started to play.

A bearded Maori man who was sitting to one side of the jukebox with his arms folded began staring at me as I paid for my beer. We listened as the poignant words of the song about aboriginal injustices in the Australian outback grew louder and louder. I knew I had stumbled into the wrong place: there was an undercurrent of unfriendliness, and one wrong move on my part might bring it bubbling to the surface.

Without a word, the bearded Maori man rose and walked towards me. His jacket carried the faded insignia of a red bulldog, which I recognised as the emblem of the Mongrel Mob. He leaned across me, stubbed his cigarette out in an ashtray in front of me on the bar and exhaled a cloud of smoke into my face. Up close, his *tā moko* tattoos made him look ferocious.

'Why don't you drink in your own bar, *pākehā?*' he said.

'I actually don't have a particular bar. I've only just arrived in Dunedin,' I said.

The other Maoris watched the encounter, their russet eyes mirroring a cry as if to right some historical wrong.

'*Pākehā*, this hotel is for family – for *whānau*.'

Dublin or Dunedin, it was all the same to him – I was a *pākehā*, a member of the race that had dispossessed his people. Without an argument, I got up, nodded to the barman and slowly walked to the door. No one followed me, although I was half expecting them to, and I imagined they were watching me as I walked away.

★

In February, I learned that the Pogues were going to be playing at a music festival in Dunedin called Febberfest 88. They had recently released a single called 'Fairytale of New York', which had gone to number two in the UK charts. The band had been founded in 1982, and had begun as Pogue Mahone, the Anglicisation of the Irish *póg mo thóin*, meaning 'kiss my arse'. The band was fronted by singer Shane MacGowan, and they had used the irreverent name to snub the authorities.

On the night of the concert, I went to the Captain Cook on Albany Street to meet some friends. They knew very little about The Pogues and gathered around to listen as I told them. My medical colleagues were impressed to learn that I had gone to medical college with two of Shane's first cousins, and that his uncle was Professor William McGowan, who had performed the first renal transplant in Ireland in 1963.

'He has another uncle, Uncle Leo, who has an Irish pub in

Frankfurt. And the taxis have stickers there with "V.I.P." – Visit the Irish Pub,' I told them.

I lifted my drink and noticed the drunken drover I had met on my first night in Dunedin. He was looking over at me, obviously annoyed at the attention I was receiving. He approached our table.

'Well Irish, do you know any New Zealand bands? Loose Change and Sang Froid are playing the Febberfest this year. I bet they're much better than these Pogue guys!'

He then pointed at the label on his bottle of Speights.

'Do you know what "SPEIGHTS"'means?' he asked.

Some of the hospital staff advised me not to bother answering him.

'Superior Piss Enjoyed In Great Hotels in The Southland,' he said, sneering.

I smiled politely at him and went on chatting about Shane MacGowan.

Soon we left for the small ballroom where the band was playing. The rafters were decked in Irish green bunting, giving the feeling that St Patrick's Day had arrived a month early.

After what seemed like a long wait, Shane, dressed in a white T-shirt and a red necktie, wandered onstage. He balanced a tin whistle with a Guinness bottle in one hand as the band started playing 'The Broad Majestic Shannon'. By the time they sang 'Fairytale of New York', the crowd was swaying to the rhythm, and I was proud to be Irish. When the concert ended, I felt tall in the crowd, trying to catch the many eyes that had shared the musical culture of my nation. On the way out, I noticed the drunken drover.

'Do you know what the Irish meaning of "SPEIGHTS" is then?' I asked him.

'Shane's Pissheads Enjoy Irish Guinness Here in The South!'

I left him without waiting for his response and went backstage, where I met Shane and partied with the band until late the following morning. Although he had a concert in Auckland the next day, to his manager's dismay, he was only too happy to stay with me in Dunedin, chatting and sharing stories about the 'old sod'.

*

I missed Trish and looked forward to the day when she would join me. At first I wrote to her and phoned whenever I could, reading her letters over and over again, delighting in each loving word and soaking up every little bit of information about home. There were times when I almost knew them by heart and they would come to mind throughout the day. Unfortunately, the longer I stayed in New Zealand, the further I fell behind in my correspondence with her.

Trish complained in one of our telephone conversations that she felt lonely and neglected and wondered why, if I loved her so much, I didn't put pen to paper. Of course, I reassured her that I still cared for her as much as I had on the day I had left, and that all of my future plans revolved around her. I may have related how crammed my days were: I had work and, on my days off, I visited Bartley or attended naval training and never seemed to have a spare minute. She seemed to accept my explanation, as long as I promised to do better in future – which, of course, I did. After I hung up, I thought no more about it. But on the other side of the world, Trish was only beginning to think.

*

As the months progressed, the high mortality rate from asthma continued to climb, causing growing concern in the hospital. It seemed that the problem did not exist in every hospital, and suspicion began to fall on a drug we were using called fenoterol, which was made by the German pharmaceutical company Boehringer Ingelheim. The Wellington Asthma Research Group was convinced there was an association, but the drug representatives said the group's studies were flawed, and the New Zealand Department of Health asked that they be repeated. Meanwhile, patients were dying. My own feeling on the subject was that, if there was doubt about a drug, its use should have been suspended pending further investigation.

One day on the wards, I was discussing the problem with my intern, Graham.

'How do you manage asthma differently in Ireland?' he asked.

'We give IV aminophylline on admission.'

'To everyone?' asked Professor Sears, who was listening to our conversation.

'Yes, to everyone,' I replied.

'And what if somebody comes in already on this medicine?' he asked.

'We give it to them as well.'

'That doesn't make a lot of medical sense,' he said. 'If the patient is already at therapeutic levels of theophylline, you're only exposing them to the side-effects of the drug. You would be better off using some beta-agonist there instead.'

I couldn't disagree with the professor – he was right. The medication we were using in Britain and Ireland had been around for more than a hundred years. It had first been extracted from tea leaves in 1888 and used as a diuretic. Hirsch, in Frankfurt, used it as a treatment for asthma just after the Great War and it survived in the role despite having many side effects. The newer beta-agonist drugs like Ventolin and Bricanyl had been in use for many years. What we didn't know at that time was that the newer German medicine we were using in Dunedin, fenoterol, was actually much more toxic than the aminophylline or theophylline that I had used in Dublin.

I'd already left New Zealand by the time the suspicions about the drug became irrefutable. When taken repeatedly, it had detrimental effects on the heart. In 1989, the New Zealand Department of Health took action to restrict the use of fenoterol. The epidemic of asthmatic deaths in New Zealand was over.

★

As the time approached for my second HIV test, I became very anxious. The test was done anonymously through the usual channels in the hospital. It would change my life if it came back positive, but I would just have to deal with it. Meanwhile, I didn't want my colleagues to know there might be a problem or to look at me differently. Trish was the first person I rang when I received the news that I was still negative. I could sense her relief and excitement at the other end of the phone. She was missing me terribly in Dublin, but didn't seem committed to travelling down to join me in New Zealand.

★

The drug companies at that time had more influence over doctors than would be allowed today. During the winter of 1988, one of them took a group of us to Hammer Springs, a town in the Canterbury region of the South Island. As part of a bonding exercise, we took a powerful twin-engine jetboat down a thirty-kilometre stretch of the magnificent Waiau Gorge. The boat followed the contours of the sheer canyon walls, passing within centimetres of the rugged cliff faces. We passed the Waiau Ferry Bridge, set against the snow-capped mountains. It was a great opportunity to see the rest of New Zealand in a way that I would otherwise never have been able to.

★

One morning in September, I got another letter from Trish. Reading it was one of the hardest experiences of my life – she wanted to end our relationship. I went through her previous letters looking for clues of when she might have made the decision. Each perusal only added to my misery, but didn't gain me any insight into why a love that had been so strong could suddenly have died. I spoke to her on the phone, but she made it perfectly clear that there was no going back. She said that she didn't want to see me and that she wanted to spend some time in self-reflection. She suggested I do the same. I wanted to respect her decision, so I decided to give her the time she needed. But I had no intention of losing her – I couldn't. I would return to Ireland.

My journey home from New Zealand took me by way of Thailand and India, countries that have given the world some of its oldest beliefs and philosophies. I would have loved to spend months travelling through these ancient kingdoms. Of course, that was my head speaking. My heart had already decided that I shouldn't spend too long, just in case Trish solidified her relationship with her new boyfriend, and I was pushed out of the picture.

10.
BACK TO IRELAND

I looked out of my hotel window in Bangkok just as the sun lifted itself out of a bed of soft clouds on the horizon, sending shafts of sunlight in all directions to awaken the surrounding countryside. This was Thailand, the former Siam, a land that had inspired one of my father's favourite films, *The King and I.* I thought about my father for a while and was saddened that he and Trish had never met. However, time moves on and the old kingdom of Siam had disappeared with the passage of time, just like my father.

The hotel concierge recommended visiting a Buddhist temple on the west bank of the Chao Phraya River, called Wat Arun. With a heavy heart, I caught the Tha Tien express ferry and made my way across to the temple. We arrived as the sun rose high enough to begin streaming over its imposing Khmer-style spire. The glistening light display could be seen from every corner of the city. The magical effect was caused by little pieces of Chinese porcelain and coloured glass which caught the light. I could see why it was called the Temple of Dawn.

Some monks in saffron robes were already up and attending to their duties. I watched them march in single file along the tree-lined riverbank. Some were carrying aluminium begging bowls, while others carried small birdcages. They clapped their hands to the rhythmical beat of a melodic mantra. This daily alms ritual, *tam bun*, is part of the Buddhist philosophy of giving and creating merit to gain good karma, and it takes place all over Thailand.

A small wind rose as I stepped off the boat and the mantra grew louder as the monks gathered around, happy to accept money from the tourists who were travelling with me. Their leader, Praydoor, greeted me in perfect English, his young face exuding an air of self-assured dignity. I felt at ease in his company and asked him questions about Buddhist philosophy. I felt that he sensed my pain. He told me that all personal suffering was caused by craving and when that stopped the pain of loss would end. He bowed and then lifted a small cage.

'Why don't you let the bird carry away your suffering as it flies to freedom?'

'How much does it cost?'

'Just a few baht.'

I was annoyed by the simplicity of the symbolism and told him that I didn't agree with caging wild birds in order to set them free. He told me that he had raised the bird from birth and now it was old enough to survive on its own. He said that if something is trapped within a cage it is good karma to release it and give it freedom. I gave him some money. I felt that he was trying to tell me to let Trish go.

I stayed for another few days in Bangkok, but soon it was time to move on.

★

On the morning I arrived in Delhi, I hired a 1950s-style black and yellow Morris Oxford taxi to take me on the three-hour journey to visit the Taj Mahal in Agra. The romantic mausoleum was built by Mughal emperor Shah Jahan in memory of his third wife, and it was one of the places Trish and I had prioritised on our list of things to see. I was apprehensive about visiting it alone, knowing it was a symbol of eternal love.

My route took me along the Grand Trunk Road, one of southern Asia's oldest and longest major highways. From the front seat, I watched the vortex of bicycles, rickshaws, bullock carts and pedestrians that formed the lifeblood of the Indian highway criss-crossing and passing us in every direction. A Krishna figurine dangled from the vehicle's front mirror, moving hypnotically to the rhythm of the potholed road beneath us. After two miles of clanking, the car gave one last metallic groan and ground to a halt. A stony silence filled the cab as my driver got out and opened the bonnet to survey the damage. A tattered strip of electrical cable hanging under the engine indicated that our dynamo was missing.

The frantic driver started pacing around the vehicle, cursing his luck and looking impatiently for the missing component.

'It cannot be far. I see one of the bolts,' he said, before tumbling into the crowd and bending down to pick something up out of the dust.

I was preoccupied with some desperate cycle-rickshaw drivers who had stopped, looking for custom, so I hardly noticed the man in the white *dhoti* coming towards the car. I suppose he could have been a Hindu holy man, but he looked too dishevelled. He walked, with a slight limp, up to where I was standing outside the car.

'Master Sahib, is this what you're looking for?' he inquired, thrusting the generator in my direction. 'My name is Chandrapal and, please, Sahib, I am travelling to Calcutta – could you aid me in my journey?'

I looked at the man, tall in the crowd, his body covered in the only possessions he owned in the world. His craggy, lined face was worn, like the sculpted staff he carried. He moved closer, grinning. His eyes were piercing and yet at peace, indifferent to the chaos that surrounded us. There was a certain aura about him, and I sensed that he would be interesting company. He lowered his head and looked over at the driver, who had taken the dynamo from him and was busily repairing the taxi.

'This taxi is fully booked out!' the driver said, without even bothering to lift his head from underneath the half-open bonnet. 'Please leave! You can see that we have no more places in this vehicle.'

I indicated that I would pay for the man's passage, but the driver's eyes widened and he gesticulated with his finger, excitedly signifying there was to be no more talk about carrying this holy man in the taxi. The driver said that he had never agreed to take me to Calcutta, which was a few days' drive away, and that he was returning to Delhi that evening.

I turned back to the poor man and said, 'Sorry, Chandrapal, but he's the boss.'

He agreed, standing away from the car in poised silence, passing no remark on the taxi driver's intolerance, which we both knew was probably caste-driven, the unspoken way of life in India.

'Here are some rupees,' I said.

'I do not want to carry money – it would buy me only trouble. If I had your money, then the robbers would follow me and I would not sleep at night.'

'But if you had my money you could pay for a taxi to go to Calcutta!' I replied.

'I never buy what kindness can give from the heart.'

'Here, take this money and get an autorickshaw to take you a little further on your way to Calcutta.'

I placed some money in his aluminium bowl. He began murmuring some Hindu mantra as I got back into the taxi. He drifted away, walking behind a passing bullock cart and timing his steps to the rhythm of the creaking wheels. From the back window of the taxi, I could see him pausing and looking into the begging bowl to count his takings. Then he lifted something high into the air and gave it a fling – my money!

★

When we finally reached it, I found that touring the Taj Mahal was very difficult for me. The symbol of eternal love only reinforced my sense of loss. I knew that if I had acted differently, Trish would have waited for me. But I had felt that I just couldn't commit to our future until I knew my own.

After visiting the Taj Mahal, I took a so-called 'super air-conditioned coach' to Calcutta. There were windows missing and although passengers had queued to receive numbered tickets, people sat wherever they liked. While there, I went to see Mother Teresa's Missionaries of Charity, and found her oasis of humanity to be a special place, where the spiritual worlds of the living and the dying met. This was a place where people crossed over to the other side in dignity and love. They cried with outstretched hands from their beds when they heard I was a doctor, each wanting to live, and I felt a great sense of empathy. It reinforced my desire to use my profession, wherever possible, for the betterment of mankind.

*

When I returned to Ireland, I began working in Our Lady's Children's Hospital in Crumlin as an accident-and-emergency senior house officer (SHO). Some of the scenes I witnessed there were truly heartbreaking, like when I watched a mother carry a dead three-year-old burns victim to his sister, so she could kiss him goodbye. Both children had been in an upstairs bedroom when a fire had broken out. Medicine can tear your heart out, but one quickly learns that the best doctors are those who remain dissociated and stoical – the next tragedy is only waiting round the corner.

When I met Trish, at first it seemed as though she wanted us to get back together, but then she changed her mind. Eventually, she left Ireland to work for the summer in the United States. This gave me a little more insight into how she must have felt while I'd been away. This was the place where I most expected her to be at my side and, if it was possible, I missed her even more now that I was back. Slowly I began to realise that it was harder for the person left behind – they met the same friends and visited the same places, only now they did it alone. The person who left was, at the very least, meeting new people, sharing new adventures and not burdened by the constant reminders of what they were missing. It was too late – she wouldn't see me.

After accident and emergency, I began work as an orthopaedic SHO. My consultants were Mr Frank Dowling and Mr Ossie Fogarty, both excellent orthopaedic surgeons who specialised in placing Hartmann's rods for paediatric scoliosis, and introducing limb-lengthening techniques to height-challenged patients. The techniques were becoming popular since the discovery that the pooled pituitary human growth hormone being used on pituitary dwarfs was infected with the HIV virus and causing deaths. It seemed impossible to escape this virus, which left a trail of destruction wherever it appeared. In that year, we discovered that babies on the hospital wards with HIV-positive blood tests were suddenly becoming negative when they reached six months old. The tests were showing false positives due to the mother's blood still circulating in the child's system. The age of antiretroviral drugs had arrived, they were being used on the newborns – and they were beginning to work.

★

In 1989, while I was working at Our Lady's in Crumlin, a number of parents asked me to accompany a group of one hundred very sick children to Lourdes, a small town in the foothills of the Pyrenees that is famous for its miraculous cures. I agreed to go because I felt it would be interesting to see the sick children I treated every day in a completely different environment. Many were dying and some had brain tumours, with large swollen heads secondary to unresolved hydrocephalus. I spent a lot of my time in Lourdes administering intravenous diazepam to fitting epileptics, sometimes treating as many as five patients at one time. It was sad to see the children suffering, but they faced their illness with resigned dignity, and their parents handled them wonderfully as well. We all knew that many of the children would not see out the rest of the year, but the parents were tireless in their devotion and never gave up their hope for a cure.

The Lourdes authorities asked me to sit on a committee that oversaw the criteria for miraculous cures. There had been about two and a half thousand recognised medical 'cures' there since 1858 and, of these, sixty-four were accepted by the Catholic Church as miraculous. I accepted their invitation and, for many years, we communicated and they sent me medical notes of potential miracles for perusal. The authorities were extremely conservative in their acceptance of any unexplained patient survival not readily explicable by medical or scientific means, and I was fascinated by the interaction of religion and medicine. It still intrigues me to this day.

★

After my six-month rotation in paediatrics ended, I decided to remain in Ireland. It was the fall of 1989, and I had established a line of communication with Trish, who had by now returned to Ireland. I wanted to give it until Christmas to see if we could put the relationship back together again.

Part of me felt that it would be advantageous for me to do the preliminary parts of General Practice, in case I decided to go overseas again; at least I would have some specialist qualifications. Eventually, I opted to do Obstetrics and Gynaecology in Our Lady of Lourdes Hospital in Drogheda, County Louth. The hospital was run by the Medical Missionaries of Mary as an international training hospital. The obstetric unit was built away from the main hospital, so it had a certain independence. I worked with three obstetric consultants: Mr Liam O'Brien, Mr Finian Lynch and Mr Michael Neary.

The actions of the latter would later cause national outrage: it would be discovered that he had carried out an inordinate number of caesarean hysterectomies. Some patients had expressed concern over their procedures to me, which I had noted in their charts. This would be used in the High Court at a later date. Michael Neary was suspended by the Irish Medical Council after an inquiry found that he had carried out nearly two hundred peripartum hysterectomies in the previous twenty-five years, often on women with one or no children. The average consultant obstetrician carries out five or six of these operations in their entire career.

I found it extremely difficult to live without Trish and every phone call just made the situation worse. It's a strange thing: sometimes the more you try to show someone that you love them, the further away you drive them. At that point, all the flowers and fast cars in the world can't bridge the gap, it's all or nothing, and women can sometimes be cruel without meaning to be. Men express their emotions differently and often carry a heavier burden as a consequence.

Trish decided to work helping famine victims in Ethiopia. My instinct was to join her and, for a while, I intended to ask her, but my friends and family could see how distraught I was becoming and didn't want me to suffer any more, advising against it. In the end, I decided to take their advice, finally drawing a line under the relationship. I still sometimes wonder if that was the wisest of decisions.

Heartbroken, I decided that I needed to leave Ireland again and continue my HIV tests in another environment. I decided to apply for a position at the PARC Irish hospital group in Baghdad, Iraq. This was a country that I had always wanted to visit, a country that was once considered to be the cradle of civilisation, home to Babylon and Nineveh.

In late 1989, while I was contemplating this move, the world around me started to change forever. During October, many Eastern-bloc citizens started to defy their Marxist regimes and strike for freedom. The movement for political change had started with Solidarity (*Solidarność*) in the shipyards of Poland and had spread from there. After weeks of mounting civil unrest in East Germany, the government there announced that it would allow its citizens to visit West Berlin, starting on 9 November. Many thousands of people gathered near the Brandenburg Gate.

As the crowds in Berlin grew larger, I knew this was a historic time and I wanted to share the moment when the people gained their freedom from the outdated communist regimes that had once ruled them with iron fists. So I arranged to go to Berlin. Just before I left, I received a letter which carried a blue-and-red official postmark from the PARC hospital complex in Baghdad. It offered me a medical locum position there for an initial period of six weeks.

I arrived in West Berlin and found a small room in a hotel on Schöneberger Strasse. The owner was a pleasant man with old-fashioned Germanic manners, slightly bent and rather aloof. Up in my room, I went across to the half-opened window and peered outside. It was freezing on the streets outside and the palm trees in the Iraqi hospital brochure that had been enclosed with my job offer made Baghdad seem like a tropical paradise. The moon had risen and a cold wind was starting to blow, biting like frozen needles into the edges of my face. It made a whistling sound and, before long, its presence had filled every corner of the small room. The night had a peculiar intensity about it, like the whole city was standing at the edge of an abyss from which there was no return. In the distance, I heard the haunting melody of Beethoven's *Ninth Symphony* and thought how appropriate it was that this work should commemorate the ending of the Cold War and, with it, the old order that had shaped the world my generation had grown up in.

Crowds were building up on the streets below and, amidst the blare of a hundred alpine horns, a few people attempted to sing the enduring Lutheran hymn *Nun Danket alle Gott*. They beckoned for me to join them in their march to the Wall and, on that freezing cold November night, I walked along the crammed pavements of Potsdamer Strasse to the green copper chariots that graced the pillars of the Brandenburg Gate. There, I climbed up on a scaffold of clasped hands and secured a foothold on the side of the concrete edifice. Somebody threw me up a small hammer and, under the glow of an array of klieg lights, I symbolically broke a piece of rubble from the wall. The people below me cheered and a knot of emotion rose in my throat as I looked out at the thousands of people below me in a sea of flashbulbs and flickering sparklers.

For a moment, the crowd became silent. In the blur of emotion, I became fearful of the new political system that I was helping to create. The Soviet Empire had collapsed, but nobody was willing to look far enough above their bottles of Sekt to care about exactly what would take its place. Below me, some people joined in the chorus of a song coming from a tape player. Their words broke into my thoughts and, like a stone dropping into the pond of life, ripples spread out as others sang loudly in the frosty night air. It was a tune of Bob Dylan's, and it seemed to capture the moment: 'The Times They Are a-Changin'.'

11.
FLYING TO BAGHDAD

Back in Ireland, I began reading as much as I could about the political situation in Iraq. Reports in the media told of a world ruled by a brutal dictator called Saddam Hussein, who had created a totalitarian society based on the ideologies of Nazism and Stalinism. His tyranny was likened to the darkest days of the Jewish ghettos, Iraq portrayed as a modern-day Nazi Germany, awash in a sea of propaganda. Amnesty International said there was evidence of civilians being tortured in vats of acid, and of parents being forced to watch as torturers gouged out the eyes of their little children. I bought a book called *Republic of Fear*, which told of secret police – the Mukhabarat – who maintained strict control of the population through disappearances and targeted assassinations. Some British papers intimated that the ruling Ba'ath Party were using chemical weapons against their own people.

Medical staff I spoke to who had lived in Baghdad during the worst years of the Iran-Iraq war tended to paint a different picture. They told of a country with modern highways and great nightclubs and hotels with seven-star ratings, a land where women had the freedom to work in high-powered legal, medical and government jobs, a place where there was a higher level of literacy than in Ireland. 'Even the poor Arabs who live in the marshes have schools and electricity,' one told me, 'and that's more than some of our neighbours in the west of Ireland.' They assured me that alcohol was freely available in Iraq, unlike in some of the other Gulf states. Most considered Iraq a modern nation, which didn't take a fundamentalist line, and this level of religious tolerance led hundreds of western Christian medical staff to practice there in the early 1990s.

I found it difficult to marry these conflicting views on Iraq, but I would see things for myself.

The journey to Baghdad found me caught in a middle seat of the Iraqi Airways plane, sandwiched between Sarah, a young Irish nurse, and a jowly Scottish engineer called Donald. The pretty blonde nurse's distinct Dublin 4 accent told me she had probably trained in St Vincent's University Hospital. My other conversationalist, by comparison, carried the more rhotic accent of Scotland's capital, Edinburgh.

Donald was a tall man with a welcoming smile, whose greying sandy hair was swept back from his face. He told me that he was a professional naval diver and spent his time searching for unexploded mines in the waterways around the southern Iraqi city of Basra. These devices had been left behind after the Iran-Iraq war and had to be cleared from the Persian Gulf in order to ensure safe passage for ships travelling upstream. It would take them years to finish the project, as many of the mines were adrift in the open sea.

'Do you want some Johnny Walker?' Donald asked, smiling as he poured some duty-free whiskey into a glass and handed it across to me. 'Take a decent wee drop. With the restrictions on foreign currency, it might be the last you'll get of any *good* Scotch whisky until you come back.'

I could see he was a seasoned traveller who had been to Iraq many times, and I took the opportunity to find out some of what he knew about the country.

'Do you ever see any of the mass public hangings?' I inquired.

'You'll never see any of that – it's all drinking and parties.'

'Surely not all the media reports are wrong?' I asked.

Softening, he poured me another whisky.

'Ah, don't believe all you read in the papers. You're going to love it out there, and just wait till you see the nurses' parties – you'll probably still be going back there in two years' time,' he said, and laughed.

Donald eased my anxiety, and I almost wanted to believe him, but I also remembered my classmate Mohammed al Sadr in the Royal College of Surgeons. He was an Iraqi political refugee who carried – deeply embedded in his back – the scars of torture inflicted by Saddam's Ba'ath regime. More than once, he had broken down in tears as he recounted how his mother had been murdered while she slept. Like many other Iraqi students studying medicine in Ireland, he would never return to his native land. For the next six weeks, I was going to live under the regime his family had fled from, so it was natural to be apprehensive – but deep inside, the prospect excited me too.

Sarah settled herself more comfortably into her seat and smiled across at me.

'Are you looking forward to working in Iraq?' she asked.

'Well, it's easy money. What about yourself?' I asked.

'The hospital staff before us worked when Iranian missiles were falling on the city. If they can do that, then we should be OK. I've spoken to some of the nurses working there at the moment, and they say it's all right,' she said.

'I suppose we'll just have to find out for ourselves.'

★

When the plane came to a halt on the runway in Baghdad, I looked through the cabin window at the twinkling night sky. After what seemed like a very long wait, we were allowed to disembark. The air outside was still. There was hardly a trace of wind to soothe the burning landscape.

We collected our luggage from the baggage carousel and joined the phalanx of people waiting for immigration officials to check their passports. Some soldiers in green fatigues eyed us warily, readjusting their guns. I stared straight ahead, trying to avoid their gazes, as my backpack contained banned newspapers and magazines which highlighted the world's growing uneasiness about Saddam Hussein. Although our colleagues in Baghdad looked forward to news from home, it was advisable not to carry it through the airport. A heavy-set man standing in front of me in the queue shifted nervously from one foot to the other, his breathing long and laboured. He frequently turned around, keeping an eye on the soldiers at all times. I put a little distance between myself and this anxious stranger.

An old man approached me. He was dressed in a loosely wound turban, and walked in slow, shuffling steps, using a wooden stick as a support. He gazed at me with feverish eyes, pointed his stick at a Californian badge that I had sewn onto my backpack and shouted, 'American!'

His aggressive behaviour intimidated me, and my pulse quickened as his voice grew louder. People began to stare. I turned to look over my shoulder in the hope that he was speaking to someone behind me.

'You're from America?' he persisted, pointing his wooden stick in my direction.

'No, I'm from Ireland,' I said, indignantly pushing him away.

A combination of exhaustion, whisky and fear made me feel nauseous. The bright lights of the airport swirled around me. If the soldiers searched and found the newspapers, my time in Baghdad could be over before it began – or I might face an even worse fate.

I lowered my head and attempted to ignore the old man in the crowd. There were tears in his eyes as he took an old crumpled photograph from his pocket.

'I am Hassan – Kurdish,' he said. 'My son is in California.'

What I had perceived as aggression was really a father's desperation about his son's whereabouts. I tried to make amends, telling him that I had once lived in Los Angeles – but it was too late. The soldiers were now walking across to see what was bothering the old man. He had spotted them and quickly turned away, disappearing into the crowd.

Sarah, who I had left behind in baggage claim, came over to me.

'Welcome to Baghdad, the cradle of civilisation and home for the next six weeks,' she said, pointing up to a colourful mural of Saddam Hussein seated on a chestnut stallion. The artist had portrayed the

Iraqi leader as a gallant Arabian knight leading his troops into battle. I later learned that this portrait remembered the Battle of
Qadisiya, during which the Iraqi cavalry brought the great Persian
army to its knees and changed the course of Islamic history. I stood
in awe of the symbolism of the picture, amazed that I had arrived in
the ancient land of Mesopotamia, home of the Hanging Gardens of
Babylon and the Garden of Eden.

The line moved again and soon it was my turn in front of the
immigration official.

'*Salaam alaikum*,' I said, trying to speak a little Arabic.

'*Alaikum as-salaam*. Papers,' he demanded, not bothering to lift
his eyes from his desk.

He was younger than I had expected, probably still in his early
twenties, and I was surprised that he was wearing casual Western-
style clothes. I handed over my passport. He fingered the pages of
the book methodically, painstakingly checking the colourful visas I
had collected from my many travels around the world.

'Have you been to Israel?' he robotically asked.

'No,' I replied as my visa had just been stapled to the page, and I
had since removed it.

It was apparent from his cold manner that there would be no
pleasantries exchanged. He looked up at me, checked the photograph on the passport, and then stamped it with the words, 'This
visa is considered invalid for entry into Iraq if the bearer obtains an
Israeli visa on his passport.'

'What are you going to be doing in Iraq?' he asked.

'I am going to work in a hospital,' I said.

'If you going to work in the hospital, you must take one of these,' he
said, giving me a slip of paper. I opened it slowly and read its contents.

Dear Passenger,
    Please note that according to the Revolutionary Command
Council resolution No 229 dated 16/4/1987 you should call within
five days of your arrival to Iraq at either Alkindi, Alkarama or
Alkadhmiya Hospital in Baghdad or the preventive health centres

in the governates for AIDS Laboratory Blood Tests. Otherwise you will be submitted to a fine of five hundred Iraqi dinars or six months imprisonment, in case of not paying the fine.

I finished with the immigration officer and went to join Sarah, who by now had got ahead of me.

'Everybody has to be tested for AIDS before they can work,' I said to her.

The test the Iraqi government was requiring me to take would establish, for the fourth time, whether I was HIV-negative. I intended to take it as soon as possible.

'Well, look on the bright side Patrick,' she laughed, 'at least you know that every nurse in Baghdad is HIV-negative.'

We walked together towards the door of the arrivals lounge, where there was another large portrait of Saddam Hussein, dressed in a red-and-white chequered *kaffiyeh*, an Arab headdress. Icons of leaders signify power in the Middle East and, if his portraits were anything to judge by, the 'Father of the Nation' was a very powerful man indeed. This was my first exposure to the personality cult of Saddam Hussein. A nearby sign read: 'Don't for one moment think that the Revolution is unaware of what you are all doing. Remember that the Revolution is everywhere and it has its eyes wide open.'

The automatic doors opened and a stifling blast of hot air hit us in the face. We said our goodbyes to Donald, who promised to meet up with us when he came to Baghdad.

A welcoming committee was waiting to meet me and Sarah. We were approached by a smiling, dark-haired guy in his mid-twenties, who shook hands with me and said, 'Hi, I'm David, one of the cardiology registrars. And this is Paul, one of the medical SHOs. I think you know each other – your fame goes before you!'

I immediately recognised an old friend I had played guitar with at college. We chatted as we walked from the airport terminal, across the parking lot.

The night air was heavy and it clung to my skin like an invisible cloth. Above us, a brilliant crescent moon hung sideways in a deep rose sky, bathing us in its light. The sweet smell of roasting chestnuts wafted from a nearby vendor's stall. A hawker exhibited piles of men's shirts on the pavement in neat rows, next to a display of cheap watches. Paul lifted one of the watches and gazed at the image of Saddam smiling from between the moving hands.

'Big ERIC gets his face on everything out here. Be careful – he misses nothing,' Paul said.

'Who's Eric?' I asked.

'ERIC – Eternal Ruler in Command,' he whispered. 'That's what we call Saddam.'

He told me that it was best to talk in code about anything that related to the Ba'ath regime or its policies, as the country was over-run with Mukhabarat, secret police, who continually listened to conversations and phone calls.

'You can't tell them apart from the ordinary man in the street, so it's best to be careful at all times,' Paul said. 'You won't find anyone willing to talk about life in Iraq.'

Suddenly Donald's conversation made more sense to me. Like a lot of foreigners living in Iraq, he had learned never to mention the dark side of the Ba'ath regime, even in drunken conversation.

Paul continued: 'I hear they're going to put you into Staff Health. You'll be given your own jeep.'

'What's it like?' I asked.

'Brilliant, it's a bit of a doss, you'll probably have every waster in the hospital coming to you looking for a day off. But at least you'll get the use of your own Nissan Patrol. It's shared between you and Patricia, the Staff Health nurse.'

We approached a green-and-white jeep bearing the Ibn al-Bitar hospital insignia. It was surrounded by a group of irate taxi drivers, as David had been parked right in the middle of one of their ranks. An unshaven man with an obvious limp approached us and begged for some dollars. I presumed he had been injured in the Iran-Iraq war; he wouldn't be the last of these people we would meet in Baghdad that year.

'Be careful they don't confiscate your jeep. Look at this new circular on parking that was sent round today,' Paul said, reaching into his pocket and taking out a slip of paper.

> To all staff, Ibn al-Bitar Hospital,
> A drive to tighten up the traffic regulations is taking place, in particular in Basra and also in some parts of Baghdad. A directive has been given to apply the maximum penalty for illegal parking, breaking of speed limits, driving through the red light and reckless driving. The penalties for expatriates could amount to confiscation of the vehicle and a ban on re-entry to Iraq. Such offences for Iraqi staff could result in imprisonment for a year. Personnel using vehicles, particularly for social purposes, are reminded of their responsibility in the event of the vehicle being confiscated, stolen or damaged.
> —Hospital Administrator

'A year in jail for parking in the wrong spot – that's a bit over the top isn't it?' I said.

'Well, just be glad we're not driving your Nissan Patrol to the airport tonight, or we'd definitely all be locked up for a year,' Paul said.

'Why do you say that?' I asked.

'Oh, it's big scandal in the hospital at the moment. Did you hear about Farzad Bazoft – the *Observer* journalist? He was caught at the airport with soil samples he'd taken from a missile plant. He was caught with your old staff nurse in your Nissan Patrol. They say she'll get a life sentence.'

I learned that Bazoft was a reporter who had arrived in Baghdad a few months earlier. He'd met Daphne Parish at the Mansour Melia Hotel, where he was staying. The two became friendly, and he used her as a cover to investigate an explosion that had occurred at the Al-Iskandaria military complex, about 30 miles south of Baghdad. Rumours had circulated that many hundreds of Egyptian technicians working in the plant had been killed.

Bazoft attracted attention to himself when he started asking the hotel staff questions about whether the facility made rockets, failing to realise that the secret police were everywhere. The nurse supplied him with sterile containers from the hospital to gather soil samples from the affected area. When Bazoft tried to leave the country he was arrested at the airport, carrying sensitive photographs and the soil samples, which bore the Ibn al-Bitar logo, and therefore were easily traced back to the nurse.

'The Iraqis now say that Bazoft is an Israeli spy,' David said. 'They came and took Dee from the hospital. I saw her leaving with Dr Raad and two dudes in black suits. Some of the other nurses have tried to get in to see her. She's in a really crap place, full of cockroaches, and nobody speaks English there. Apparently she made a Christmas tree out of old copies of the *Baghdad Times*.'

'At least it's putting it to some use,' Paul said, laughing. 'The Nissan Patrol you've been allocated has the most famous licence number in Iraq!'

We made our way to the centre of Baghdad on a modern highway, which we shared with tooting Toyota pickup trucks and orange-and-white taxis, all frantically jostling and competing for more favourable positions. As we reached the suburbs, the landscape changed. Old men wearing long white *dishdashas* wandered along the streets and chatted to hawkers selling cans of Pepsi and packets of Marlboro cigarettes from little stalls illuminated by chains of flickering bulbs. At last we crossed the Tigris, passing over the Al Sinak Bridge, and entered the sector that was to be our new home.

The expatriates had nicknamed this area of the city 'Saddamsville'. It was comprised of many rows of twelve-storey apartment blocks with neatly landscaped gardens and date palms. Soldiers on sentry duty outside a nearby military complex watched our vehicle as we drove along the broad boulevards of 14th of July Street and made our way along the edge of Zawra Park towards the impressive concrete structure of the Al Rashid Hotel, where I was to stay during my locum.

'Wait till you see this place,' Paul said. 'If most big hotels in the West are five stars, then this is seven stars!'

The Al Rashid was set amidst twenty acres of lavishly manicured gardens. My friends told me the building was designed by Swedish engineers to withstand a bomb attack, and its eighteen storeys pivoted on an oil suspension system, so finely balanced that the manager could tell when uninvited guests were staying over in some of the top floors.

A gentle breeze blew as we entered the courtyard. It was hot that night in February, and a wedding party sat under the shade of some acacia trees. The women's outfits were especially elaborate, with large hoop skirts and long veils. The people were friendly and soon we were dancing with them under the bright Iraqi moonlight to the rhythmical sounds of musicians with small reed flutes and hand drums. The music reminded me of my time in Istanbul, but the tone was Arabic and mysterious.

'Patrick, you'll have to meet The Hajj – he's a legend,' David said, pointing to a tall European man in the distance.

He explained that the friend we were meeting had earned his nickname while working in Saudi Arabia, where he had gone on the pilgrimage to Mecca disguised as a Muslim, wearing white garments called *ihram* that pilgrims donned as part of the tradition of shedding signs of their wealth while undertaking the journey. Only Muslims are supposed to enter Mecca, and it was said by hospital staff in Baghdad that an English traveller, Richard Burton, was the only other non-Muslim European known to have performed the feat – nearly one hundred years earlier.

'It's amazing what you can do with a split tablecloth and a jeep fan belt if given the chance,' The Haj said in the bar later, laughing.

★

The next morning I got up and made my way across to the nearby hospital, a whitewashed, low-slung building set in a small garden lined with pomegranate trees. There was a tiny open courtyard with a tiled pavement that led to the Staff Health Clinic. The morning started easily. Pauline, the staff nurse, had already dealt with the trivial problems concerning staff.

Once we had introduced ourselves and she had shown me

around the clinic, she took a deep breath, smiled and opened a door to show me where a group of Indian porters sat shivering, their faces peering out at me from the depths of the woollen blankets they had wrapped themselves in. This was a common occurrence, even when the outside temperature climbed over forty degrees Celsius. There were about ten of them, waiting for some antibiotics and hopefully a day or two off work. During my time in Baghdad, I grew used to their contrived performances, and even found a certain charm in the way that different cultures portrayed their illnesses.

That day, one of them actually had a fever. His name was Anwar, he was an assistant chef, and he had severe Giardia gastroenteritis, which required his immediate release from work and a hefty course of Metronidazole. This taught me to examine everybody and not to stereotype the different nationalities too easily.

Part of my duties was working in a walk-in casualty service, seeing Iraqi patients who had previously been admitted to hospital. Late in the afternoon, the first of these patients arrived: a couple from Najaf, a town south of Baghdad. The husband, a slight man with refined features, introduced his wife and told us she had previously been one of our renal dialysis patients. His English wasn't good, so we needed the assistance of Nadia, our interpreter. His wife, clearly uncomfortable, deferred lying down, preferring to remain in a distorted position in front of my desk. I noted how she tried to smile, but looked too exhausted even to let go of the black handbag she grasped with the fingers of an older rheumatoid patient.

'She can't open her mouth,' her husband said in broken English, gesturing to her face, his loving eyes filled with sadness.

'How long has she been like this?' I inquired.

'For a few days – they just drove up from Najaf,' Nadia replied.

I was told that her face had gone numb the night before and that at one point she had been unable to breathe or see properly.

'Can she open her right hand?' I asked, realising that she couldn't let go of her handbag.

'No,' he answered.

'I think she's got tetanus,' said Pauline, mentioning a previous case.

I had to admit that it certainly looked like tetanus, but the patient hadn't had any fever, malaise, or even headache prior to the symptoms appearing. It was a baffling case.

'Has she any numbness around her lips now?' I asked.

The patient nodded and I realised that she also spoke some English.

I asked Pauline to draw some blood and to ask the lab, which was only next door, to get the results back to me as soon as possible. I thought I knew what was happening, but didn't want to say, as I was only starting my medical rotation and my diagnoses would be under scrutiny.

When the bloods came back my suspicions were confirmed. The patient was suffering from reduced levels of calcium in her blood, causing the nerve endings to fire continually, producing a constant spasm of the muscles around her jaw. I wondered whether the condition would have been easier to diagnose in Dublin, where I could have got a better history of the problem from the relatives. I informed the renal registrar, who agreed that we should give her some calcium gluconate. The effect was immediate, and the patient regained her normal countenance within a few minutes.

Pauline looked over at me and her thumbs-up suggested that we would work well together over the next few months.

★

I returned to the Al Rashid Hotel that evening, excited after my first day at work. David had agreed to collect me and bring me along to 'The Villa', a sort of Irish social club in the Mansour area of Baghdad, where hospital staff went to relax in the evenings. He said that we could catch a coach there from outside the Commissary, a small shop on the complex that sold Irish provisions. After we got there, a blue-and-white Mercedes coach pulled up. In the distance, a forlorn mullah struggled to communicate to the city through a faulty microphone. The coach's driver, an elderly man, descended and started talking to my friends. I guessed, from his black-and-white turban-like head wrap, that he was not Arab – possibly Kurdish.

'This is Hassan,' said Paul, introducing me.

The driver smiled.

'*Choni?*' I said, greeting him in the forbidden Kurdish tongue, which I had learned from friends in Istanbul.

'*Bash'm supas ey to?*' he replied, astonished and smiling, returning my greeting.

He gripped my hand firmly. I instinctively knew that we would be friends.

'Where are you staying Patrick?' asked Hassan.

'I hear they might be moving you to Room 908 in one of the residential apartment blocks,' David said.

'Oh no – not 908!' Hassan said, holding his hands to his head and laughing loudly about the apartment's infamy. Apparently it was a shared apartment and my new roommates were party legends in Baghdad.

On the way to The Villa, David told me that Hassan had lost his sons in the Iran-Iraq war. They had been forced to fight for Saddam and, as a consequence, he hated the Iraqi Arabs. I knew from a *Sunday Times* article that I had smuggled into Baghdad from Ireland that the Iraqi air force had dropped mustard gas on the little town of Halabja and killed thousands of people, while the watching world said nothing. Part of the reason was because the US initially tried to blame Iran until ITN television footage showed this not to be the case. I wanted to travel to the Kurds' homeland in the northern mountains and learn more about their culture, but Paul said that was considered dangerous and was actively discouraged by the hospital authorities.

That evening, after spending some time in the Villa, we all went to a party in Block 2 of the residential apartment complex. It seemed that everyone from the hospital was there, and they had gathered huge platters of pizzas, samosas and chicken legs, cooked up in the hospital canteen earlier in the day. The haunting melody of Sinead

O'Connor's 'Nothing Compares 2 U' was playing loudly from a CD player. Some innovative people had chopped up large blocks of ice in the bath to make a modified fridge.

'So, you're joining the Ba'ath Party!' said one of the male nurses, laughing.

The party was soon in full swing. Most of the people present were Irish and British female nurses, and David was correct when he said they outnumbered the males by about ten to one. During the evening, I again met Pauline, the Staff Health nurse with whom I would be working for the next few weeks.

'Don't sleep in tomorrow morning,' she said. 'I wouldn't like you to miss those Indian porters with their "total body pains". They'll be lining up for a day off work at eight o'clock.'

Pauline told me that most of the hospital porters were Christians who came from Goa in India. An enterprising lot, they ran the black market in currency at the hospital.

'We have to stay on the right side of them to get a good deal, but you can't be too soft or they'll skive off work at any opportunity,' she said. 'I hear you might be staying in Room 908. Those guys are the hardest drinkers in the block. When they throw a party, it usually lasts all week.

'Did you hear what they did the other day? They say Pat McGlynn found a donkey wandering in some fields beside Block 34 and brought it up to his apartment in the lift. When Chris Duckling – aka "the Duck" – found it, he fed him enough gin and tonic to get the poor donkey drunk and then rode it through the hospital court-yard.

'Actually Pat's here at the party – come on over,' Pauline said.

Pauline introduced me to Pat, a likeable male nurse from County Donegal, in the north-west of Ireland.

'What's this I hear about you keeping animals in the apartment?' I said to him.

'Which animals do you mean?' he replied.

'I heard about the donkey getting drunk up there,' I said. 'Is it true?'

'Oh God yes – for a minute there I thought you meant the chickens.'

'Chickens!'

'Yeah, we had two chickens, called "Curry" and "Supreme", living outside on the corridor for a while. They were leftover extras from last year's Christmas party. The hospital management made us get rid of them, so we gave them to Hassan, the bus driver.'

I left Pat and wandered around the room. My eyes fell on a printed notice displayed in a prominent position on one of the walls.

All Residents Blocks 34 and Block 2

- All staff holding parties have a responsibility to ensure that attendance is by invitation only
- No amplification is to be used outside the apartment
- Apartment occupants have a responsibility to keep the noise level at parties at an acceptable level
- Any damage to apartments is the responsibility of the occupants

All social notices must be cleared by the hospital administration before they are placed on the notice board.

Signed: John Duffy, Hospital Administrator, Mrs Anne Morgan, Director of Nursing, Mr Joe McMullan, Medical Director of the Ibn al-Bitar Hospital.

It was the first time I had seen a directive on the official way to party, signed by such senior hospital staff. While I was reading the notice, Sarah sneaked up behind me and whispered in my ear, 'Fancy meeting you here.'

Sarah told me that news was breaking on the BBC World Service that Nelson Mandela had just been released from Victor Verster Prison in South Africa. In the '80s, like many other students, I had joined the anti-apartheid demonstrations outside South Africa House in London and protested for his freedom. I took Sarah's hand and we danced for a while before moving outside to the balcony, where we sat chatting and listening to the loud music. I pushed all thoughts of Trish to one side and, a little while later, we left the party and went back to the Rashid to have a few drinks in the residents' lounge before going to bed.

Morning came early, and I read Sarah's note on my pillow, explaining that she had gone back to her apartment to change for work. I got up and made my way along the busy streets to the Ibn al-Bitar Hospital. A small group of barefoot children played together on the side of the road, while a little boy carried a glass of sweet tea, in a pear-shaped Turkish glass, to an old man seated on a shabby armchair by the side of the road. The old man nodded to me serenely, and I responded with the traditional greeting, '*Marhaban. Kayf haluk?*'

That evening, David and Paul arrived at the Rashid to bring my luggage over to Room 908, and then took me downtown to have a closer look at the city before sunset. We passed through narrow streets, which were full of toothless old men sitting and chatting together, through shabby areas with flaking plaster shopfronts and alleyways full of young children playing and vendors selling mangoes from little stalls. David and Paul pointed out Saddam's Presidential Palace; a group of Northern Ireland lads had constructed the fine fretwork on the building. From the outside, it looked like an ornate mosque, with neat rows of sandy bricks laced with intricately carved arabesque portals and windows. On the roof, there was a blue-and-white tiled dome that exuded the grandiose ethos of the Ottoman Sultans.

Underground, the building was completely different. It was, in effect, a vast underground command structure, designed by Swiss engineers to house a communications centre, a generating station and a barracks for hundreds of men. It stretched eighty feet into the ground and was supported on a hard rubber foundation with springs, designed to withstand the shock waves of enemy bombs. This nation was preparing for an invasion.

As we approached Al Kindi Street, a jeep-load of armed soldiers swerved in front of us, forcing us to pull over. David cursed under his breath. They jumped out and surrounded our vehicle, looking at us through narrowed, suspicious eyes. The soldier in charge lowered his Kalashnikov and approached the passenger-side window.

'Papers!' he demanded.

David passed his residence permit to me, and I obligingly passed it on to the soldier at my window. His dark, unwavering eyes looked at me for what seemed like a long time. I had seen that look before – a mixture of edginess and suspicion, hate and fear – at British roadblocks in Northern Ireland. He glanced at the permit, slowly looked at each of us in turn, as if memorising our faces, and then silently passed the papers back. I thought he tried to smile before waving us on, but I may have imagined it.

'Just say nothing – *ciúnas!*' Paul said to me, meaning 'quiet', invoking the way Irish people over the centuries spoke together whenever they didn't want other nationalities to understand them.

David took his residence permit from me and stuck it into the pocket of his shirt. He turned on the engine and moved back onto the carriageway.

'I hear they're restricting the import of Heineken into Iraq again,' he said, as if nothing had happened. 'If we don't book some this evening at the Commissary, we'll have to get some crates of that Shahrivar piss instead.'

We followed the highway for a while before approaching a grotesque monument straddling the highway. It consisted of two gigantic crossed sabres made of cement, held in an upright position by clenched fists pointing in opposite directions. From the apex of the structure, an Iraqi flag fluttered in the gentle wind.

'This is the Iraqi Arc de Triomphe,' said David. 'It was built to commemorate the so-called victory over Iran. The hands are modelled on those of Saddam himself.'

12.
ROOM 908

The door to Apartment 908 was open and music was playing loudly inside. It was early evening and there was no one at home. I assumed my roommates were downstairs with friends. The apartment looked like it hadn't been cleaned for years. There were unwashed cups and plates everywhere. Surprisingly, the same level of squalor didn't extend to the toilets or shower area, where the smell of cologne made it seem like a real bachelor pad. This was it – Room 908, with its abandoned frying pans and empty beer bottles, another enchanting abode in the ebbing hourglass of my life. I left my luggage beside an empty bed and waited for my flatmates to return.

Chris arrived some time later and opened some beers.

'What's with all the black PVC tape on the windows of my room?' I asked, pointing to the criss-crossed duct-tape strips, which looked like leftovers from a previous party.

'That's to stop the glass shattering down on top of you if you're hit by a stray missile in the middle of the night,' he replied. 'It was needed during the War of the Cities, at the end of the Iran-Iraq war, but everyone feels it's better to leave it up, as you never know what could happen here.'

A mosquito whined above my head and the black-and-white television in the living room, showing Ba'ath propaganda, flickered on and off to the rhythm of the air conditioner.

'Have you brought over any Irish papers?' he asked, looking at my luggage.

I opened the backpack and dumped the contents on the bed.

'Good lad, well done! How the hell did you get all that lot through?'

He brought the papers into the kitchen, where he cleared a space on the table. My eyes fell on the story about Saddam gassing the Kurds in northern Iraq.

'Have any of you lads heard what happened up in Halabja?' I asked.

'Never heard of it, what's that about?' he answered.

'It's a small town up in Kurdistan, near the Iranian border, and Saddam has apparently killed a lot of people there.'

'Never heard of it, but he's always fighting with the Kurds,' Chris shrugged. 'Ask Hassan, the bus driver – he's Kurdish.'

He then started to read the article about Halabja aloud.

'By all accounts, a combination of mustard gas and other, more instantly fatal, chemical agents caused the massive carnage at Halabja. The injured survivors that reporters saw being treated in hospitals in Tehran and elsewhere last week showed the classic symptoms of mustard-gas poisoning – ugly skin lesions and breathing difficulties. As well as progressively affecting the lungs and skin, mustard gas also impairs the bone-marrow function,' he read.

'I actually heard about this,' he said, tapping the paper with his finger. 'They say we're treating some of the survivors down in the ICU of the hospital.'

★

Sunrise came early, its radiant light splintered into shafts by the tape on my bedroom window. From the courtyard below, some schoolchildren began singing a patriotic verse, probably extolling the virtues of their 'Great Leader'. As I listened, their young voices gained vigour and strength, and the revolutionary verses continued for nearly thirty minutes. Over the coming days, their patriotic singing became my second alarm clock in Baghdad.

I got up and made my way to the hospital. It was already hot outside and the streets were busy, despite the early hour. White taxis with orange panels stalked me, looking for business, while old men on the sidewalks lazily trailed their long *dishdashas* through the dust.

I passed the International Communications Centre, a military complex strategically situated across from the hospital. The building was guarded by a group of young soldiers who stood aloof and neatly dressed, their black boots glinting in the bright sunlight, their red epaulets defining their status as members of the Republican Guard, an elite unit tasked with protecting the president and the important military buildings in the capital.

The day at the hospital began with the usual plethora of staff health problems. One had to be extremely careful regarding confidentiality, because if the wide-ranging blood screens in Baghdad showed any communicable diseases, especially hepatitis, it would compromise a career back in Dublin.

That afternoon, I ran an outpatient emergency-room clinic for Iraqi patients who already had been patients of the hospital and who might require readmission. One of my first patients was an Olympic gold-medal winner. He was an older man who was once a weightlifter. Grateful to discover that his abdominal pain did not require admission, he presented me with a large Arabic ring before leaving. Maybe it was a morning for Iraq's unusual personages to grace my clinic, but the next case proved equally interesting.

Before me sat a well-built woman with delicate bone structure and skin that had the smoothness that comes from years of care. She wore a padded red dress and imitation jewellery; her well-combed hair fell seductively around one shoulder.

'I've come for my injection,' she said.

The nurse had left the room, and I searched through the patient's chart for some reference to her malady. The nurse returned with the patient's medicine and proceeded to inject her. As she left, the patient embraced me a little too warmly. I looked at Pauline, hoping for an explanation.

'Well now you've met Mary,' she said, smiling. 'Do you know who she is?'

142

'Haven't a clue, but she appears a little strange.'

'Mary is Iraq's only transsexual – she comes here every few months for her hormone injections. She had the job done in London but, God love her, she must have an uphill battle existing in Baghdad.'

After the clinic ended, I walked through the hospital, looking for one of my room-mates. Sarah came up to me and guided me towards a new item that was pinned on the noticeboard, saying, 'It's pretty heavy stuff.'

On Friday, 16 February 1990, the Iraqi Ministry of Foreign Affairs informed the British Ambassador in Iraq that Mrs Daphne Parish is to be charged with espionage against Iraq. She is to be tried on 26 February before a Revolutionary Court. The Iraqi Ministry of Foreign Affairs has said that the same charge is to be taken against Mr Farzad Bazaoft. He will also appear in front of the Revolutionary Council on 26 Feburary. The British Ambassador was assured that full legal access would be granted to Nurse Parish's lawyer, and that a representative of the British Embassy would be allowed to attend the trial.

Sarah and I decided to get a taxi and travel to the Saray Souk, in the old city. She was shaken by the development and very concerned about what might happen to her colleague.

'Some say she'll get twenty years or more,' she said. 'And Bazoft could be hanged.'

The driver was friendly and spoke in broken English. I was very much aware that he might report our conversation to the Mukhabarat.

'Ná bí ag caint,' I said, indicating in Irish that she should stop talking.

She remained silent for the rest of the journey.

The sun sank into a swirling canvas of saffron and Jaffa-orange hues, adding a wonderful sense of romance to the evening. The souk was packed with people, who lingered by open hemp sacks of cinnamon, tobacco and turmeric. We walked for about an hour through the labyrinth of mysterious sunlit alleyways and narrow stone streets. Every now and then a bearded barterer would call out to the crowd, in an attempt to be heard above the noise of the clinking tinsmiths. It was exciting to ramble through this mystic terrain teeming with open stalls selling pictures of painted sultans and delicate little filigree silver dishes garnished with etched steel knives and daggers.

However, amidst the bustle and chatter, the buying and selling, there was also suspicion and uneasiness. Occasionally, I saw fear in the eyes of the friendly stallholders who implored us a little too desperately to buy quartz watches emblazoned with the latest propagandist portrait of their Great Leader.

★

Over the next few weeks, I went travelling as much as I could through the little villages that surrounded Baghdad. I had long been fascinated by the memoirs of the Ethiopian-born British explorer Wilfred Thesiger, who had travelled through this area in the 1950s, on the way from his homeland in Ethiopia to Afghanistan. Aristocratic by birth, educated at Eton and Oxford, Thesiger was a self-confessed romantic and traditionalist. His adventures fed a deep-seated desire within me, especially his stories of the Marsh Arabs and the rise and fall of Babylon. The ancient city, which has haunted European imaginations for centuries, was only about eighty miles south of Baghdad.

In Devenish Primary School, Mr Regan had taught me how its hanging gardens were once considered one of the wonders of the ancient world, but I had never imagined that I would visit it one day. The Bible stated that Babylon would be destroyed and never rebuilt, a Christian prophecy that Saddam Hussein had been unable to resist proving wrong. When he rose to power in Iraq, he said that Babylon would once more rise again from the dust. He conceived a grandiose scheme to reconstruct the ancient city, even building on top of the foundation stones of King Nebuchadnezzar's Palace. Archaeologists worldwide were horrified, and said that to rebuild on top of these ancient artefacts didn't preserve history – it disfigured it.

On my second weekend in Iraq, I visited the ancient city and sat for a while alone, reading the inscription that Saddam had had embossed into the brickwork: 'In the era of Saddam Hussein, protector of Iraq, who rebuilt civilisation and rebuilt Babylon.' Babylon had long been associated with the anti-Christ, and was said to have been the seat of power for the tyrant of the world. Maybe, I thought, this was history repeating itself.

*

Sarah and I spent most of our free afternoons in February soaking up the sun and lazing beside the swimming pool in the Mansour Melia Hotel. After a hard day's work, it was a welcome change of environment – the landscaped garden filled with flowering bougainvillea was like an oasis. The hospital staff relaxed by the poolside, tanned their torsos and fanned themselves with the latest edition of the *Baghdad Times*. For a nominal fee, hotel waiters in light-brown uniforms carried drinks to the guests. These facilities were available exclusively to privileged Westerners, some of whom exuded an air of pretentiousness. Donald joined us there on a few occasions and laughed about how apprehensive I had been on the flight over.

Since Farzad Bazoft's arrest, hospital staff had become more aware of their own security and were careful about what they said in front of others. As the date of his trial approached, the atmosphere in Baghdad changed and everybody was on tenterhooks, waiting to see what would happen to the prisoners.

There seemed to be growing antipathy towards the hospital staff, and I perceived animosity in the eyes of the patients in the hospital wards. Even the sickest amongst them clicked their tongues in feigned intolerance at the very suggestion that anything was wrong with their country. From morning to night, the indoctrination of the masses continued, through the two television channels which every home in the city received.

International appeals largely fell on deaf ears in Iraq. At one stage, Saddam Hussein personally tried to calm fears by assuring British Prime Minister Margaret Thatcher that the journalist would get a fair hearing.

★

The morning of 15 March started like any other Thursday. The usual patchwork of cotton cumulus clouds hung along the horizon. By mid-morning, the sun was climbing in the sky and promising temperatures well in excess of forty degrees Celsius.

Everybody at the hospital was looking forward to the 'Spring in the Air' party at the British Club in a few days' time. Some of the hospital staff had formed a rock group called the Baghdad Blues Band, which would play at the party. The local expatriate Hash House Harriers were getting record attendances at their weekly fun runs and had to increase their alcohol supplies for their post-run festivities.

In the late afternoon, I wandered through the bazaars, hoping to get a watch repaired. I left it with an old Egyptian jeweller and headed off to a little restaurant for something to eat. Normally we went to the 'liver souk', an area of the bazaar where tasty delicacies were sold from modified wheelbarrows. On this occasion, I decided to try out a newly discovered eatery, nicknamed by hospital staff 'the Hole in the Wall Restaurant', because it had a gaping hole – from a missile attack – near its front entrance.

The restaurant was crowded and quite loud. After a while, some Iraqis, who spoke good English, joined me at my table.

'What do you think of the news?' one of them asked.

'Why, what's happened?' I said.

'They hanged Bazoft, and the nurse was sentenced to fifteen years imprisonment.'

I was incredulous – so much for Saddam allaying fears. I knew that life in Baghdad would never be the same again. Despite the opportunity for Iraq to show leniency, Bazoft had been sentenced to death and had already been executed in Abu Ghraib prison. His body was placed in a wooden coffin and left outside the British Council, which was right beside the hospital.

I listened to their feeble justifications, namely that Bazoft had made a confession of his own free will on Iraqi television, and found it difficult to believe that they were thinking clearly. They had been subjected to a substantial propaganda campaign, but perhaps they thought the same of me. We were different people seeing opposite sides of the same coin. I was outnumbered and felt it was useless to argue. The fact that Bazoft had an Iranian background made the execution easier for the Iraqi people to accept. They also seemed proud to have a strong leader who would not waver in his decisions, even with world opinion against him. I thought Saddam was poorly advised in deciding to hang Bazoft. By doing so, he had played into the hands of the Israelis, who wanted to portray him as a dangerous monster who could not be trusted, especially as he had used poison gas on his own people.

My head started to spin. I could only surmise that propaganda and malice was being spread from the nearby minaret. Had I judged the population of Iraq so badly? Was it possible that Bazoft could be an Israeli spy?

Suffering from an acute loss of appetite, I made my apologies and wandered back over to the old jeweller's shop. He had repaired the watch while I was away but tried to convince me that he had replaced two of the main bevel wheels. The fact that one of the wheels he said he had taken out of the watch was nearly as big as the back of the watch only infuriated me. Many Iraqi people considered the Egyptian craftsmen to be deceitful, and I had little difficulty in expressing my predicament to some local militia. It was gratifying to see the soulless old watchmaker grovel at the soldiers' request to hand over the time-piece without charging me. Suffice it to say, he got his revenge when the crown wheel fell out of the watch about ten days later.

Back at my apartment, Chris was distressed by the news about Farzad Bazoft and Daphne Parish. He told me that some of the staff had seen Bazoft's body being unceremoniously deposited in a coffin from the back of a pickup truck outside the British Council. There was a derisory note in Arabic attached to the remains. It said something to the effect of, 'Thatcher wanted him back – she can have him back in a box.'

Chris also told me that Donald, the Scottish engineer who had been on the plane with me, had been arrested in Basra and charged with being a British spy. The Iraqi authorities had decided that, in addition to removing dangerous mines, he was actually placing new detonation devices in the shipping channel on behalf of the British government. Chris, who was English, surprised me when he said, 'He was ex-British army, so who knows who is telling the truth. The best thing is to keep your thoughts to yourself out here.'

The government-run *Baghdad Observer* reported that the verdict passed on the captives was just, and that the court had given Bazoft and Parish proper, legal trials. Minister for Information and Culture Latif Nsayyif Jassim stated that the international outcry over the sentences was blatant interference in Iraq's internal affairs. We were warned not to attend the party scheduled to take place in the British club that night. Two nights later, hand grenades were tossed over the wall of the club, and a Polish boy was seriously injured. Only seven years old, he was admitted to Ward E with extensive leg wounds. This ward was reserved for the treatment of Westerners and visiting Iraqi dignitaries.

My room-mate Pat was working on the ward, and I took the opportunity to visit him. The child appeared to be in good spirits and had been inundated with well-wishers. I wished our young victim well and told him I would come back to visit him again.

'Do you know who just vacated the bed he's in?' asked Pat.

'No – anybody important?' I replied.

'An Egyptian pilot accidentally shot down over the Tigris during the air show last year. He was piloting an Alpha jet, which they'd never seen before, and they thought it was the Israelis coming to attack Baghdad,' Pat said.

'Oh I heard about him. Didn't one of the nurses shake his hand and tell him how lucky he was to be able to "ejaculate" out of his aircraft?' I replied.

★

There were definite signs of a shift in Western media opinion about Iraq after the hanging of Bazoft. For many in the Middle East the image had changed from 'Saddam the protector' to 'Saddam the tyrannical monster'. The following week, the BBC World Service informed us that Dr Gerald Bull, a Canadian ballistics expert working for the Ba'ath regime, had been assassinated in Belgium. The assassination had the hallmarks of an Israeli Mossad killing. Then news broke that Bull had been developing a new Iraqi 'supergun' capable of launching nuclear warheads thousands of miles, deep into the heart of Israeli territory.

Some days later, British Customs confiscated forty nuclear trigger devices from a wooden crate at Heathrow Airport being loaded onto Iraqi Airways Flight 238, bound for Baghdad. It was apparent that the Western powers were intent on commencing a battle against the Iraqi regime. But Saddam remained belligerent. On Iraqi television news, he spoke of an Israeli conspiracy. He threatened that he would use his weaponry to drive them into the sea. What the Ba'ath regime really needed was a Western public-relations department.

Night after night, we watched in awe as the heavy artillery on the roofs of Baghdad's highest buildings lit up the night sky with bursts of practice tracer fire. The hospital authorities told us that the Iraqi government had evidence that Israel was going to attempt a surprise air strike. It would be modelled on their 1981 attack on the Osiraq nuclear reactor, but this time Iraq would be prepared. There were rumours that an Israeli jet had been shot down over the Tigris, but it may have been the poor Egyptian pilot in his Alpha.

Before long, political demonstrations were being organised in downtown Baghdad, and the Iraqi media whipped up the populace by claiming that the Israeli secret service was plotting with the West to attack them. I watched many of these agitated meetings from a safe distance, feeling it was better not to show my face, as the pent-up anger in the crowds rose to the surface and overflowed.

I must admit, I found it rather difficult to believe the Western media, which was suggesting that Iraq was positioned at the centre of some great secret doomsday project. There was suggestive evidence that there was another hand at work: intelligence reports leaked from Tel Aviv were probably influencing the Baghdad government's decisions. Whatever criticism could be levelled at Saddam, his activities were now creating a flurry on the world stage.

As the tension grew in Iraq, I heard about a British worker from Northern Ireland who had been found dead in a hotel room. It was alleged that he had worked for Matrix Churchill, a British company based in Coventry, which was rumoured to be involved in the 'supergun' project. The company apparently had been bought by the Iraqis as a front for making components, which would allow them to bypass the paperwork required for procuring sanctioned technological materials. They were now targeted by Interpol and some of their products had been confiscated from Hungarian lorries at the Haydarpaşa customs, on the Asian side of the Bosphorus, in Istanbul.

The British worker had been discovered in suspicious circumstances after sustaining a fatal head injury. The preliminary medical report stated that his death resulted from a skull fracture sustained during a fall from his bed while having a heart attack. His co-workers thought differently. There were accusations that a taxi, which collected him from a local bar, had been driven by members of Mossad, and that people had seen him being bundled into the back of it. Rumours also circulated that he had presented to an Iraqi hospital the previous night after receiving a head injury. X-rays taken at that time showed no evidence of a skull fracture.

The dead man was transferred to the Ibn al-Bitar Hospital for a post-mortem. The pathologist normally in charge of performing this duty happened to be a patient of mine and had suddenly become ill. I had to decide whether he was fit enough to perform his duties. If I deemed him unfit, a replacement pathologist would have to be flown in from the United Kingdom. For purely medical reasons, I decided that it was preferable that he did not perform the autopsy. Because of the intense suspicion surrounding the death, it was a difficult call to make. His fellow workers were convinced that their friend would not get an objective autopsy and that there had been a dark hand involved in the proceedings. My decision could only add to the controversy. It was the first time that my medical opinion had played a role in politics, and I felt uncomfortable with the responsibility.

Although my involvement in this case was small, my administrative position gave me access to some conversations with official parties about another reason why Bazoft had been so readily executed. My diplomatic sources claimed that within a few days of Bazoft's arrest, Mossad had contacted the Iraqi embassy in Holland, stating that Jerusalem was willing to make a deal for *their* man. This alleged conversation convinced the Iraqis that they were dealing with a real spy, and sealed his execution. All Mossad had to do was sit back and watch as Saddam proved to the world what a monster he really was.

★

I was reaching the end of my locum job in Baghdad, and I decided to return to Dublin, where I would take the opportunity to do a repeat HIV test. If things did not deteriorate in Iraq, I might take another locum position there, which would allow me to work until the beginning of August, when I would take up a GP registrar position in Scotland. I had selected Broxburn, a small agricultural town in West Lothian, about five miles from the Edinburgh airport.

One Tuesday night before I left Baghdad, a group of hospital staff decided to go to the disco in the Palestine Hotel. We were enjoying ourselves until one of the men from a party beside us began hassling one of the nurses in a very unpleasant way. His unruly behaviour continued until, eventually, I went over to confront the man, warning him to leave the young woman alone. Everybody at the table went silent, and it was only then that I noticed some of them were wearing pistols.

The person in question let go of the nurse and looked at me coldly for a moment. Then he got up, brushed himself down and – unexpectedly – shook my hand, apologised and promised to behave himself in our company. I returned to my own table, but my friends had seen what had happened and had become very subdued. The other party left shortly afterwards and, as soon as they were gone, my friends began to babble excitedly.

The person I had just confronted was apparently none other than Uday Hussein, the feared son of Saddam.

13.
THE APPARITION

I returned from Ireland after spending a few weeks in Dublin as a locum Medical registrar. It had taken all of my powers not to phone Trish, but I had thought about her every day while I was there. My new duties were more varied than before, covering all hospital departments, including Intensive Care at weekends. I made it a habit to go to ICU for a personal briefing and learn about the patients who were critically ill. This tended to leave me better prepared for unexpected middle-of-the-night phone calls.

One night, I was called to the wards, where one of the SHOs was having difficulty controlling an asthmatic patient. She was obviously afraid of the cannula needle, probably because she had seen the half-terror in the eyes of the inexperienced doctor holding it. Although he was older than some of the other SHOs, the doctor had recently been an intern at a hospital in Belgium and was finding the rigours of a busy tertiary referral centre in the Middle East rather daunting.

'She's very excited and won't allow me to put a drip in her arm,' he said dejectedly.

The patient was surrounded by female family members, all dressed in black *chadors*, who were squabbling with the nurses. Some Iraqi hospitals didn't have a developed nursing system, so the females in the family often acted as nurses. Consequently, they treated our female staff with some condescension.

'Get the family out of the room please,' I said, trying to take control of the situation.

Hospital security arrived and took the family into one of the side rooms. With the help of the nurses, I managed to get the hysterical young woman into a supine position and prepared an infusion bag of aminophylline and steroids. It is often preferable to go ahead and insert an IV cannula into the patient to gain access in case of emergency and worry about the legal consequences later. I had learned that nearly all the patients in Baghdad screamed while having cannulas inserted, but that they quickly settled on receiving their drugs. Their protests were not about infringement of their personal liberties, but rather a genuine cultural needle phobia. I inserted the cannula with minimum objection and got the patient settled quickly.

I called into ICU, where there were five patients, including two renal transplants and two small children recovering from cardiac surgery. A recent spate of post-operative paediatric mortalities had affected staff morale, and the nurses were sombre and withdrawn. Dealing with hysterical parents who blamed them for their children's deaths was taking its toll. Furthermore, one of the nurses had received a needle-stick injury from a child who had Hepatitis B.

'What about the patient in the corner?' I asked.

'We don't know much about him. Apparently, he's a twenty-four-year-old transfer from the Rasheed Military Hospital. He's suffering from right and left heart failure. Dave is going to phone us later with all the details about him, but he's chatting away to us at the moment and in great form. His folks are wandering around here somewhere, so you had better get out of here before they nab you as well,' one of the nurses replied.

Later that evening, I was called back to ICU. The nurses were concerned about the young soldier who had been transferred from the military hospital earlier that day. He was standing on his bed, naked and drenched in sweat. He had removed the fluid line from his arm and bright red blood was pouring onto the white sheets beneath him and down onto the floor below. The spectacle verged on a surrealistic scene from a Ken Russell movie. There was a look of sheer terror on his young face; his pupils, in full dilation, were focused right on me. He pointed and shouted – a confused tirade in my direction.

I couldn't understand how I had evoked such fervour in a patient whom I had seen for the first time earlier that day. At the same time, his family surrounded me and his mother threw herself on her knees, beating her head with a closed fist in a wildly excited state. I fumbled my way through the melee to reach the nursing station. The wailing of the haggard old women around the bed had a foreboding rhythm, and the whole scene began to take on the cast of a tribal ritual rather than a high-technology intensive care unit.

'What the hell is going on?' I asked one of the nurses nearest to me, who seemed to be getting more afraid for the safety of the other patients by the minute.

'Apparently he's seen an apparition. St John the Baptist says he is going to die if he doesn't leave the hospital.'

'And can we not sedate him?' I said.

'He'd already been given twenty milligrams of Valium by IV before he pulled out his drip,' she sighed, frustrated. 'They want to bring him to Karbala, a town about sixty miles from here!'

'Where the hell is security when we need them?' shouted one of the nursing sisters, who had come to see what all the noise was about.

'They've already been here and have gone to the blocks for reinforcements,' one of the staff answered.

'Do we have an interpreter with us?' I asked.

'Yes, Maria is here.'

Maria, an Iraqi Christian, seemed to be at a loss as to what was going on. She looked at me in astonishment, her eyes searching mine for some solution to the problem.

'These are crazy people – they think their son is going to die at eight o'clock tomorrow if he is not brought to Karbala,' she said.

From the nursing desk, I could see the patient, who continued to bleed from the Venflon still stuck in his vein. I noticed that he remained fixated on a spot in the room; presumably he was looking at the apparition.

'What is the significance of Karbala?' I inquired, knowing that I had heard the name before.

Maria explained that for Shi'ites Karbala is one of the holiest places on earth. A famous battle had taken place there in 680 AD, between the supporters and relatives of Muhammad's grandson, Hussein, and the forces of Yazid, the Umayyad Caliph. Hussein and all his supporters were killed. Shi'ites still commemorated the Battle of Karbala each year in the Islamic month of Muharram. It was a ghastly sight: they mourned by flagellating themselves with whips until they bled. Saddam Hussein eventually banned the practice.

These people were fanatical and each and every one believed the patient was seeing a vision of St John the Baptist, who predicted he would die at eight o'clock in the morning if he didn't go to pray at Hussein's Shrine before then. I asked Maria to tell them this wasn't possible – the patient was sick and couldn't be transferred.

'Patrick, don't you think I've already done that?' she sighed.

'You'll have to phone Medical Director Joe McMullan immediately and tell him about this, because there's a crowd of them gathering outside and security can't hold them,' one of the nurses said.

I had just managed to contact him when one of the security guards arrived to tell us that about ten people had broken into the hospital grounds and were heading for the intensive-care unit. We could hear scuffles and loud voices in the corridors outside.

'You'll have to contact Dr Raad, the Iraqi director of the Ibn al-Bitar Hospital, as this sounds like it could become quite serious,' Mr McMullan advised.

I had a mental image of what might happen to the defenceless sick children lying in intensive care if these religious zealots broke through the doors. Their assault on the hospital was a dangerous development. A nurse told me that Dr Raad knew about the situation and had decided to call in the army to protect us.

Objects were thrown onto the roof and the noise outside grew louder. Dr Raad phoned to say he had come to the hospital and attempt to negotiate with the fanatical mob gathering on the streets outside.

The noise outside began to reach fever pitch. We could hear women chanting in shrill tones as stones rained down on the roof of the hospital. There was a genuine fear that a riot was going to ensue and, before long, other wards started phoning the unit for information. Word started to spread around the hospital that something big was happening outside the gates. The staff coming on duty relayed developments to those still working inside.

The anxious patient remained standing on the bed, continually repeating that he was going to die at eight o'clock. The relatives left to speak with the other members of the Shia sect outside, giving us some respite. The crowd grew louder and more vehement, and each new wave of protest seemed to agitate the patient more. For a long time, we stood listening to the conflict, then a volley of shots rang out and there was silence.

A while later, we heard footsteps approaching the unit and we were asked to open the locked door. Dr Raad entered with an army officer and stood looking at us silently for a moment before speaking.

'This is Colonel Adnan, and he has ordered the army to fire shots over the crowd outside to disperse them,' Dr Raad began. 'A judge in a court of law will have to decide tomorrow morning whether the patient can leave the hospital, but until that time he will stay here. You are not in any danger from these people tonight.'

They both turned to the soldier and spoke a few words to him. He appeared to be a little less agitated, but there was a fear in his eyes that even they couldn't remove. One of the nurses managed to get the Venflon out of his arm and apply a small compression bandage. Two armed guards were placed outside the unit.

Taking advantage of the temporary lull, I retreated back along the outside courtyard to my bedroom in the doctor's residence. Patients' relatives were sitting under the palm trees, chatting and smoking below the bright stars of the Baghdad night. A few soldiers with Russian AK-47 assault rifles slung loosely from their shoulders stood by the perimeter walls. There was no sign of any of the soldier's family members within the compound.

I found it difficult to get to sleep knowing that I could be called at any moment, and for a long while I lay and listened to the crickets singing in the long grass outside. From time to time a muezzin on a minaret wailed into a microphone and woke the sleeping city.

The phone rang – cardiac arrest in intensive care. I looked at my watch. It was twenty to eight in the morning. As I struggled to put my clothes on, I heard the cardiac beeper of my colleague sounding in the room next door. I wondered which of the patients had crashed and decided it was probably one of the little girls again. I ran out the door, pulling on my white coat, and narrowly missing a pair of veiled Muslim women who were walking along the path. A group of nurses were returning from an all-night party in one of the blocks and watched me running across the courtyard. Their early morning revelry was changed to concern as they watched my sprint. I took a shortcut, jumping over some shrubs to reach the door of the unit, and arrived on the ward out of breath.

One of the nurses was bent over the body of the young soldier, compressing his chest in a valiant effort to maintain his vital functions. I looked at the cardiac monitor and saw the trace was wildly erratic – the patient was in ventricular fibrillation.

'Ah no, draw us up 100 milligrams of lignocaine and some adrenaline,' I called to the nearest nurse.

'It's already drawn up and ready to push,' she answered.

'How long has he been like this?' I asked.

'Only about three or four minutes. I called you immediately,' she replied.

'We just *can't* lose him,' I said, as if my voice could defy the heavens above.

'Right, charge the defib at two hundred, we'll have to shock him . . .'

I pushed both drugs into his cannula, which one of the ICU nurses had re-sited during the night.

'OK, stand back everyone,' I said, placing one of the paddles over his breastbone and the other to the left side of his chest wall.

I pressed the button and the electricity discharged into his contracting body. For a moment, we stood frozen and waited for the response to register on the oscilloscope. The jagged lines slowed down to a more decipherable pattern, but then continued to change – into an almost lethargic pulse.

'He's going into asystole.'

'Give me some more adrenaline and some atropine,' I called, grabbing a laryngoscope and attempting to put a small tube into the patient's throat to allow him to get some oxygen.

'Who is the anaesthetist on call?'

'Gerry is – he's coming in,' one of the nurses replied.

Eventually, I managed to get an endotracheal tube into the soldier's throat, which is never an easy task in the best of circumstances. The patient had vomited and had to be attached to suction apparatus. We turned him on his left side and I listened to his lungs. The fine crackles in both bases told me he was full of fluid and showing signs of very advanced left heart failure. The other SHO had joined us, and I instructed him to give the patient some Lasix, a drug which would clear some of the back pressure on his dying heart.

'Will I continue CPR?' asked the nurse who was manually compressing the patient's heart.

'No, stand back and let's see what we have. He's had three lots of adrenaline and atropine and remains in asystole. He's been like that now for nearly twenty minutes. If there's no response soon, we'll have to consider calling it a day. I'll try some intra-cardiac adrenaline,' I said, asking a nurse to hand me a long needle.

I pushed the needle into the patient's thorax, but couldn't find any heart muscle, which would have been indicated by the immediate rush of blood into my syringe. The patient looked at me. There was no fear or pain in his eyes. We both knew he was being taken away by a power bigger than my little needle. I tried again, aware that his heart chamber must be distended and at least twice the normal size. I realised at that moment that I should respect the inevitability of death and was withdrawing my needle when the anaesthetist arrived. We reviewed the situation and agreed that the patient had been given every chance but was not going to recover. The arrest was called off. It was just after eight o'clock – the very time that he had predicted he would die unless he was transferred to Karbala. The court would not sit in judgment for another hour.

What power of belief had influenced this patient to predict his own demise? How could we face his family and tell them we thought we knew better, but we were wrong? The great Western concept of pharmaceutical healing was beginning to look a little tattered.

As I was leaving the unit, the young soldier's relatives began to enter. His parents fell on their knees by his bedside, bowed their heads and touched his body. There were no emotional scenes from any member of the family. No one pointed the finger of blame. Their response to his death was dignified, as if it was an order from the heavens. They simply unfolded a large carpet and rolled the soldier up inside it. Without uttering a word, they carried the body outside to a waiting taxi. They attached the corpse to the roof of the vehicle and disappeared into the dawn.

14.
THE MARSH ARABS

To the south of Baghdad lay the reed marshes of Al-Qurnah, which had formed between the deltas of the Tigris and the Euphrates rivers. This watery realm was first brought to the attention of the world in Thesiger's memoirs, which instantly enthralled me when I came across them in the school library when I was about thirteen. His adventures fed a deep-seated desire within me. He amazed me with his stories of villages on small islands in the bulrushes, giant wild pigs and herds of water buffalo that apparently swam in the shallow waters. He discovered tribesmen miraculously untouched by Western civilisation, who managed their environment in much the same way as their forefathers had done thousands of years earlier. The inhabitants of the marshlands still caught fish with five-pronged spears and poled their canoes through the shallow waters of the reed beds. After Thesiger published his personal experiences of living amongst these people, they became known to the outside world as the Marsh Arabs. His fascination captivated my imagination.

Working in Baghdad, I was excited at the prospect of travelling to a place I had read about in my childhood. I revisited Thesiger's work and viewed it with a more adult eye, but with possibly no less romantic an outcome. One weekend in early May, I caught a flight south to Basra, Iraq's second-largest city and only substantial seaport. The white-brick houses reminded me of those I had seen in Istanbul, with latticed wooden balconies and high windows. A few merchant ships were tied up in safe anchorage, waiting to go downstream. Crewmen stood around chatting on the banks of the river as they watched the fast-flowing, brownish current make its way to the sunny waters of the Persian Gulf. At the railway station, I found a taxi to take me to the little town of Al-Qurnah, where I asked for directions to get to the Amarah marshes.

'Just follow the mosquitoes and you'll find the marshes,' joked a local man, who was among several casting small nets from the river-bank.

One of them added something else, and then two small boys appeared and introduced me to Sayid, who had once lived in the marshes and had a *mashuf*, a canoe for tourists to rent. He spoke some broken English and for a nominal amount, he agreed to take me in a canoe upstream to the village he grew up in, near the town of Huwair. Sayid laid some cushions on the floor of the craft, in an effort to make our journey more comfortable. He then stepped into the stern and, using a long pole, steered us gently into the heart of the reed beds.

We travelled gently upstream for about an hour or two as evening fell. I remembered that Thesiger had written about wild boars goring people in the marshes, but had read that as a result of a recent drainage scheme, it was becoming increasingly rare to see them.

'Are there any wild pigs in the marshes?' I asked.

He didn't understand, so I imitated the noises of a wild boar. He pulled his pole out of the water and stopped the canoe. He probably thought I was afraid of large animals in the marshes, and it was getting too dark for travelling. He pulled the canoe into the shallow water, and I was a little disappointed that we didn't travel any further that day.

I could see that a lot of the marshland around us was being drained. Recently, the Ba'athist government in Baghdad had acceler-ated this process by constructing a large canal through the Amarah marshland, which diverted the waters from the Euphrates else-where. The local people called the canal 'the third river'. This project had been started by British engineers in the 1950s, and the regime said they were just awakening a dormant agricultural project that had run out of capital. However, many people in Baghdad felt that Saddam had another reason for draining the marshes.

Down through the centuries, the marshes had become a place of sanctuary for escaped slaves and serfs, as far back as the Zanj Rebellion in Basra in 869 AD. Now, they provided shelter for the fleeing Shi'ite deserters who had been told by Iran's Shi'ite Ayatollah Khomeini to lay down their arms. The Marsh Arabs were playing a dangerous game when they hid the deserters, who were shot on sight if they were discovered.

Sayid and I made a small campfire, communicating as best we could.

'Soon marshes here all gone,' Savid sighed, flattening his outstretched hand as if to show that the shallow waters of the region were steadily getting lower and lower.

'Saddam take water out, he not put back. Everything now dies here,' he said, gazing out over the water as if afraid it might disappear before his eyes.

We sat in silence for a few moments, paying our respects to a landscape which, if Saddam had his way, would soon be no more.

'What religion are you?' I asked.

'Shi'ite,' he said, throwing back his shoulders and raising his chin as he spoke.

'What do you think of Saddam Hussein?' I continued, probing a little deeper.

'Saddam – he very big man,' he said, with a reserved look that probably hid his true feelings.

It was not safe to be critical of the Iraqi leader. He had spies everywhere and nobody knew who to trust, as even children told their teachers about what their parents did at home.

'And Khomeini?'

'Khomeini people fighting, bang-bang,' he replied, lifting the long pole out of the water to show me his skill with an imaginary machine gun.

I suspected he was also amusing himself, giving me the sort of answer he imagined an innocent tourist wanted to hear.

★

The next morning, we left early and Sayid took us further out into the reeds, the thrusting swing of his body silhouetted against the rising sun as he navigated the craft with ease. It was so peaceful travelling through the reed beds, listening to the calls of the pygmy cormorants as they dive-bombed the busy waters, searching for their next meal. The orange rays of the morning sun danced lazily with the mists of the delta and seemed to set fire to the Iraqi landscape.

We reached a part of the marshes where great herds of black water buffalo grazed indolently in the shallows. It was fascinating to see how they formed the basis of the marsh economy. They seemed to be everywhere, and grazed freely on the bulrushes that grew along the edges of the waterways. They swam with their heads above the water and were guided along mostly by the village children, who rounded them up in the evenings.

Near a division in the waterway, Sayid pulled the *mashuf* over against the riverbank and looked for a place to disembark.

'Are we stopping here?' I asked.

The sun was pouring golden footpaths along the narrow reed beds as Sayid edged the *mashuf* closer to the shoreline. I began to see the humpbacked houses of his village through the blanket of fog that had settled along the island. A pied kingfisher rose from the rushes and warned the inhabitants of our approaching craft. As we neared the settlement, I could see how the wispy white smoke rising from little flickering fires in their doorways mixed with the marsh fog and hung like a murky mist above the island.

We landed the craft beside a fleet of other small *mashufs* laden with green grasses and fodder for the village animals, which were still grazing in the shallow waters. A small boy appeared from the twilight shadows of the reeds and helped to pull the prow of the *mashuf* ashore.

'*Salaam alaikum*,' I ventured feebly, unsure of what language they spoke in the marshes.

'*Alaikum as-salaam*,' he replied, eyeing me with some curiosity.

Sayid disembarked and pulled the front of the small craft a little further into the vegetation. The marsh boy then bade us goodbye and hastily scrambled onto the back of a nearby water buffalo, calling to the others to follow him home for the night. The morning air was scented with the bitter smell of roasting coffee. I walked with Sayid towards his dwelling, which lay at the near edge of the marsh island.

'You know, the Ma'dan are still like the Bedouins Arabs – they gather together in the mornings to drink strong coffee and talk about their problems,' Sayid said. 'They have the traditions and religion of the people from Arabia.'

I was aware that the Marsh Arabs, despite what Sayid thought, had closer connections to the culture of the ancient Sumerians who had lived several millennia earlier in what is now Iraq.

We entered a dwelling through a small platform that had been constructed from fence poles and bundles of reeds. There was a woven-reed partition hanging above the doorway that appeared to separate this structure from the sleeping and cooking quarters within. I imagined that this flap could be tied in position in the wintertime, to resist the icy winds that would blow south from the snowy Hakari Mountains in Kurdistan.

The interior of his *sarifa* was much smaller than I had expected, and I began to wonder where I was going to spend the night. Two women stood to greet Sayid as we entered.

'This is my mother – and my sister Nadam,' he said.

Sayid's *chadored* mother approached me, devotedly kissing the back of my hand and repeatedly gripping it against her wrinkled forehead. His sister, an attractive young woman, was baking bread in a small pan by the fire.

She smiled at my embarrassment and continued stoking the glowing fire. The yellow flames jumped and twisted, casting golden reflections on the olive skin of her face and hands. I watched her as she kneaded the bread, and the time slowly ticked away between us to the sound of the crackling embers. She returned my gaze, blushing as she stopped to put more fuel from a pile of buffalo dung on the open fire, before returning to her bread-making duties.

I am sure Sayid saw my horrified expression as I considered my next meal.

'Eet's very good, burns smoky and keeps the mosquitoes away,' he explained.

He could see that I was not convinced and then he jokingly continued in a vein that reminded me of the remarks of the fishermen in Basra: 'My friend, thank Allah that we didn't bring our camels from Arabia to the marshes of southern Iraq!'

I had lost my appetite!

★

I found the Ma'dan a fascinating group of people. In retrospect, I'm sorry I only made one journey to their delta home and didn't find more time to share with them. I could never have imagined while sitting on the wall outside our house in Garrison that I would one day see the reed beds that Thesiger had described, and meet descendants of the people he had met.

15.
JOURNEY TO KURDISTAN

Many of the patients on the oncology ward at Ibn al-Bitar Hospital were suffering from aplastic anaemia, a rare form of bone-marrow cancer, which left them unable to make mature blood cells. It did not go unnoticed that the majority of patients suffering from this condition came from the north-eastern area of Kurdistan, where Ali Hassan al-Majid – acting under direct orders from Saddam Hussein – took the decision to use tabun nerve agent and mustard gas against the Kurdish population during the Halabja attack about two years earlier. A video team from the Iranian army had captured the grotesque horror of this bombing attack. Five thousand people, mostly women and children, had been killed in the first two days, and nearly ten thousand others suffered from injuries that took their lives later. These wretched patients presented in Kurdish hospitals around Sulaymaniyah, and future problems associated with cyanide poisoning caused by tabun went mostly undocumented.

Mustard gas was first used effectively in 1917, by the German army against British and Canadian soldiers near Ypres. Since that time, it has been used in several wars. Doctors discovered as early as 1919 that it caused decreased counts of white blood cells, and it was trialled as a therapy for Hodgkin's lymphoma and other types of lymphoma and leukaemia. The mutagenic and carcinogenic effects of mustard agent mean that victims who recover from mustard-gas burns have an increased risk of developing cancer in later life. It was impossible not to feel the deepest of sorrow for these poor people.

In hindsight, it was probably during an arduous night taking blood cultures on the oncology ward that I made up my mind to visit the area where the nitrogen mustard gassing had occurred. I had always had a sense of adventure and a desire to experience historical events at first hand. But I was also aware that travel to that part of Iraq was forbidden.

When I floated the idea with my colleagues who had been in Iraq longest, each and every one of them considered it too dangerous to attempt such an expedition in the aftermath of the trial of nurse Daphne Parish. Many Iraqis were already pointing fingers at British hospital staff, accusing them of being spies. Perhaps it was the experience of growing up in Northern Ireland that spurred me on, as I had been raised in a place where propaganda reigned supreme, and sometimes it was difficult to tell fact from fiction unless you witnessed it with your own eyes.

In late June, I started to put my plans in place. With a camera and four rolls of film in my orange backpack, I went to the taxi rank outside the Alawi al-Hilla bus station, looking for an English-speaking driver to take me to Mosul, in the heart of Kurdistan. I wandered amongst the drivers at the station, chatting and trying to glean as much information as possible; the secret police came in many guises, so I had to be careful about my choice. I was hoping to meet a Kurdish-speaking driver who wouldn't be afraid to take me from Mosul across the backbone of the mountains to the cities of Erbil and Sulaymaniyah when it was required. In this way, I hoped to avoid drawing the attention of the secret police to my final destination: Halabja.

Eventually, I found a friendly young driver, Mohammed, who appeared to possess the right credentials. 'You want to go to Kurdistan?' he asked, in disbelief, when I told him my plan. I chatted to him for a while, trying to gauge his interest in making the journey north. Then we haggled over the price of the trip. I was carrying more than a thousand American dollars, but the cultural norm was to bargain, and I felt it was important to follow tradition. We agreed to travel to Mosul, Erbil and Sulaymaniyah for four hundred dinars. I decided not to mention the visit to Halabja until later.

Mohammed took me back to his house, where he said goodbye to his family and collected a change of clothes. I felt apprehensive about travelling to northern Iraq without telling my friends at the hospital where I was going. It was a conscious decision, though: I didn't want anybody in Baghdad to know about my journey. The larger the number of people who knew, the greater the chance of being caught by the secret police.

I had a strange sense of elation as I left Baghdad behind. The apparatus of the state was everywhere, and the Mukhabarat ruled a nation where violence was legitimised by a network of informers who accepted the situation as some sort of 'necessary evil' on the road to progress. As hired workers in this realm, we doctors and nurses at Ibn al-Bitar stood idly by and helped the regime perpetuate this system. Like many other Westerners, we justified it to ourselves, even as the smell of the bodies of so-called 'enemies of the state' grew stronger by the day. Although we distanced ourselves from it, we were really prostitutes in the cradle of civilisation, selling our souls for blood money supplied by the black gold that lay under Iraq. In my own way, I was finally rebelling against the regime, standing idly by no longer.

I peered out the window at the countryside as the taxi followed the signs towards the town of Tikrit, the village of Saddam Hussein's birth. Most senior members of the Iraqi government came from Saddam's own Tikriti tribe, the Al-Bu Nasir, and bore the same surname, 'al-Tikriti'. The village of Tikrit was special to the Kurds, because it was the birthplace of the famous twelfth-century Islamic leader, Saladin, who was Kurdish. Saddam Hussein frequently compared himself to this great leader, but at the same time openly commanded genocide against the sultan's descendants.

As we progressed north, I played my cassette tapes, a mixture of U2, Bob Marley and John Lennon. They brought a sense of comfort as our journey brought us through the fertile plains of Samarra, where we passed fields of golden wheat and farmers harvesting their crops. As evening fell, we reached the mud-walled buildings of the village of Ash-Sharqat, where Mohammed pulled the car over to a little roadside garage. The town had an Arabic feel, with palm trees overlooking single-storey homes, each of which had a little courtyard. The main street was quiet, and there didn't appear to be any soldiers in sight. To the east lay Kirkuk and the oilfields. To the north, one could see the low banks of white clouds that hung around the eastern foothills of Kurdistan.

The garage owner, a jovial man with red capillaried cheeks and a flowing handlebar moustache, appeared. He approached us with welcoming arms, emitting a string of salutations in both Arabic and Kurdish. He told his son to guide Mohammed's car up an elevated concrete ramp and proceeded with the oil change. When that was finished, he gave the young boy a few dinars to go off to a tea shop for three glasses of sweet, blood-red tea.

'*Ingelterre?*' he asked, as he passed me a glass.

'*Irlanda!*' I said.

'*Ah, Irlanda,*' he said, and struck his right fist against his heart. 'Bobby Sands!'

He shook my hand firmly, as though he admired my nationality, or saw us as sharing a common history of oppression and suffering. In many ways, the feeling was reciprocal, and was possibly the reason that I was going to visit Halabja. I thought about Bobby Sands and the injustices of Northern Ireland, aware that the British had a long history in this area. Only seventy years earlier, the Royal Air Force had shot and bombed the Kurds as they worked in their fields, in an attempt to gain control of the new oilfields in nearby Kirkuk.

We continued on to Mosul, a major trading city and home to more than a million people. It was late in the evening when we reached the outskirts, where we found a hotel near Babatub Square. The city lay on the ancient caravan route that ran between Europe and India, and Marco Polo passed through on his way to China. However, its importance declined with the opening of the Suez Canal, which made it easier to transport goods east from Europe by sea. The discovery of oil in Kirkuk had somewhat restored Mosul's fortunes, and a new pipeline had been constructed to carry the crude product to the Mediterranean ports by way of Turkey and Syria.

Although it was late in the evening, there were a lot of old men still sitting around the square chatting. The narrow streets were bustling with people dressed in Kurdish-style baggy trousers, gathered at the waist and tapered at the ankle. The women were mostly dressed in Anatolian costume, although many of the older ones wore black *chadors*, highlighting the large number of Sunni Muslims who inhabited the area. The restaurants were already full, mostly offering helpings of a rice dish. When I saw it was *pilav*, I realised that we were only about fifty miles from the Turkish border.

Everything was peaceful in Mosul. It somehow seemed devoid of the petty pressures and suspicions of downtown Baghdad. With a few beers on board, I decided it might be a good time to approach Mohammed about the delicate subject of Halabja. He told me he had been brought up in Sulaymaniyah, about fifty miles from the town.

'Have you ever been in Halabja?' I asked.

'Yes,' Mohammed said, beginning to look uneasy.

'Can I go and see it?'

'No, it is not allowed,' he said, waving his finger in the air in front of me. 'It is forbidden to go there!'

I felt it was better not to pursue the subject. We chatted for a while longer, and then I made my excuses and said goodnight. I had completed the first part of my journey and spent the rest of the evening carefully updating my diary.

★

Mosul sprang to life in the early morning. People gathered in little groups outside open-fronted bakeries to buy fresh flatbread, and the smell from the long flat ovens reminded me of eastern Turkey. This was a city that had existed two thousand years before the birth of Christ, and I was humbled to be in the presence of such antiquity, as my guidebook indicated that one of the gates of Nineveh was close by. Mohammed and I went to a bus garage, where we saw some mud-brick towers and reconstructed stone walls, probably the Shamash entrance to the ancient city.

After Nineveh, we left for Sulaymaniyah and the endless expanse of inhospitable, colourless hills where it was nestled. We passed young shepherd boys tending to their flocks as we travelled further east into the low foothills of the mountains. Every now and then, as sunlight reflected from the blue-green tiles on the dome of some local village mosque, Mohammed would laugh and say, 'Kurdistani telephones!' and point to where the last flash had occurred. He was referring to the fact that the Kurdish *peshmerga* often used mirrors to signal messages from one village to another in the days before mobile phones. The barren landscape grew more desolate as the daylight colours started to fade, and the hillside anemones faded into the treeless slopes.

We drove through the low mountains, past a succession of little villages, towards the outer boundaries of Erbil, the fourth-largest city in Iraq, stopping for a while near the Kaisary market to take some photographs. The journey to Sulaymaniyah took us about two hours along a two-lane highway, skirting the city of Kirkuk. We passed some checkpoints near the oilfields in the Baba Gurgur region, where we could see long yellow flames emerging from along the pipelines. Historically, the Kurdish people saw the area around Kirkuk as theirs, as they had lived there for over a thousand years. However, the recent government-planned Arabisation of the area had successfully diluted the Kurdish population.

We reached the town of Sulaymaniyah as twilight approached, and rented rooms in a modest hotel on a small square in the heart of the bazaar area. The hotelier was a Kurd called Zamo. Pictures in the hotel of the Imam Mosque in Isfahan suggested that he had close affiliations with Iran; we were getting close to the border. We talked for a little about Halabja, although I was careful not to disclose my interest in the town.

The next morning, over breakfast, Zamo and I got into conversation about how Saddam was not the first to use gas against the Kurds. It came as a surprise to me when he told me that the British had once ruled the area, and that Winston Churchill was the first to use gas against the Kurds.

'Have you been up to see Halabja?' I asked.

'No. No one is allowed in, but I've heard there's nothing much to see. The Iraqis have removed all the evidence,' he said.

Over breakfast, I decided to come clean with Mohammed, and told him that I was a doctor. I explained that I had treated many patients from the area who had presented with blood diseases and cancers. It was important, I said, that the outside world hear about what had happened in Halabja. He was obviously frightened but, nevertheless, I could see he was giving it some thought.

'Only *peshmerga* can take you over the hills to Halabja,' he whispered. 'It's not safe and they will need money.'

He left to make some phone calls, and I considered my position with some trepidation. If I were caught travelling with *peshmerga*, Kurdish rebels, into a restricted area, I would probably receive a long jail sentence.

When Mohammed returned he said, 'It's settled. I'll take you to meet them and they will take you to Halabja.'

He said he would wait at the hotel in Sulaymaniyah for two days and, if I had not returned by then, he would leave without me.

We set off, heading due south for Arbat, hoping to make the mountainous village of Darbandikhana before evening. We stopped for lunch at a restaurant where many Hino and Mercedes trucks were parked, painted brightly in the Baluchistani fashion. The entrance was lit by rows of little red light bulbs strung around the tree trunks. I stood in the park admiring the vehicles, each with its own regional decoration, with images that probably signified memorable events in the drivers' lives.

It was a tranquil afternoon, and the sound of Kurdish music lingered in the still air. Several men, who I assumed were truck drivers, were seated around a table drinking tea and playing cards. The one nearest me carried a small, bent knife tucked into his *peshtwen*, that broad plaited sash that Kurdish men use as a belt. They began laughing loudly at one of their group, who I presumed was losing, as he banged the wooden table repeatedly in frustration. The waiter showed us to a table by the window and offered us some sweetened tea in two miniature tulip glasses.

'I can take you no further,' Mohammed said. 'You must wait here, and I'll go get some friends.'

One of the card players stared at me for a few minutes, as if suspicious of my presence. I realised that he had probably never seen a European traveller this deep into Kurdish territory before – but he didn't seem particularly unfriendly. He smiled at me through a mouthful of decaying teeth.

Mohammed drove off in the direction from which we had come. I waited alone at the restaurant for several hours.

16.
VISITING HALABJA

Evening came and still there was no sign of Mohammed. Strangely, I felt no fear, but rather a sense of living in the midst of history and experiencing for myself what had happened there. Dusk was already falling when he returned with two men, both dressed in loose Kurdish clothes. They shook hands with the waiter, as if they already knew him, before joining me at the table.

'These are my friends – they'll take you to Halabja,' Mohammed said casually.

'Hello, my name is Jamal,' one of the men said, stretching out his hand to greet me.

'And I am Soubhi,' the other said. 'Would you like to eat? Those deep-fried *kibbeh* look good,' he continued, pointing to some food on display.

The waiter brought us bottled water and a plate of Kurdish flat-bread.

For a while we chatted about David O'Leary and Ireland's chances of winning the World Cup in Italy, before Jamal got to the point.

'You want to go to Halabja?' he asked.

He leaned back in his chair and gazed at me as though making a private assessment.

'The army has roadblocks around the lake and it is forbidden to go there except with special permission,' he said. 'You cannot take photographs or you will be arrested.'

He looked at me closely, obviously unsure whether to be amazed at my tenacity or my naiveté.

I leaned forward to meet his eyes and said, 'Do you think it's possible? How much would it cost?'

'It's possible. Two hundred American dollars.'

I agreed to the price, but felt embarrassed as I had told Mohammed I only had Iraqi money.

Jamal then opened a small bag, revealing some grey-and-white striped traditional Kurdish clothes. I would have to travel in disguise.

Mohammed changed his mind and said he would drive us to the lakeshore and leave us to walk the rest of the way.

'It's only about fifteen kilometres – two hours across the mountains. It is better we don't sleep tonight and go into the village in the morning,' Jamal said.

★

We drove about ten kilometres up the road to a hydroelectric project called the Darbandikhan Dam. The dying sun gently ended the day, casting weary shadows on the surrounding hills. We waited at the hydroelectric dam until about two o'clock in the morning and then Soubhi advised Mohammed to take a desolate southerly route that ran across the river, in order to try and miss the army patrols. I wondered whether his friends were actually *peshmerga*. It surprised me how focused they were, not allowing themselves to indulge in small talk for long, and continually watching the hills around us.

On a deserted part of the road, Mohammed stopped the car and opened the boot to get my knapsack. Jamal retrieved a large assault rifle from the boot and slung it over his shoulder. It was only then that I realised the great risk we were taking. If an Iraqi patrol had opened the boot, we'd have been arrested and they'd have thrown away the key.

Mohammed's friends had seriously escalated the danger for me, but I said nothing, knowing the rifle gave us a level of respectability in the mountains. He didn't speak as he handed me the orange knapsack and camera.

'I'll see you back at the restaurant,' I said, and he nodded.

Jamal sensed my apprehension.

'Have courage,' he said.

The lake beside us supplied a large part of Iraq's fresh water and electricity. It was a strategic location, and the thought struck me that Iranian forces might have crossed the border into Halabja in order to take over the power station. Maybe Saddam had used poisonous gas to try to force the Iranian army to retreat.

Trekking in single file, we travelled deeper into the mountains. Jamal stopped to have a cigarette, and I noticed the way he covered it with his hands, not wanting to send out a signal. Even in the moonlight, one could see a long way. We walked slowly, passing some herds of black goats, but no words were spoken.

Eventually we reached a collection of shacks on the outskirts of Halabja, where we sat on a stone wall and waited for the dawn. Some dogs barked, and I felt they would surely give away our presence. The sun rose in a blaze of orange and saffron and lit up the surrounding countryside. In daylight, one could see that many buildings had been razed, while others had half-built block walls with sheets of galvanised iron to give them stability.

When the sun was fully up, one of the men went ahead to see if it was safe to enter the town. He returned after about twenty minutes, and we went to meet the wakening townsfolk. On the way into the town, Jamal pointed to an old rusted iron casing. It was about three or four feet long, with a long barrel and a conical top.

'Gas shells!' he said, and spat in disgust.

I took a photograph of the casing, amazed that something so crude could wreak so much destruction. The photograph would provide evidence of Saddam's inhumanity to his fellow man.

'There are many cases here, some unexploded,' Jamal said.

It seemed that some families actually used these unexploded shells as roof supports when building their houses. I thought of how hard it must be to raise a child in this environment, as every day one was reminded of the scourge of war. Jamal hung his rifle on his back as we approached a small hospital near the centre of town.

'Can we go into the hospital?' I asked Jamal.

'No!' he said, wagging his finger in the air. 'Saddam's men there!'

We had breakfast at a little restaurant, where people were reticent about interacting with us. I felt quite foolish making an appearance dressed in Kurdish gear. After about thirty minutes, we met someone who was willing to talk about the gassing but said he didn't want to be photographed. The old man was hesitant at first, but later talked freely.

'They started shelling early in the morning,' he said. 'Everyone was frightened and all the children were crying with the sound from the aircraft overhead. Then a smell of garlic filled the shelter and everyone knew it was a chemical.'

He took a deep breath and allowed it to escape slowly, as if remembering took an act of tremendous will.

'My eyes were burning and they bombed us for hours. When it was over, I discovered my family were dead. The next day, we found my brother with his skin blue.'

I looked into the old man's eyes and realised that I had heard enough. Whatever urgency had brought me here to share this experience was now gone. I was frightened by the horror of it and wanted to get back to the safety of the Ibn al-Bitar Hospital as quickly as possible. This man had looked death straight in the face, and I didn't want to join him.

The sight of demolished buildings in the hills around me bore testimony to what had happened during Saddam's Anfal Campaign, also known as the Kurdish Genocide, of which the Halabja chemical attack was only one small part. I took some photographs as mementos, and we left the town to make our way back along the mountains, moving at a more hurried pace. My guides pointed to small empty hamlets in the far-off hills. The villagers, they said, had been brought by lorry to 'resettlement camps' near the towns. We walked back along the lake to the village of Darbandikhan, where a car was waiting to bring me back to the restaurant.

At about one o'clock, Mohammed returned to the restaurant as promised. I was never so relieved to see anyone in my life and greeted him like a long-lost friend. We started our journey home, following the road back to Sulaymaniyah mostly in silence. The track was narrow, lined with hillside hamlets where children played with their dogs in the dust. Sometimes the road curved, and I glimpsed herds of goats and sheep in the valley below.

Mohammed seemed very apprehensive, his eyes fixed on the rear-view mirror. I glanced over my shoulder and, through the dust in our wake, saw what was causing his concern. There was a green army lorry coming at speed behind us.

'Do you think they're following us?' I asked.

'I don't know – I think so,' he stuttered, shaking his head as though trying to clear it.

We drove onto a narrow dirt track which led to a village. The lorry was still there. There was now little doubt that it was following us.

We cut back onto the main road at the next intersection. Mohammed accelerated in a frenzied attempt to outrun them. Another lorry appeared on the far-off horizon, blocking our path. My skin crawled as we neared it, and the soldiers got out on the road with an array of machine guns slung carelessly around their necks.

I felt goose pimples break out all over my body. We were the only vehicle on the road, and I knew there would be no witnesses if anything should happen to us. Frantically, I pulled off my Kurdish clothes, realising that a European in this attire would only arouse more suspicion. A black-and-grey petrol tanker was parked up ahead, and I shouted at Mohammed to stop the taxi. I jumped out and hid the rolls of film on a small side-rail, which carried the fuel hosepipes.

A jeep shrieked to a halt in front of our car, blocking our exit should we decide to make a run for it again. Three young soldiers jumped down and approached us. One of them opened Mohammed's door, screaming as he pulled him from the vehicle. A second soldier pointed his rifle at me through the open door, while a third opened the passenger door and hauled me outside.

My bundle of Kurdish clothes were taken and thrown on the road. They found my camera, and some rolls of undeveloped film, lying on the back seat. These were snaps I had taken of the flames in the oilfields and of a large, brightly lit bridge outside Sulaymaniyah. The oilfields were in a strategic location, and I knew they could be interpreted as evidence of military espionage. This would be indefensible in an Iraqi military court. Similar cases had been punished with penalties of up to ten years imprisonment.

The soldiers proceeded to dismantle the taxi, taking out the back seats and tossing them by the roadside. Their painstaking inspection continued for about thirty minutes before they bundled us into one of the jeeps. Thankfully, during the inspection, the driver of the petrol tanker returned and unwittingly drove off with the pictures I had taken in Halabja.

Mohammed tried to plead with the soldiers, but they were not sympathetic. At one stage, the exchange became heated and he was punched viciously in the face. I found myself willing him to be quiet so they wouldn't kill him for talking back.

My father and mother with (from left to right) Raymond,
Bernadette, Sean, Anne, me and Brian

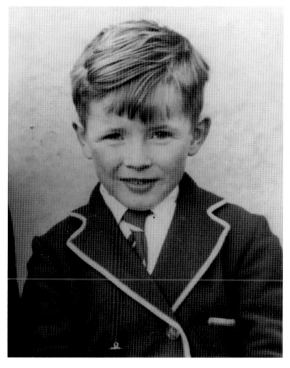

Attending Devenish
No. 2 Primary School

Graduating (centre) from Queen's University, Belfast, with (from left to right) Raymond, Sean, Mo, my mother and my father

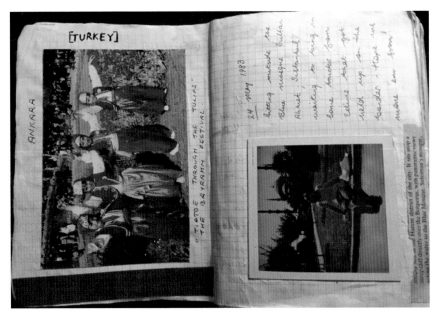

Pages from my travel journal,1982-83

In Istanbul on a Turkey Run in 1983

Graduating from the Royal College of Surgeons
with a medical degree in 1986

On holiday with Trish in Cahors, France

On the South Island of New Zealand in 1988, near Dunedin

At the Taj Mahal, while traveling back to Ireland
from New Zealand in 1988

In 1989, working as an orthopaedic SHO in
Our Lady's Children's Hospital in Crumlin

In 1990, with Chris Duckling (standing, centre) and others
in Room 908 at Ibn al-Bitar Hospital, Baghdad

In northern Iraq in 1990

In Erbil, northern Iraq, in 1990, on the way to Halabja

Fermanagh Herald

No. 4,416.   SATURDAY, 20 APRIL, 1991   PRICE 30p

(30p in Republic of Ireland)

LOCAL DOCTOR'S FRIENDSHIP WITH THE KURDS

'WEST INDIFFERENT TO THEIR MISERY'

THE PLIGHT of the Kurds fleeing the troops of Saddam Hussein as seen in newspaper and on our television screens has horrified people throughout the world. As the refugees die in their thousands attempting to reach safety over the Turkish border, we publish exclusively in the 'Herald' the thoughts of a local doctor who has travelled this area extensively and lived amongst these people in the Summer of 1990, often evading capture in his attempt to document and photograph their way of life.

Dr. P.J. Treacy, son of Mrs. Sheila Treacy and the late Patrick

In Moscow after the dissolution of the USSR in December 1991

In the Ngorongoro Crater in 1992, with local Masaai people

In Bulawayo,
Zimbabwe, in 1992

In the Okavango Delta with Richard, before the rugby match

Wiith Nurse Judy on the Carnival Cruise Lines ship *Jubilee* in 1992

Wiith Julianne (left), who was born aboard the *Jubilee,*
and her brother, in New York for Julianne's Communion

In 1996, with the Royal Flying Doctor Service
in Broken Hill, New South Wales, Australia

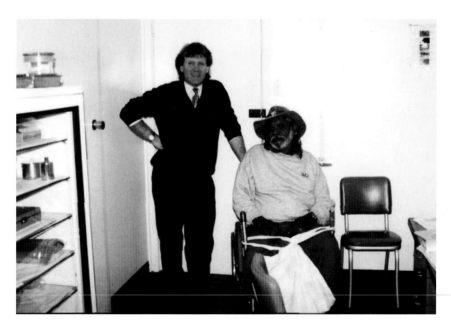

With a patient in 1996 at the hospital in Willcania,
New South Wales, Australia

At Ground Zero in New York, two weeks after
the terrorist attack of 11 September 2001

Outside Neverland on the day of Michael Jackson's funeral in 2009

Outside the Cathedral of Our Lady of the Assumption in
Port-au-Prince, Haiti, not long after the 2010 earthquake

With Bishop
Pierre Dorcilien
on the Doolough
Famine Walk in
2011

in Monrovia, Liberia, opening an orphanage for
the organisation Michael Jackson's Legacy 2012

With Botox pioneer Dr Jean Carruthers (left),
and Dr Tim Flynn, one of America's top dermatologists

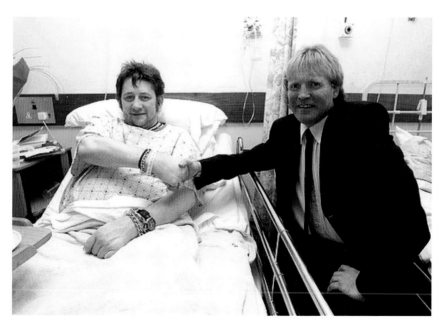

With Shane MacGowan of the Pogues
in St Vincent's Hospital, Dublin

With Jay-Z at the United Nations Association
awards in New York

With Bono at the United Nations Association
awards in New York

17.
PRISONER OF SADDAM

After about thirty minutes, we reached an army complex with a heavily fortified front entrance. The soldiers brought us out into a central courtyard, where we were separated and led to different buildings. We were to be interrogated independently. In all our careful planning, we had not discussed what we should say if we were caught. I was brought down a short corridor to a little cell, about six feet square, which contained a small bed with a filthy mattress. The steel door was locked, and I was left alone. I sat on the bed and tried to gather my thoughts.

The soldiers had taken my passport, camera and film, but left my watch. I was concerned that it had only been a short time since Daphne Parish had been sentenced, and soon they would realise that I was working at the same hospital. They also had my rucksack and would certainly have my pictures developed. No matter how I tried to organise the thoughts in my head, I kept coming to the same conclusion – I was in trouble.

I could hear noises, as if people were walking outside in the corridor, but no one entered my cell. The time passed slowly, and I knew it must be getting dark outside, but still nobody came to interrogate me. I must have fallen asleep because the next thing I remembered was an old man, dressed in a long white *dishdasha*, standing over my bed. He carried a tray with some jam and flatbread and encouraged me to eat.

'Do you speak English?' I inquired.

He put his hands to his lips and shook his head, indicating that he could not. When he left, the door was locked under the careful scrutiny of the soldiers on duty outside. I sat down on the mattress and started to eat. Once I had finished, I lay on the bed for a long time, trying to get back to sleep. Night fell and, with it, darkness entered my spirit. I had read of horrific acts performed in Iraqi prisons, and I prowled the room in silence, wondering what to do next, realising there was absolutely nothing I *could* do. I knew I had to be strong and face the consequences of my actions. Knowing what time it was brought me some small comfort, and I was thankful they had let me keep my watch.

During the night, there was a lot of shouting in Arabic, and the agonising screams of a prisoner being beaten. My heart hammered in my chest and I hoped it wasn't Mohammed. At one stage I thought I heard my name being called, and feared the worst. What devastation had I brought on this man by my decision to travel to Halabja? Over the next three hours, the steel doors along the corridor banged open and closed, as other prisoners were arrested and interrogated.

Morning came and the sun shone through a slit in the passageway under my door. At about ten o'clock, the door of my cell opened and two men entered. They escorted me down the corridor to a room where a group of soldiers sat smoking around a small table. My passport lay open beside them, and my camera was propped up with the lens facing the ceiling. One soldier spoke to me in perfect English.

'What are you doing in this area? What kind of pictures have you taken?' he asked.

'Mostly farmers in the fields, and a group of Kurds I met in Sulaymaniyah.'

'How do you know the driver of the car you were travelling in?'

'I met him today in a restaurant in a little village near here.'

'Who were the other people who were travelling in the taxi last night?'

I shrugged my shoulders and did my best to look confused.

They had found my Kurdish clothes in the back seat, but they had no way of knowing I had been to Halabja, unless Mohammed had talked. On balance, I decided he would never admit to organising my trip, or to any wrongdoing, as he was only too aware of the consequences of such an admission. They continued their interrogation, but I wouldn't admit to being in the taxi the night before.

'Why are you taking photographs in Iraq?' he asked.

'I like the country and the people,' I replied, 'trying to look as innocent as possible.

'Where are you working here?'

'At Ibn al-Bitar Hospital. You can ring them to check if you wish.'

The exchange continued and, as it progressed, I felt less intimidated by the interviewer, although I worried about being lulled into a false sense of security. I told him again that he could verify my story if he phoned the hospital, and hoped in doing so that he would let people know where I was.

'What part of England do you come from?'

'I'm an Irish citizen,' I said. 'You have my passport.'

'Where did you go to college?'

'In Dublin.'

'Do you know Trinity College?' he continued.

'Yes, very well, but I didn't go to college there. How do you know Trinity College?'

He stood up abruptly and folded some papers in front of him. He looked at me and said, 'We already know that is where you are working, but we will have to check some other things later in the day.'

The preliminary interview ended abruptly, and an escort took me back to my cell. I was gratified things had gone so easily and sensed that the interviewer had been trained in the West, possibly even in Dublin. There had been no mention of the photograph that I had taken of the bridge, and I could only suppose they were waiting for the film to be developed. Maybe that was what he meant when he said they would be checking out some things later.

The day dragged on slowly and nobody bothered about me for many hours. I realised how hard it would be to serve a jail sentence and thought of all the poor prisoners languishing in jails up and down the country. During the day, I heard the sound of a man sobbing and felt it was only a matter of time before the soldiers inflicted this level of interrogation on me. My thoughts turned to Mohammed and what was happening to him. Only my jailer broke the monotony that day, bringing me food on three occasions and allowing me a visit to the outside toilet on another. The soldiers in the corridor never smiled, looking at me as something of interest rather than of concern. I read some of the graffiti on the walls, each word a protest in another language. This was not the script of drunken prisoners, but of those threatened with extinction by the state apparatus of Saddam Hussein.

When night fell, the lights went out and again I was alone in the darkness. It is easy to become hopelessly lost in the silence and isolation. It was important not to allow guilt to take over – that would ensure the absence of objective thought. I wondered if they were playing a game with me and if the level of interrogation would increase with each passing day. They could easily find my driving licence, associate me with the Nissan Patrol that Daphne Parish had driven, link me to the journey to Halabja, and I could end up with a lengthy sentence as a spy – or worse. I wondered what had happened to Jamal and his friend, and remembered his words before we started the journey: 'Have courage!'

My mind raced. After a while, I fell into a sort of trance, somewhere between waking and sleeping. I began dreaming about a priest who had taught my religion classes at St Michael's in Enniskillen when I was a teenager. In my dream, he spoke to me in a soft Monaghan accent. 'What is courage? Is it the absence of fear? No, it is the ability to stand up against things that are unjust, knowing that the consequences of your action might be physical injury.' My mind swirled, following the different experiences in my life and taking me right back to where I had started.

I awoke in a sweat and looked at my watch. It wasn't yet six o'clock in the morning, and already there was the noise of people washing themselves in the bathroom area outside. A cockroach scurried across the floor. Normally, I would have killed it, but some-how I felt guilty taking the life of the only other living thing in my cell. After a few hours, I was allowed to wash and was given a light breakfast, before the soldiers brought me back to the interrogation room. This time there appeared to be a judge at the table, and I was given the impression that a court was in session.

'How did you get to Sulaymaniyah?'

'I took a taxi.'

'Where did you get the taxi?'

'From the Alawi al-Hilla bus station.'

'Where did you go to?'

'To Mosul,' I said.

'And then where?'

'I got another taxi to Erbil.'

'And from there?'

'I got a taxi to Sulaymaniyah.'

'All different taxis?'

'Yes, all different taxis.'

'And where did you meet this driver?'

'I met him in that small village.'

'Then how do you explain this?' the judge said, sliding a picture across the table that I had taken of Mohammed with the garage owner outside Tikrit.

My heart sank. I had forgotten this photograph. Trying to stay focused, I wondered how many photographs they had developed and what Mohammed might have told them. I decided to say the photo-graphs were not mine, but I didn't know if some of the other pictures on the roll could incriminate me. Was I in any of them? I remem-bered changing a roll of film at Nineveh and another at Halabja.

'That picture must belong to the taxi driver,' I said, with what I hoped was conviction.

'And these?' showing me the pictures of Nineveh.

'They are mine,' I replied, hoping there were no photographs of myself and Mohammed together. I didn't think there were, as my camera was complex and I didn't trust anyone else with it.

'The taxi driver says he brought you there,' the judge said, fixing me with a stare.

'Why would he say that? I only met him this morning,' I said.

'What did you talk about in the taxi?'

'We talked about Kurdistan.'

'What did you say?'

'I told him it is not a real country and it is not recognised in the world.'

My answer resonated with a colonel beside me, who seemed to stand a little taller as he puffed out his chest, giving me an indication of the way they expected their questions should be answered.

'Have you been to Israel?' he asked, raising an eyebrow.

'No,' I answered.

The judge then produced the *Sunday Times* article about Halabja that I had carried with me on the journey from Baghdad, as it contained the names of people who I wanted to interview.

'Where did the driver get this?'

'I don't know – what is it?'

'It is an English newspaper not allowed in Iraq. You must have given it to him.'

They passed the paper over for my perusal.

I tapped the left-hand corner a few times with my finger and noted that the date on it was Sunday, 27 March 1988.

'It has nothing to do with me,' I said. 'Check my passport – I was in New Zealand then!'

'What were you doing in New Zealand?' the judge asked, clearly unimpressed.

'I was working as a doctor.'

'And why did you come to Iraq?'

'I was always fascinated by the Iraqi people, especially the Marsh Arabs.'

'Have you been to the marshes?'

'Yes, I have been to the marshes.'

'What do you think of Saddam Hussein?' the judge asked, changing tactics.

'I think he has brought a lot of literacy to Iraq, even to the people in the marshes.'

'Is this your photograph?' he said, showing me the picture of the bridge.

'Yes.'

'You will receive one year's jail sentence for this photograph.'

'Why?' I asked in astonishment.

'We think you are a spy, and this is a military bridge.'

'I am not a spy! The bridge had nice lights so I just took the photograph.'

'Do you think we are stupid?'

'Well, if I was a spy, surely I would have better photographs than these?' I said, becoming agitated.

The soldiers beside me moved in a little closer, in case I tried to do anything rash, I surmised.

'What type of photographs?' the judge asked.

'I don't know – ones of the army and things I suppose.'

The interrogation continued for another hour, covering the same topics. Why had I come to Iraq? Why was I taking photographs of sensitive military structures? Did I know the driver? Was this my newspaper?

I was returned to my cell, confident that I had stood up to the constant barrage of the interrogation, but shocked by the sentence of one year for taking a photograph of a bridge. If I was jailed in Iraq, how would I get my HIV tests, and what if they were positive? Where would I get treatment?

My thoughts turned to Mohammed. Because of me, they had arrested him and found the *Sunday Times* in his possession. Some of the photographs of the oilfields in Kirkuk were on the same rolls as the 'garage man', and his taxi had also been identified as being near the hydroelectric dam the night before. I knew he was in bigger trouble than me.

Evening came and, with it, the reality that I could be in prison in Iraq for the next year. I would have to forgo my GP registrar year in Scotland and would have to dig deep in the coming weeks to find the mental strength to face the sentence. Surely, the administration at the hospital would come looking for me and get the Irish embassy to secure my freedom. The next morning the questioning continued.

'The driver says he brought you to Halabja.'

'I was never there.'

'We have witnesses who saw you there.'

'Then bring them here.'

Jamal and his companion were perfectly at ease in Halabja. They only objected to visiting the hospital, which, when I thought about it, was understandable. At least some staff there had to be involved in the cover-up operation following the gas attack. I was pretty confident that no witnesses would come forward, unless they were forced by the army to do so. However, the Mukhabarat had deep tentacles, and anything was possible.

I thought of the advice my father had given me in Northern Ireland: 'If you're going to say anything – say nothing!' Remembering made me think of home, of how my mother would worry about me. Tears filled my eyes, and the interrogator, misreading the signals, increased his questioning, confident of a successful outcome.

'Where did you meet the driver?' the judge asked again.

I said nothing.

'Answer!' a soldier shouted, hitting the back of my head with the butt of his rifle.

I put my hand behind my head and felt the trickle of blood.

'There is no need for such things,' said the judge. 'I am sure the doctor will tell us everything he knows.'

'I've told you everything already,' I said, holding my head in the knowledge that this was only the beginning.

If Mohammed talked, I would probably be sentenced to many years in jail – or worse, be hanged like Bazoft. It was imperative that they didn't discover that the Nissan Patrol on my driving licence was the one used for the journey to the Al-Iskandaria military complex. It would be one coincidence too many. Strange to think that my future could be dictated by a penny-pinching accountant's refusal to scrap the car.

The questioning continued. Over and over they asked the same questions. They were trying to cloud my judgment. The judge seemed quite civilised, but I knew that if I diverted, even a little, from a previous answer it would be enough to hang me.

My mind was foggy as I tried to remember the information and my head hurt where I had been hit. They were trying to wear me down, slowly, bit by bit, day by day, and I knew it was going to get worse.

The soldiers returned me to my cell, and I was left alone for a few days, except for the delivery of food and trips to the toilet. At first I was relieved, but relief was quickly replaced by thoughts of what might happen to me. When I was brought back and forth to be inter-rogated, I at least felt I had some say in my own future. I could put up a good fight. Alone, I could only imagine what my fate might be.

Sometimes I would think of Mohammed, and I would be over-come with guilt. Had I followed my own lust for adventure to his detriment? These and many other thoughts were still racing through my head on the morning of the fifth day, when the door of my cell opened. A colonel, carrying a small handgun, came into my cell and sat on my bed. He left the gun between us, which immedi-ately aroused my suspicion.

My God, this is it – I'm going to be shot by the Revolutionary Council, I thought.

'What do you think of Iraq?' he asked.

I said nothing, just kept my eyes on the gun, wondering if this was some kind of test. 'You think we're all barbarians?' he said.

'No I don't,' I promptly replied, feeling that denial was in my best interest at this stage.

'Yes you do – but I know James Joyce and I know Trinity College.'

He replaced the gun in its holster, roughly pinned my arm behind my back and frog-marched me out of my cell. *He's leading me away to be tortured*, I thought.

We passed the soldiers guarding the cells and made our way down the corridor. I could almost feel his anger as he bent my arm into a more painful position. What had happened? Had they finally come across my driving licence in the little red pouch I'd carried?

The colonel marched me to the end of the building, opened a door with his key, and forced me outside. There was a stone path through the centre of a courtyard in front of me, although it seemed like a long way to walk with my back turned to an armed guard. I stood and looked back at the window in the door where the colonel was standing. He stared back at me but didn't speak. Then, through the bars of the window, he handed me the red pouch. There was some film in it, which they had exposed – and my driving licence. They hadn't put two and two together. He stared at me with cold, indifferent eyes, as if the life had died within them many years before.

'What about Mohammed, my taxi driver?' I asked.

He just stared at me without responding. I turned to walk down the long path, holding my breath, suppressing the desire to run. Would I be shot in the back as an escapee, or had I genuinely been released? The courtyard was empty except for a few soldiers guarding the entrance with Kalashnikovs slung over their shoulders. At the far end of the gate was a portrait of Saddam Hussein in traditional Iraqi dress, greeting Kurdish peasant women. In the distance, I could hear shots being fired, but the casual glance of the soldiers in that direction persuaded me it was probably of no consequence. In a few minutes I was through the outer perimeter and making my way back down the road. As I reached the end of the path I thought, *I'm free – I'm out of here.*

Eventually, I reached a taxi rank, where I found a driver who was willing to travel the four hundred kilometres back to Baghdad. Nobody at the hospital knew where I had been, and my immediate reaction was not to go back there. What if the secret police were watching me in order to see where I went or who I met up with? I decided to take the first flight out of the country.

When I reached Baghdad, I phoned Chris and told him to collect my belongings and meet me at the Hole in the Wall. He knew he would have to move clandestinely in order not to arouse the suspicions of the Mukhabarat. After I had recovered my possessions from him, we had a farewell drink, and I asked him to say goodbye to my friends.

'It's been good fun mate, stay safe. I just can't believe we nearly had another Dee Parish on our hands!' he smiled, shaking his head.

Then I went to the airport and caught the first flight to Europe.

★

In August, I met Hajj and some of the Ibn al-Bitar nurses at the Galway Races. We were in the bar, catching up and watching some horse racing on television when the programme was interrupted by a breaking *BBC News* bulletin.

'Quiet, everybody, and listen to this!' said Hajj.

The newscaster said, 'More than a hundred thousand Iraqi soldiers backed up by seven hundred tanks invaded the Gulf state of Kuwait in the early hours of this morning. Iraqi forces have established a provisional government and their leader Saddam Hussein has threatened to turn Kuwait City into a "graveyard" if any other country dares to challenge the "takeover by force".'

The Iraqi army had just invaded Kuwait, stating that it had always been a part of the Ottoman Empire's province of Basra, something that made it rightfully Iraqi territory; the British had made it a separate emirate after the First World War.

Tensions had been simmering for some time. Iraq had accused Kuwait of stealing Iraqi petroleum near the border through slant drilling. Kuwait said it was doing this to compensate for more than $80 billion it had loaned to Iraq to finance the Iran-Iraq war and which Saddam was refusing to pay back.

★

I later discovered that my roommate Chris and his girlfriend, Dr Mary O'Loughlin, had returned to Baghdad from a holiday in Turkey just as hostilities had commenced and had been held there as prisoners, unable to join the overland exodus through Syria. They were among many Western hostages held by the Iraqi regime during this time. In fact, all 450 of the hospital staff – British, Irish, Danish and American – were held, and Saddam threatened to place them in areas of military importance if Iraq was attacked by the West.

In the coming months, celebrity statesmen made their way to Baghdad to try to secure the release of these hostages. Photographs of Saddam with Jesse Jackson were splashed across the newspapers of the world. The singer Yusuf Islam, formerly known as 'Cat Stevens', secured the release of a trickle of hostages, but it was the former German prime minister, Willy Brandt, who scored the biggest success, when he landed in Frankfurt Airport with 174 freed hostages on board.

Around the time of the Gulf War, there was a series of popular rebellions in the northern and southern Iraqi provinces, which were referred to as the Sha'aban Intifada among Arabs and as the National Uprising among Kurds. After the war ended, Saddam Hussein's forces, spearheaded by the Iraqi Republican Guard, sought a terrible revenge on the Kurdish people for this uprising, and the streets I had walked in Mosul, Erbil and Sulaymaniyah ran red with their blood.

The vanquished people gathered in the tens of thousands and formed a haunting column of men, women and babies, all blindly stumbling through the snows of the Zakho Mountains, at the mercy of the wolves and the pursuing Iraqi army. Their anguish made the world listen, and my article about my journey to Halabja made the front page of the *Fermanagh Herald*.

18.
SCOTCH, WHISKEY ON THE ROCK AND WHITE RUSSIANS

A letter from Chris arrived for me in Scotland:

Truth is we have no problems (except for leaving!) and are free to move all over the country. Unfortunately it's not the same for some other companies, who have either taken up residence on the embassy lawn or are languishing in the local power station, etc., but by all accounts being well treated – food, four beers, two boxes of cigs a day, and all for free!

Mary Mac got trapped here when we came back from Turkey. She was at the end of contract and came back for luggage on 31 July. All is much as usual. Fr Pat is on the dry (except for gin + tonic) but your replacement is very inferior. Mary Mac is doing a clinic on the embassy lawns once a week, and it's one of the best parties going. Have fun in E'burgh – the street behind Princes St is wall-to-wall pubs, but I suppose you've found that out already.

Keep in touch. Pat says 'On-On', in memory of the call sign of the Baghdad Hash House Harriers that we used when out jogging together.

—Chris (Happy Hostage)

What a role reversal! Just a few weeks earlier, we had said goodbye to each other in a pub in Baghdad, and now he and Pat McGlynn were prisoners in Room 908. I was surprised the Iraqi government had allowed him to get a letter out.

*

I was settling into the life of a Scottish general practitioner, under the tutelage of Dr Nigel Woods and Dr Fergus McRae. Both men worked hard to provide the community with a good level of service. The practice had an on-call room in nearby Bangour General Hospital, which I shared with a doctor from India and another from Nigeria.

General practice was a new way of life for me, and there were some funny incidents. On my very first evening on call, a distressed mother rang and spoke to me in a thick Scottish accent.

'Cud ya cum outa the house? Me bairn's grating,' she said.

'Your bearing is grating?'

'Yes, me bairn's grating terribly all day!'

'Sorry – this is the doctor's – are you sure you don't need a mechanic?' I innocently replied, remembering all the grating bearings I'd replaced in my father's garage in Garrison.

Lindsey, a nurse who also stayed at Bangour, informed me that a 'grating bairn' was the Scottish way of saying a 'crying child'. We laughed about the peculiarities of the Scottish language.

*

I soon got a letter from the chef at Ibn al-Bitar, Robbie Sweeney, who updated me on what was left of the Baghdad Blues Band.

> The Baghdad Blues Band now consists of Sean, Carl, Declan, Serge (Italian guy!) and Neil from the lab on lead guitar and he is good. Carl got a visa, thank God, for we're getting fed up listening to Declan trying to sing. Luke had joined the band, but, as you probably know by now, he ran out across the border, thank God. We are hoping to be home on 15 Dec as PARC have proposed this. I'm hoping to buy a pub in Drogheda. Any word from Trish or could you be bothered?
>
> —Robbie

Robbie sent me photos of him and the former world heavyweight champion, Muhammad Ali, sparring together in Baghdad. This hero of my father's bicycle shop had gone to Iraq and secured the release of another fifteen hostages. One by one, my colleagues from the Ibn al-Bitar hospital started to arrive home, beginning with the transport manager's family and some of the nurses. As Christmas approached, there were 270 Irish Ibn al-Bitar hospital staff still being held in Iraq or Kuwait.

★

In Britain, the winter of 1990 was one of the worst on record. The snows began in early December and caused havoc, bringing down power lines and disrupting electricity. There was an enormous rise in call-outs for patients with respiratory illnesses. The very young and very old were most susceptible to the flu viruses of that year. By the time the snow ended in February, the severe weather had led to the deaths of about ten people.

In early 1991, it was decided that Bangour General Hospital should finally close and its services should be moved to a new facility in Livingstone. The new hospital had many teething problems. Some were quite simple, like the beds being longer than the curtains. Others, like the nurses' strike for more handover time, created problems for the doctors.

One evening, I visited a sick child in a house near Broxburn, whom I believed had meningitis. As the child was deteriorating, I gave her an injection of penicillin and, deciding not to wait for an ambulance, I drove her to the new hospital in my own car. The child lay in accident and emergency for quite a long time. The paediatric registrar helped me perform a lumbar puncture, which confirmed my diagnosis, and Andy Woods, the emergency-room SHO, decided to transfer the sick child to the paediatric hospital in Edinburgh. It was the correct decision, as the child deteriorated in the ambulance on the way.

The next day, her sister presented with similar symptoms during a lunch-hour call, and I drove her to the hospital too. My quick action on their behalf was kindly rewarded with free beer by an ever-grateful father during my tenure in Broxburn, which I happily imbibed at the Volunteer Arms public house in East Main Street. Although happy to be accepted within the wider community, I often felt slightly on edge in the bar, as this part of Scotland retained traditions similar to Northern Ireland's, and proudly sent loyalist flute bands across the water to march on 12 July.

In March of that year, I received a letter offering me an accident and emergency registrar's position in St Bernard's Hospital in Gibraltar, a British overseas territory located on the southern end of the Iberian Peninsula. It suited me as I was due to finish up my GP registrar position in Scotland at the end of the year. I ruminated on the possibilities of working in Gibraltar for a while: from there I could travel through Africa and eventually work in Cape Town, where I had already registered as a doctor, now that Mandela was free. In the months before my departure, I started dating a design student named Hazel. I asked if she would like to join me in Gibraltar and she agreed.

Dr McRae laughed when he heard where I was thinking of working.

'You'll spend your time there treating tourists for monkey bites!' he joked.

Towards the end of July, some of my patients organised a 'Rock rave' in one of the local pubs as a farewell party for me and Hazel. One of my patients, Doris Wilson, made up an elaborate yellow-and-white cake in the shape of a suitcase, with baggage tags saying 'Scotland', 'Gibraltar' and 'Ireland'. Then we packed our belongings into my car and set out for the three-day journey to the bottom of Spain.

On our way through France, we stopped over in Montauban to see my brother Raymond, who had recently bought a small farm near the banks of the river Tarn, just off the motorway between Toulouse and Bordeaux. The cold winter of 1990 had killed off his apple crops, and he was finding it difficult to make ends meet. It was great spending time with him, and although I wished I could stay longer, we had a long journey ahead of us. Two days later, we reached the small Spanish border town of La Línea de la Concepción, on the eastern flank of the Bay of Gibraltar.

Gibraltar wasn't like anywhere I'd ever been before. The name of the promontory was derived from the Arabic name 'Jabal Tāriq' or 'Mountain of Tariq', and it reflected an earlier period when the Moors had ruled this part of Europe. The Rock had been of vital strategic importance to Britain during the Napoleonic wars, a role it maintained during the two world wars, when it was a location for British operations against the Germans. As we crossed the border, we were told to wait as two policemen placed barriers on the road. I was amazed when a Boeing 737 landed a few minutes later; the airport runway intersected with the road we were driving on. I had never seen anything like it. Our route took us by the Shell filling station where members of the SAS had shot the three IRA volunteers a few years before.

St Bernard's Hospital was built on the top of a hill, with a medical history dating back to 1567, when it was used to treat syphilis. The elevated location meant that it was well away from the town, but it also meant that after we visited the bars and restaurants in the town, we had to walk up hundreds of steps to reach our accommodation in the doctors' quarters. However, we were richly rewarded for the climb, with balconies that provided the best view across the strait to the northern coastline of Africa.

Hazel and I shared the quarters with three doctors: Lisa Penrice from Manchester and Ian Franklin from Avon, as well as Marcel and his wife from the Transvaal in South Africa. My Casualty registrar position in St Bernard's was straightforward, and Dr McCrea's prediction that I would spend my time treating tourists with monkey bites proved quite accurate.

In the evenings, my colleagues and I chilled out in the pubs around Irishtown, and discussed the events of the day. We often sat out on the balcony of the doctors' accommodation and watched the setting sun spill orange and purple rivulets of colour into the far-off deserts of Morocco. I told Marcel that I was registered in South Africa and discussed the possibility of working at the Groote Schuur Hospital, in Cape Town, where Professor Christiaan Barnard had performed the first human heart transplant in December 1967. This was where Marcel had his next rotation, and Hazel wanted to travel down to South Africa.

At the beginning of September, Hazel and I went on holiday to Tangier in Morocco, staying at the Europa Hotel. For her, it was an incessant hassle – 'official guides' walking after her, vying for her attention. For me, it was great to be back in the Arabic world, with its dagger and tin markets, watching the old men spinning cotton with the help of bicycle wheels. I had to laugh when one of the more persistent local hagglers began speaking to Hazel in Irish.

Towards the end of the month, the nurses in the hospital decided to stage a walkout over conditions, and felt that the junior doctors should support them. It is always difficult when medicine becomes political, because one has to continue working with one's colleagues when things settle.

In the midst of the negotiations, an elderly Moroccan man was admitted through the accident and emergency department. He had been found lying in the street, semi-comatose, unkempt and smelling of alcohol. At first, everyone assumed that the patient, who was well known to them, was just drunk. Although his initial neu-rological observations were entirely normal, I had a bad feeling about the case and decided to admit him to one of the surgical wards, where I put him on an hourly examination and requested a skull X-ray.

During the early hours of the morning, the patient developed 'racoon' signs around his eyes, and his skull X-ray showed evidence of a fracture. I transferred him to the intensive-care unit and informed the locum consultant that we had a possible intracranial bleed and base-of-skull fracture. Over the next hour, the patient's right pupil stopped reacting to light and became fixed and dilated. The consultant agreed that the most likely cause of the patient's dilated pupil was a massive bleed in the subdural part of the brain, which was compressing the oculomotor nerve. In the absence of a brain scan to confirm, we had no choice but to bring him to theatre and drill an emergency burr hole to relieve the pressure. When we opened the surgical instruments, I remember my surprise at seeing how similar they looked to a carpenter's swivel drill and bits. The consultant separated the temporalis muscle before cutting into the periosteum.

'Get the drill bit and start screwing it about two centimetres above and behind the orbital process of the frontal bone,' he said, as I injected more adrenaline into the skin to prevent fresh bleeding. 'Just about there – but be careful, this patient has a much larger skull fracture than we saw on the X-ray.'

I started boring into the patient's exposed skull with a large conical bit. As the bit drove deeper, I became ever more cautious not to burst through and damage the brain underneath. The technical practicalities of being accurate while drilling into somebody's skull were, in all honesty, not very different from what I had learned in my father's garage, and I switched over to the cylindrical bit while my colleague teased the 'freed-up' skull fragment from the delicate dura matter underneath. We removed a large clot, covered the brain with antibiotics and got him back to the intensive care unit. The next day he developed a fixed pupil on the other side and had to go back to theatre.

Meanwhile, word arrived at the hospital that the Moroccan patient had been assaulted by a local Gibraltarian, who had gone into hiding somewhere on the Rock. Moroccans were Gibraltar's underclass, and many of them lived in squalid, cockroach-infested slum hotels in an area of town called Casemates. They were forced to pay tax, but were not allowed to enjoy any of the benefits of citizenship, and if they lost their jobs they were deported back to their homeland. It was later discovered that the poor man had been battered over the head with a shoe until he became unconscious. His attacker came from a good family, and subsequent rumours indicated that this man had already left Gibraltar and was being treated in a psychiatric hospital in England. The patient lived through most of the following week, but eventually succumbed to his injuries.

In every moral sense, this situation regarding these immigrants was grossly unfair. These people had saved the Rock with their labour in 1969, when the Spanish dictator, General Franco, decided to close the frontier, preventing Spaniards from working there. Almost five thousand came during that period but, as the years passed, the Rock of Gibraltar became their prison cell. The authorities even confiscated the passports of their wives and children whenever they stopped over on the evening ferry that ran from Tangiers to the Spanish port of Algeciras.

Another disturbing aspect of life in Gibraltar, at least in 1991, was the government's apparent willingness to turn a blind eye to tobacco smugglers, who were known locally as the 'Winston boys'. The smugglers operated openly, using speedboats to cross the strait between Morocco and Spain, with Gibraltar as their base. On any given evening, one could wander amongst the black Phantom speedboats in Gibraltar's extensive harbour and see young men loading cartons of Winston cigarettes, preparing for the run across to Playa de la Atunara. The Spanish Guardia Civil abhorred this smuggling, and often chased the Winston boys with helicopters and speedboats.

★

One of the most interesting people I met on the Rock was Dr Cecil Isola, a sixty-three-year-old politician, whose wife was Irish. He had been born into a political Gibraltarian family, and his ancestors had been on the Rock longer than the British. Cecil was a larger-than-life character, a product of his upbringing at Stonyhurst College in Lancashire, the alumni of which included three saints, seven Victoria Cross winners, two prime ministers and one signatory of the American Declaration of Independence. He had studied medicine at Trinity College Dublin, but after many years of service as port medical officer was getting too old for climbing the sides of ships in the middle of the night to see sick patients on board, and he had handed over this duty to the junior doctors in St Bernard's Hospital.

One evening, I was standing on the balcony, enjoying the fiery sunset and thinking about Africa. Marcel joined me, and we talked for some time about my plans to travel overland from Kenya to the southern tip of Africa. Then, my beeper sounded for an emergency. It was a call from the harbour master, asking me to attend a possible heart attack aboard a Yugoslavian tanker.

'Are you on call?' Marcel asked me. 'I hit my nose on the side of a big Indian cargo ship last Tuesday when I was climbing up the rope ladder. A massive wave threw me against her side, and Dr Isola's black bag fell into the water!'

We all knew the dangers of climbing on board these ships late at night with only a small torch to light the way. Often, the crew spoke no English and commands were mistaken. A Russian crew once brought me down into the lower decks to fix an engine while their first mate lay upstairs suffering from an angina attack. However, it was also quite a lucrative business, which we all participated in, so we protected each other on that rare occasion when we were required to attend both the hospital and a naval emergency at the same time. We had a small car at our disposal, which I drove down to the Waterport Gate, where a pilot boat was waiting to take me out to sea.

'What is it?' I inquired in Spanish.

'Chest pain,' the captain replied, indicating that we had better hurry.

The craft thrust its way into the darkness, and before long we were alongside the tanker. It was a calm, starry night, perfect for alighting, and after the crew had thrown down ropes to haul up my equipment, I climbed aboard. The vessel's captain was first to meet me. He walked awkwardly, as if his leg had been injured, and ushered me into a little room.

'This young man is very sick, and I don't want him aboard my vessel,' he began. 'I want you to find bed for him in the hospital – please, you find bed for him?'

I was worried that the patient was seriously ill and indicated that we should go to see him immediately. Lifting my bag from the table, I made my way towards the iron door. It became apparent that the captain had other ideas. With a gesture, he signalled for me to sit down again. From the cupboard, he produced a bottle of Johnnie Walker whiskey and filled up two glasses.

'*Zivjeli*,' he said, handing one to me. 'Please you find my man a bed, we will sail tonight.'

After we emptied our glasses, we descended into the cramped lower part of the ship, passing through different stairwells until we reached the patient. He was Yugoslavian, probably in his late thirties and dressed in white overalls. Another crew member lay on the opposite bed, anxiously watching. Some others emerged from the shadows, eager to see what was happening. I thought it unusual that the captain allowed them to congregate in this fashion, and searched my bag for a stethoscope – my gavel, my truncheon of authority. The patient began writhing and spoke to me in a faint, apprehensive voice.

'*Ulcera*,' he said, pointing to his stomach area.

I noted how his flickering eyes were fearful as he grasped my shirt, as if his life depended on my getting him out of there. He spoke to me in a tired, pleading voice as I felt his abdomen. On examination, nothing seemed to add up. His basic observations were normal, and his pulse rate ticked along at normal speed. As each moment passed, he seemed to be getting worse, the pain increasing.

'*Ulcera*,' he sobbed again.

I began to wonder whether there was a cultural aspect to his pain, but remained suspicious – the degree of pain and fear in his voice, the symptoms which were allegedly bothering him, just didn't match my findings. Although I didn't want to miss a perforated ulcer, my sixth sense made me consider whether I was being sub-jected to an elaborate hoax. The captain seemed to share the patient's anguish, something obviously beyond the comprehension of my medical experience, and he signalled for me to take the patient ashore. I thought about it for a while and then said to a stretcher party he had assembled, 'OK, we'll have to take him to the hospital.'

The crew members lifted him onto the stretcher, and I followed them to the gangway. On the way, the captain ordered someone to collect the patient's personal belongings so that they could be brought ashore with him. He turned to me and said, 'When you are finished, you fly my man to Dubrovnik.'

'Yes, captain,' I replied cautiously. 'But what's his real problem?'

The captain took me back to his cabin and, in the dim light, opened his coat and offered me another glass of whiskey.

'He is a Croatian on this Serbian ship. Yesterday his family were killed and he wants go back to fight in the war,' he said, shaking my hand and thrusting the remainder of the bottle of whiskey into my red life jacket. 'You see, I am also Croatian.'

Croatia had just declared independence, dissolving its association with Yugoslavia. Two months before, the border city of Vukovar had been besieged by Serbian troops, and the population suffered extreme hardship, with as many as half a million refugees holding their ground against the elite forces of the Yugoslav People's Army.

I learned a lot that night. Although my position as a doctor had been abused by the captain, sometimes a greater human need may transcend our professional ethics. This is a judgment call that each doctor has to make from time to time, and live with.

The patient had his gastroscopy a few days later, which proved normal, as expected. He hugged me goodbye before leaving for the airport.

★

In early November, I noticed a spectacular yacht, the *Lady Ghislaine*, moored in Marina Bay. For some reason, I was impressed enough to take a photograph of it and show it to my colleagues in the apartment. It belonged to British media mogul Robert Maxwell. His naked body was found a few days later, floating in the Atlantic Ocean.

Rumours abounded that he had fallen overboard near the Canary Islands, and some speculated that the Israeli intelligence service, Mossad, was involved in his death. He was eventually buried on the Mount of Olives in Jerusalem, across from the Temple Mount, widely discounting that theory. During his eulogy, Prime Minister Yitzhak Shamir broadcast to the world, 'He has done more for Israel than can be said today.'

During December, the commissioner of police asked me to train some of his officers in basic life support. However, the position gave me no special status when the British aircraft carrier *Ark Royal* visited Gibraltar en route to the Gulf War. It had been deployed to the Mediterranean area to monitor Libya, which had proclaimed support for Iraq's actions. I was unsure whether to be proud or embarrassed when word came back that I was the only doctor in the hospital not to be given security clearance to visit the ship. The long arm of Britannia was in action again, and somebody somewhere was working overtime.

I had more luck when the *QE2* arrived en route from Southampton with a sick passenger for disembarkation. The journey only took a few days, and I was always surprised by the number of people who developed the need for specialist help during that short period. The principal medical officer on board the *QE2* was from Staffordshire, a graduate of King's College Hospital, and he had an Irish mother. We bonded instantly, and he gave me a signed copy of his book, *Doctor of the Queen Elizabeth 2*.

'This would be a perfect career for you,' he told me. 'You've accident and emergency, cardiology and orthopaedic experience. However, it's not for the faint-hearted. You'll be on your own at sea, but you'll have the happiest memories of your life!'

I took the idea a little further and, during the Christmas holidays, went to the London office of Carnival Cruise Lines, to meet Randy Coldham, to seek opportunities as a ship's physician, working from the United States. He thought my CV was perfect and immediately offered me a ship from Miami. However, I still wanted to visit Cape Town, so I decided to wait on another liner leaving from Los Angeles, sailing along the Mexican Riviera the following June.

In the meantime, Hazel went back to college in Edinburgh, and I applied for a six-week tour from Nairobi overland to Johannesburg with a group called Truck Africa. I wrote a letter to Trish to ask if she wanted to join me on the adventure. It remained unanswered, but I was glad I had at least made the effort to see how she was.

★

That Christmas, the famous hammer-and-sickle emblem of the Soviet Union was lowered for the last time. I had witnessed the fall of the Berlin Wall in 1989 and the slow disintegration of the USSR. History was being created before my eyes, and now that I had some time on my hands, I thought it would be a shame not to witness the beginning of a new Russia, finally free of communism.

The nation had always fascinated me, right from the earliest days of my childhood, when I would take down the school atlas from the top of the teacher's press, and trace the winding path of the Trans-Siberian Express from Moscow to Vladivostok. When I grew older, my mother told me that the vast landscapes that my dream-train traversed were dotted with prison camps and the people were detained against their will behind a great Iron Curtain. Later, at St Michael's College, I discovered the music of Tchaikovsky and Rimsky-Korsakov. Now I wanted to go and experience Russia for myself, especially at this time of political transformation.

The Aeroflot jet landed at Sheremetyevo Airport as the evening snow fell outside my window. After an hour's wait, I cleared customs and found the official state taxi that was to take me to the city. The service was provided by Intourist, a travel agency founded by Stalin, and I felt his long shadow hanging over me: an unusual sense of secretiveness prevailed in my conversation with the driver.

We travelled for about twenty minutes before silhouettes of buildings began to appear through the smoggy haze of the city's chimneys. The streets we passed were surreal, with wrapped-up traders and cheap wooden stalls that contrasted with the architectural splendours behind them. Their products appeared to be mostly traditional – Russian cigarettes and vodka – but there also seemed to be quite a lot of Western merchandise. The taxi driver told me some jokes, but they went over my head.

My hotel was a large, nineteenth-century, cast-iron and brick building situated near the street where Boris Yeltsin had climbed up onto a tank to protest the attempted coup by hard-line Communists, just a few months before. I made friends with some guests from Minsk, and we dined together that evening. The waiter was unacceptably rude, but this was something I grew accustomed to experiencing in the dying days of the Soviet Union. The next morning, there were noisy Communist demonstrations outside. As the protest progressed, windows in the hotel and nearby parked cars were smashed by people nostalgic for the old days and resentful of losing their privileges.

I left the hotel and took photographs of the ragged lines of Russian soldiers who huddled together in the chilly air outside empty supermarkets. They looked uncertain and dejected, and it was difficult to imagine that these men were the remnants of the mighty Red Army, which had stood against Nazi fascism and whose May Day parades had sent shivers down Western spines. Throughout this great nation's history, authoritarianism had always been the rule, but after seven decades, the whole system was collapsing from within. Yet, the citizens of Moscow whom I met still seemed to be the cheeriest of souls and displayed little of the xenophobia that I had imagined they would have. In fact, the opposite was true: everybody smiled when they met me.

I wandered the streets to the banks of the Moskva River, where featureless proletarian apartment blocks rose high into the far-off skyline – the dying symbols of a social experiment soon to be lost and gone forever. Enveloped in thought, I followed the sloping cobblestone streets to a great bridge across the river to west of the walls of the Kremlin. A soft snow fell as I entered Red Square and, for a moment, I thought about how Batu Khan, the grandson of Genghis Khan, had burned Moscow to the ground – just as his cousins would do to Baghdad a few years later.

I made my way to St Basil's, a cathedral built in classic Russian style. When Ivan the Terrible completed it in 1561, legend states that he blinded the architects so they could never recreate it. Napoleon allowed his troops to stable their horses there, but his attempt to blow up the building was, tradition has it, prevented by the townspeople, who extinguished the burning fuses during his retreat. I remembered again the missionary priest who had visited our school, and told us that the pagan Russians had no religion and were all destined to go to hell. I did not fail to notice the irony of being surrounded by gilded cupolas, elaborate frescoes and all the iconography of these allegedly pagan people.

It was still snowing when I left the building. A group of soldiers approached me, their jackboots grinding the snow beneath their feet, their greatcoats swishing with each purposeful stride. They questioned me for a moment before posing to have their picture taken. Although we could only communicate in words of two syllables, they seemed very open and friendly, curious about Ireland and what the weather was like there.

I caught a taxi with my friends to Belorussky railway station. The dreariness of the building and its dilapidated surroundings reminded me of Kreuzburg, a graffiti-scarred sector of Berlin. Nearby, I noticed a large number of people queuing outside an empty supermarket. There were easily a hundred ragged people, standing in an untidy line outside a shop that was protected by metal grilles. Every now and then, an unseen hand lifted the grille from inside and, as the shoppers exited, more were allowed through.

I stopped by the queue to take a photograph. Most ignored my camera, turning their backs and concentrating on their places in the queue. I spoke to a female straggler at the end of the line. Her name was Olga Stawislavna and, unlike me, she was dressed for the Russian weather, with her hat pulled well down over her ears, and her heavy coat stretching almost to her toes. A woollen scarf obscured the lower part of her face and, as a result, accentuated her warm, friendly eyes. Olga's English was good and, even if her heavy Russian accent was a little difficult to get used to, I liked its cadence and tone. I found out that she was a doctor who specialised in HIV/AIDS in children, and that she worked in a nearby hospital. I considered having one last test before going to Africa, although my chances of conversion at this stage were considered fairly minimal. I was surprised when Olga told me that HIV was reaching epidemic levels in Russian cities. It seemed that nowhere escaped the tentacles of the virus.

Having found a shared interest, we talked for some time as the line of people slowly moved forward. I told her that I wanted to experience what life was like for ordinary people in Moscow. To my amazement, Olga invited me to stay in her apartment. She explained that she shared it with two engineers, one male, one female, and dismissed my worries that they might object. When it was her turn to go inside, she seemed to take it for granted that I would accompany her and, of course, I was curious to see the whole process.

We entered what can only be described as a type of supermarket, crammed with empty shelves and small display freezers with nothing inside. It was a bizarre sight. The citizens of Moscow were queuing for basic commodities like bread and sausages. They moved forward in a giant, silent conga line, compliantly awaiting their turn. There was no jostling or shouting, just the occasional soft murmur of complaint at the meagre amount of food available. People come together in times of need, I supposed, recognising the ineffectuality of creating a fuss – surviving as best they can.

Olga collected some bread and salami, sighing, no doubt embarrassed that these scanty supplies would have to feed an extra guest that night. We found a map and she showed me where her apartment was, on a street called Shirokaya Ulitsa near the Metro terminus Medvedkovo. It might seem unusual that somebody would invite a complete stranger to share their home, but those were different times, and travellers were often met with great kindness.

Olga's spartan apartment was large and airy. The cold wind whistled through cracks in the wooden sash windows. The building harked back to a more lavish time, with little reminders scattered here and there, like opulent cornices on the ceiling, now crumbling in places due to neglect. Olga and her friends welcomed me into their home, apparently one of the better places to live in Moscow, and I smiled and hid my astonishment that three professional people should live in such a place. There was nothing wrong with it, they had all they needed, but I couldn't help contrasting it to the homes of those with similar educational backgrounds and work experience in the West.

Olga had appeared full-figured in her outdoor clothing, but was actually quite petite. She tied her brown hair back from her pale face into a utilitarian bun at the nape of her neck. She didn't use any make-up, except for a little lipstick, and her well-worn clothes would have been thought old-fashioned, even by women of my mother's generation. This obviously wasn't a deliberate choice on her part, as her roommate dressed in much the same way, and both women immediately apologised for their lack of sartorial elegance. It surprised me how much they knew about Western fashion and exactly how far behind they were, so I just said, 'Neechevo, neechevo – pazhaloosta' ('It's nothing, it's nothing – please'), which I believed was expected of me. This was my first introduction to 'real' Russian women, and I discovered that I had unwittingly harboured preconceived notions that the communist ethos meant that they wouldn't care about such things.

In the West, we knew little or nothing about 'them' except what we had heard on the news. In the days that followed, I discovered that they had no hostility towards us. Olga and her flatmate both wanted to leave Russia at the first opportunity and work in the United States. It was the first time I had given much consideration to how citizens from other parts of the world aspire just to embrace the life we tend to take for granted.

The next day, while Olga was at work, I paid a visit to Lenin's black labradorite mausoleum. Under the direction of the Soviet leadership, this political theorist had been transformed into an 'immortal', his cadaver displayed in Red Square like some holy artefact. As the years passed, he became a largely fictional, god-like figure who served to legitimise both the state and those who claimed to be carrying on his original mission. By the time of my visit, the Russian people were confused – documents had been released that implicated Lenin in countless acts of revolutionary terror and barbarity, including his bloody campaign against the clergy and the kulaks. His mausoleum had become a symbol of the hopes and ambitions of a proud race who mistakenly thought they might provide a better life for their people. For more than seventy years, Russian people had stood in lines that often stretched along the length of the square, hoping to view his body. Now, as the wheels of history locked the cult of Lenin and the Soviet state together in a binding embrace, they both spiralled downward, leaving the revered mausoleum an unwanted reminder of a bygone era.

Evenings at Olga's were mainly spent in conversation after meals of salami and bread, their staple diet. My new friends felt that the West looked down on them, viewing them as inferior, not only in dress but in education and science. I told them that their scientists were respected and the Kirov and Bolshoi ballet schools were also world-renowned. My small revelations pleased Olga and her friends. These people loved their country and they were aware of the pitfalls of communism.

After spending a month in their company, it was time for me to travel to Africa. I had secured a job as a registrar in a hospital in Cape Town, and was going to travel there from Kenya overland with Truck Africa. I was due to leave from Mombasa in late February. Thesiger had been fond of Kenya, having spent many years there as a game warden, trying to control poaching. He had been fascinated by its varied wildlife and distinctive nomadic tribes, and had made a series of long journeys on foot with camels to Lake Turkana and Marsabit. His description of tribal warriors dancing by moonlight, and the Maasai initiation ceremonies, recounted in his memoir *My Kenya Days*, was one of the things that made me want to travel through the country.

19.
THE MAGIC OF AFRICA

I flew to Nairobi, where the lonesome whistle of the cold Moscow winds was replaced by the orchestral sound of a million crickets. It was early February and the temperature was just below thirty degrees Celsius, so I felt less annoyed about having my best leather jacket stolen on the bus from the airport to the city.

It was almost dusk when I finally arrived at the camp where the trucks we were using to travel across Africa were parked. The place was buzzing with activity as safari drivers from Australia and New Zealand repaired and replenished their vehicles by the flickering yellow light of diesel-generator-powered electric lamps. I stood and watched as two men changed the broken back spring on a Leyland army truck that had seen better days. The scene reminded me of a summer evening at our garage in Garrison for a moment, but then the smell of grilled steak and sausages mingling with the scent of hibiscus shrubs brought me back to Africa.

These were entrepreneurial people, making a living amidst the harsh economic realities of Africa, and they knew the value of keeping their trucks in good working condition. An arid, picturesque landscape in the wild can quickly turn hostile for a traveller unused to the terrain.

Having introduced myself to the other travellers, I met our driver Alex, who had been living in Nairobi for the previous two years. Although raised near the sloping vineyards of the Yarra Valley in Australia, he had adapted well to life in Africa. His girlfriend,

Karen, was also from the Melbourne area, and both seemed driven by an indomitable spirit of adventure. In the course of conversation, they told me that they had seen many of their friends die from cerebral malaria, septicaemia and injuries, and were constantly aware of the inherent risks that travelling through Africa entailed.

Alex told me we were going to dine that night at a restaurant named The Carnivore, and he promised it would be a unique experience.

'We have to be careful,' Alex said. 'The whole city is in an uproar and people are rioting. If the tribal violence continues, we won't be going anywhere – they'll have to close the border.'

Apparently, rioting had ensued when it was discovered that Kenyan political activist Wangari Maathai and other pro-democracy demonstrators were on a list of people targeted for assassination. They had then been arrested and charged with spreading malicious rumours, sedition and treason. International organisations and eight US senators (including Al Gore and Ted Kennedy) said that unless the government of Kenya dropped the charges, it would risk damaging relations with the United States. Maathai was released on bail.

On 28 February 1992, while she was out on bail, Maathai and others took part in a hunger strike in part of Uhuru Park, which they labelled Freedom Corner. After four days, the Kenyan police forcibly removed the protestors, and Maathai was knocked unconscious in the process, and hospitalised. Protestors rioted, and the streets of Nairobi were turned into a giant battlefield, littered with the smoking debris of burnt-out buses and shattered shopfronts.

We took the Toyota truck to Gimomba bus station, where the road was barricaded, and walked closer to survey the damage. Black smoke billowed from burning tyres, and rioters had overturned telephone boxes and cars, using them to block the streets. Fires burned all along Tom Mboya Street, and looters were everywhere.

Alex smiled at me. 'Welcome to Africa!' he said.

★

There was an enormous charcoal pit right at the entrance of the restaurant, and the aroma of cooking meat filled the air. Bustling waiters brandishing huge Maasai swords, which they used as skewers, mingled with the diners, serving ostrich, impala, zebra and every other type of meat imaginable. Most of the diners seemed oblivious to the violence in the city streets – glasses were raised and clinked while they chatted and feasted, a real contrast to my month of austerity in Russia.

This was my second visit to the southern hemisphere, and as we made our way back to camp, I searched the night skies for the friendly stars of the Southern Cross. Despite the emerging violence, I felt I would sleep peacefully under a southern sky that night.

Despite an early start, it was nearly evening when we reached Tiwi, a small settlement and beach about eleven miles south of Mombasa. While in Scotland, I had been invited to join the Corstorphine Round Table, a non-sectarian, non-political group of professionals who met every few weeks to combine their resources for the betterment of the community. We maintained strong links with other Tablers and consequently, I had arranged to meet some members of the Kenyan Round Table at the Castle Hotel in Mombasa the next day. They were part of a larger regional body called the Association of Round Tables in Eastern Africa, and their leader was an Indian businessman who lived in the city.

I went with Alex to the old hotel, which had high ceilings, historical pictures and ceiling fans in a dining room that exuded a colonial charm. After about thirty minutes, we were joined on the veranda by another driver, Steve, a New Zealander, who although small in stature, appeared battle-hardened by tough terrain. He had worked as a paramedic in Christchurch, and I was glad we had something in common.

Steve called us over to the balcony to see something that was happening on the street below. Alex looked aghast at the possibility that the tribal protest was now spreading to Mombasa and that we could be trapped in the city.

A convoy of five black Mercedes pulled up outside the hotel.

About ten men in black suits stepped from the cars and entered the hotel. Some walked to the door of the bar where we were sitting, and one seemed to communicate, by walkie-talkie, to a team below. I thought I saw the handle of a gun under his jacket.

'It's probably President Moi arriving,' Steve said. 'There's so much trouble brewing among the tribes that he'd have to travel about in a cavalcade.'

We grew alarmed when the men came onto the balcony and two of them approached our table.

'Which of you is Dr Patrick Treacy?' one asked.

'I am,' I said.

'No need to be upstanding,' the first man said, as he warmly extended his hand.

I now saw that the two men wore Round Tablers' badges on their lapels, and we laughed heartily together when we realised the mistake we had made. Then they got some of the other men to bring in ten crates of Tusker lager.

'You'll need these. There is no good beer before you reach Malawi.'

'It's true,' Alex said, shaking his head in gratitude. 'It's mostly little shebeens on route, and wait until you get to Zimbabwe, where they drink that bloody Chibuku.'

★

The following morning, we set out for the Tanzanian border, stopping at Taveta to stock up on supplies. The market was a mixture of magic and madness, staffed by well-rounded women who sprawled lazily by their stalls and appeared uninterested in selling their dried fish, mangoes and bananas. Bedraggled children with mischievous eyes followed us, giggling, while men in long *kikois* fought battles with swarms of flies who settled on the hairless cow heads they were selling.

We got back on the truck and followed the tar-sealed roads onto little red murram tracks where the gentle breeze smothered the countryside in the perfume of flowering acacia. We passed through villages where barefoot women with brightly coloured *kangas* and wooden creels balanced on their heads watched as we passed. Karen and I sat on the roof of the truck, where a welcoming breeze blew as we pitched and rolled in the afternoon heat, a cooling salve amidst the sun-bleached savannah grasslands.

After travelling a few hundred miles, dusk began to fall and a bloated orange sun spilled onto the skyline, silhouetting the surrounding hillsides. For a while, it hung like a fireball just above the horizon, lighting up the edges of the cotton clouds as if to set them on fire. I had never seen a sunset quite like it before and, for a moment, I wished Trish could be with me to share the beauty of Africa. Slowly and deliberately, I pushed all thoughts of her out of my head. This was my time. I had had my seventh negative HIV test and, for all intents and purposes, had beaten the virus. My future now stretched out before me. Already the beauty and vastness of the African continent made me pensive, and I wondered how much I still had to learn about life, and about myself.

As darkness fell, we pulled off the roadway and into the bush, and set up camp under a grove of coral trees. The setting was ideal – well hidden from any prowlers who might wish to steal our supplies while we slept. We hammered bent tent pins into the dry, unforgiving soil, constructing our green-tarpaulin village. Hungry mosquitoes quickly discovered our habitat and began to bother us. The scented air was sticky and humid and gripped me in a breathless torpor.

'Watch out for ants on the grass when you're laying those groundsheets,' said Steve. 'And close your tents while you're sleeping – the monkeys above us will steal anything that isn't bolted down.'

Some of the girls set up a small slatted-timber table, and began to prepare a meal of fresh meat and vegetables, while a couple of the guys lit a fire with twigs and branches scattered under the trees. We listened to the latest report from the BBC World Service. The increasing tribal violence in Kenya made it imperative that we cross the frontier into Kenya the next morning.

'Don't worry about the fighting, it happens in Africa all the time,'

Alex said, realising that the situation was beginning to trouble some of our female passengers.

Then, laughing, he told the rest of us: 'We don't expect any trouble until we get down to Mutare on the Zimbabwe border – there *is* a possibility that the guerrillas may take the truck from us there, and then we'd have a real problem.'

Alex's control of the situation impressed me, and I recognised the leadership qualities he obviously possessed. We would need them in abundance over the next six weeks. There were another twelve passengers on our truck – from Australia, New Zealand, Canada, Britain and Ireland – whose paths had merged, united by a common language and a desire to explore Africa. Our group mostly travelled alone, meeting with the other trucks only at campsites and in tourist areas.

I teamed up with Richard, one of my fellow travellers, and we took an axe and went to find some more firewood in the scrubland below the camp. Richard came from farming stock in Wanganui in New Zealand, but had been working in London for the last year. After his 'walkabout' was finished, he intended going back home to settle. We wandered about half a mile from camp, uncertain of the bush and the growing stillness of the evening.

In the distance we heard faint voices, which we assumed were coming from a nearby village. The sound of barking dogs disturbed the tranquillity. The voices gradually became louder as we walked. Through a small clearing ahead of us, we could see a large thorn-branched, perimeter fence, which Maasai villagers had probably erected to protect their cattle from lions. Beyond the fence were ten or eleven dome-shaped huts arranged in a circle. In the dying light, they looked like overturned curraghs, those hide-skinned boats popular in the west of Ireland.

Children were playing near the front entrance of one of the huts, and a little boy carried a small brown-and-white goat in his arms. Two or three golden dogs skulked around, but they didn't catch our scent. A young mother in a red-and-yellow sarong played with a small child who took a few hesitant first steps. I watched her pride in her child's unsteady gait, the cherished hope of a race of people who once controlled a kingdom larger than England, the once great Maasailand.

We stayed a while before returning to the encampment, gathering whatever small branches were at hand. The aroma of freshly cooked food hung in the air, and the glowing embers of the campfire soon crackled and jumped into the night sky. We gathered around, laughing and joking, and I considered how a twilight evening spent on the Kenyan savannah could instil such a sense of camaraderie amongst a group of young people. Unlike Thesiger, I embraced the company of other travellers, but I also recognised that satisfaction in attaining a goal was directly in proportion to the hardship and challenge involved in getting there.

Someone caught a glimpse of a shadow moving amongst the trees, and we realised that some children from the nearby village had joined us, but remained a safe distance from our camp. As the evening passed, they crept forward, no doubt enthralled by a rousing chorus of 'Hotel California' beat out on a guitar bought in Mombasa a few days earlier. Soon they were dancing around the blazing campfire – courtly young figures silhouetted against the yellow flames, displaying a captivating grace of movement.

Mothers stood under the coral trees near the edge of camp and watched as their offspring danced in the moonlight. One of them, who appeared older than the rest, walked forward. Her earlobes carried little silver arrowheads, which glinted in the moonlight as they dangled over the tips of her shoulders. Slowly, she began to sway to the rhythm of the music and, before long, we were all dancing together. It was a moment that caught the free spirit of Africa, transcending the boundaries of mistrust, and touched the deeper need for collective equanimity. It was probably worthy of the daydreams of Africa that were Thesiger's means of escape throughout his unhappy days at Eton and Oxford.

One of the women then asked if we were carrying any medicines on the lorry. She said there was a sick child in the village, and asked if I would be willing to examine him. The next morning we went to the village, where I saw a small, sickly child of about three. There were no obvious signs of organ enlargement or infection, but he was wasted and undernourished and probably had been failing to thrive for a long time.

'Has a doctor seen the child?" I asked a villager who could speak English well.

After a prolonged period of hand-waving in Maasai and English, I gained the impression that his mother was dead and his father was not in the village. As I further examined the wasted child, a strange feeling came over me. Could this be a case of HIV/AIDS? I looked across at Steve, who nodded back to me in politeness to the family. There was little I could do, but I left them with a small bottle of Amoxil and paracetamol, to use if he got a fever.

'Do you think he has HIV?' Steve asked me, as we left the village. 'One in five of the truck drivers in Mombasa is HIV-positive and the village is only a short distance from the main roadway to Nairobi.'

I looked across the open savannah. I may have freed myself of the virus, but here it was all around me, growing in strength and stalking the very heart of the continent.

Steve told me about the other African sicknesses, and two New Zealanders who had died on the last trip after contracting a fatal strain of cerebral malaria.

'The problem is that the malaria here is resistant to chloroquine,' he said. 'And the bloody stuff rots your liver after six months, so none of the expats take it. Vicious circle. Take your choice – you can die of the disease or the treatment!'

Alex was already up and preparing breakfast over an open fire and bantering with some black-faced vervet monkeys that had joined him from the trees surrounding the camp. The monkeys gave me an opportunity to meet my second patient, a fellow passenger, an English teacher called Joe, who had been bitten by one of the mischievous primates. Having worked as Casualty registrar in Gibraltar for six months, I felt like a world authority on simian bites. As my fellow travellers gathered around to watch me treat Joe, I couldn't help thinking of the locals and the brave African trekkers who had colonised the continent, facing charging elephants and lions with single-shot rifles, and immediately realised that this epidermal nip would not rank alongside their hardships.

We broke camp and followed a good tar-sealed road to Arusha, halfway between Cairo and Cape Town, with the foothills of Mount Kilimanjaro keeping us company for most of the trip. Children ran after the truck shouting '*Jambo!*' (Swahili for 'hello') at us and imploring us to supply them with pens so they could go to university. At first we couldn't see the famous mountain, as it lay camouflaged behind the fleecy skyline. Suddenly it appeared, an immense snow-capped cone looming majestically out of the cotton clouds, towering into the cobalt blue of the Tanzanian sky, a symbol of harmonious constancy in the changing landscape. Much of eastern and southern Africa was in the grip of the worst drought for decades, and the boiling sun rendered the nearby wheat fields a bleached barren waste.

The truck progressed at a steady pace, climbing ever higher through the steep tree-lined foothills, on the winding path to the Ngorongoro Crater. The cab had been modified to allow three people to sit on it, enabling them to view the African countryside as it unfolded ahead of us. This was the most coveted place on board, but one had to be mindful of the branches of overhanging sycamore trees and dangerously low-hanging telegraph wires when approaching small towns. Richard and I, fortunately, saw most of the continent from this vantage point. We had a magnificent view of the lush blue-green hills that merged gently, as if flowing eastwards, into a purple haze near the Tanzanian frontier. It was a scorching afternoon, and it was evident from the cracked earth in the dry riverbeds that no rain had fallen in this area for a long time.

We reached the rim of the crater, a vast plain set seven hundred metres into the centre of a volcano whose caldera had formed three million years earlier. The wildlife was everywhere: to the left, roaming herds of wildebeest; ahead, pools of bathing hippos and lakes shimmering with pink flamingos. We drove slowly towards the centre, passing Maasai tribesmen as they wandered alongside their herds of cattle, seemingly oblivious to some lionesses resting under a nearby acacia tree.

I remembered that in April 1961, Thesiger had travelled in Tanzania and walked for a month through the crater with donkeys hired from local Maasai people. It was a great feeling to know that he had been there before me, had witnessed the same views and sunsets. Maybe, in some way, we were connected through time because we both shared a desire to live and travel with people less influenced by Western culture, and to get a portrait of their way of life before it was gone forever.

After exiting the crater, we started on the two-day journey to Dar es Salaam, Tanzania's largest city, skirting the edges of Tarangire National Park, by way of Dodoma. About twenty miles from the city, we came across a large truck lying precariously on its side. Its cargo of fruit, mostly mangoes and pomegranates, had spilled from its crates and was scattered all over the roadway. A man had been thrown to the ground as the vehicle rolled, and he appeared to be bleeding profusely from a head injury. Brain tissue protruded from an open skull fracture – a substantial injury which would test the most competent neurosurgeon. I was anxious to help the accident victim.

'You'll see lots of these before we hit Harare,' said Alex. 'These people all have the AIDS virus and you'll learn to drive on by.'

After I protested, and promised I would try not to touch the dying man, we stopped. Thankfully, Susie, an Australian nurse, was willing to assist me. We looked at one another for a moment – it was evident that the victim would never recover from his injuries, lying out here in the bush. I satisfied myself that his prognosis was zero, whispered a soft prayer into his ear and drew up enough morphine to ease his suffering. Other lorry drivers en route to the capital had pulled over to offer assistance and comfort. He died about half an hour later, but at least he didn't die alone.

For a long time, nobody spoke. We were not only shaken by the death of the African driver, but also by Alex's apparent indifference to the event. It went against my deepest ethical judgment not to help somebody just because they might be carrying HIV. I couldn't just close my eyes to the suffering and walk away. Obviously, others didn't feel that way, and cracks began to appear in the group. Maybe our attitudes were based on inexperience, but I was a doctor, trained to remain objective and non-judgmental.

We made camp just east of Dodoma and planned to drive the next five hundred kilometres to Dar es Salaam early the next morning and visit the island of Zanzibar. I was soon to learn that not only was HIV rampant in this part of Africa, but it was considered by many of the white population to be a black person's disease. This meant that the standard methods of controlling the transmission were almost non-existent.

One of the big problems in African hospitals was the knowledge that needles, which were used for taking blood samples, were reused on many different patients. For this reason, I always carried a box of needles while on the continent. There was also a cultural perception amongst many blacks that condoms were a white man's ruse, foisted upon them to control their spiralling population. I discovered that this attitude was particularly prevalent in the townships of South Africa.

The next day, we reached Dar es Salaam, where there was something very different about the sunset. Maybe it was the smell of turmeric or cinnamon that lingered in the still-humid air, the call of a muezzin coming from some far-off mosque or the buzzing noise of a motorised dhow as it drew closer to the shoreline. Either way, the essence of this dusk was Arabic.

★

Zanzibar lay in the middle of an archipelago about thirty-five kilometres off the coast. For many centuries, Arab and Persian traders had sailed these waters, arriving with the winter monsoons, and returning home – their ships laden with gold, ivory and slaves – when the winds changed direction. Some said it was the fabled land of Sheba, and that the tales of Sinbad the Sailor were based on Arab sailors' adventures along this part of the African coastline. Freddie

Mercury was born here in 1946 and lived on a square behind the post office. I recalled the Islamic influence in many of Queen's songs, especially the word '*Bismillah*' in 'Bohemian Rhapsody'. It was taken from the longer sentence, '*Bismillah ir-Rahman, ir-Rahim*', which occurs at the start of nearly every chapter in the Holy Qur'an, and means 'in the name of God, the most gracious, the most merciful'.

The explorers David Livingstone and Henry Morton Stanley had both used Zanzibar as a base from which to start their inland expeditions through Africa. Some of Livingstone's legacy still remained there, a small wooden crucifix fashioned, it was said, from the wood of the tree under which he had died in a village near the edge of the Bangweulu swamps in what is now Zambia. Apparently, Britain wanted to bury Livingstone with full honours, but the local tribe refused to give up his body. In the end, they relented, but insisted that, even if his body was taken back to Britain, his heart belonged to Africa. So they buried it under an mvula tree near where he died. The rest of Livingstone's remains were buried in Westminster Abbey.

We crossed over the Malawi border near Lponga at early light. There, the Malawi police lined us up for inspection, as an authoritarian dress code had been put in place by President Hastings Banda. This meant that the women on the truck had to wear sarongs, as it was forbidden for them to bare their thighs, and a few of the men had to get their hair cut short by the border guards. The president's rather eccentric ethics apparently also extended to the arts – no movies showing couples kissing could be viewed in his country.

In Malawi, I found some of the most affable people that I had ever encountered. I could see that Irish people had passed through before me, due to the proliferation of Kerry GAA football jerseys and Concern T-shirts, which many of the small children were wearing. One of these children, possibly only three or four years of age, struggled valiantly to keep up with the other children who were running after our truck. When we stopped, he reached us, and gave me a laugh. As he stood there, with green-tinged mucus running down his nose, I noticed that his white T-shirt was emblazoned with red lettering that said, 'I'll never catch AIDS.' As he turned, I saw the back of it, which read, 'Because I'm a little wanker.' I'm sure the designers of that T-shirt never imagined it would be worn by a sickly child in sub-Saharan Africa.

We followed Livingstone's path, crossing the shores of Lake Malawi, which had signs warning of the risk of contracting bilharzia from the schistosome worms that lurked in its waters. However, this disease was the least of Africa's infection problems, as it was along some of these wilderness tracks across the border in Zambia that we encountered abandoned villages, a testament to the rising HIV epidemic. They were eerie: one expected to hear barking dogs or small children playing, but there was nothing. The nearby cities of Lusaka and Kabwe had the highest HIV infection rates in the world. Zambian President Kenneth Kaunda's own son had died from the disease four years before. One in five adults in the country had the virus, and the rate was particularly high amongst the casual labourers who worked in the copper mines. I thanked God every day that he had saved me from the virus that now lurked in the shadows all around me.

As I stood by the waters of the mighty Zambezi and watched it flow over the edge of the Victoria Falls, it was easy to see why it was known as one of the most spectacular natural wonders of the world. Amidst the cavorting rainbows, the capering cascades and the deafening roar of the largest curtain of water on earth, I felt at home with the real spirit of Africa. We stayed there for a week. In the evenings, we dined in the Victoria Falls Hotel, an opulent building in the grandest colonial style. I felt at home there, amidst the camphorous scent of flowering leleshwa, with the tawny vervet monkeys playing along the rooftop. Nobody wanted to leave that hallowed place, but eventually we did, travelling onwards to Zimbabwe.

★

The 1992 drought in Zimbabwe was horrific, the worst in living memory. The newspapers carried articles daily about children fainting from dehydration in the primary schools, and the nation once famed as the breadbasket of Southern Africa was experiencing food riots in the streets. I was sorry to see the fledgling nation in such a terrible state. It had always been special to me, even before independence, when it was still known as Rhodesia.

My interest started when I shared a house in Dublin with my Rhodesian medical-student roommate, Greg. It was also influenced by Bob Marley's protest song 'Zimbabwe', which he released on the 1979 album *Survival* and played during the independence celebrations one year later. Because of these experiences, the tales of the old Rhodesia and the spirit of the new Zimbabwe had equal shares of my heart.

Whilst there, I wanted to immerse myself in the culture as much as I could. This meant I wanted to visit the grave of Cecil Rhodes, the person for whom the nation was originally named. Few of my friends shared my sense of nostalgia and, in the end, I decided to go to the Matopos Hills and see Rhodes's grave alone, cushioned by the promise that Richard and Victoria would meet me at the Selborne Hotel in Bulawayo a few days later.

The Selborne was the epitome of the former colonial era. With its carved arches and wide balconies, it was affectionately known to expatriates as 'the Grand Old Lady of the South'. It was there that I met an old couple who owned a tobacco farm some miles from town. Timothy drove a vintage green Austin 40 Farina that had caught my eye on the pavement outside the hotel. It reminded me of one driven by Johnny Keenan, back home in Garrison when I was young.

'Has she the 948cc engine?' I asked him.

'No, she's got the larger 1098cc,' he replied, with a warm smile.

The old farmer, whose grey hair fell over a cragged face, flickered to life as he spoke about his car. Our friendship grew over a few beers in the Selborne bar, and a fuller flush seemed to settle on his tanned face when he told me that he had been born on a farm about fifteen miles from Bulawayo. While the Johnnie Walker flowed, he reminisced about his childhood, fondly remembering journeys into town with his father.

'Africa was very different then,' he said. 'The streets of Bulawayo were beautifully decorated with hydrangeas and jacaranda, and everything and everybody had its place! Now the country is destroyed with bloody commie crooks in charge. The Zim dollar is worthless and half the kaffirs have AIDS!'

Timothy reminisced about a time when Rhodesia was called the 'breadbasket of the world', and his father would pay the staff by the light of an old hurricane lamp on the veranda. He introduced me to his wife, who was from further south, near the gold fields of Mafikeng in South Africa. She told me she still remembered the day she arrived with her father on a steam train from Mafikeng, to find work at Timothy's farm. I loved their stories. For me, it was a privilege to be able to share an insight into their disappearing world.

They took me to see Rhodes's grave, and on the way we visited the grave of their only son. He had died on bush patrol, fighting 'terrs' down on the Mozambique border some years before. Looking at their broken-hearted faces as they stood by his graveside, I knew that part of their spirit had died with him. I watched as Timothy sprinkled wild flowers on the ochre rocks around the grave, a symbolic action recognising those daring men who had fought in this inhospitable landscape to forge a new home. Now, President Robert Mugabe had threatened to send them all back to England.

That afternoon, the Zimbabwean newspapers carried headlines of a South African referendum, which promised to finally end apartheid and lift the ban on the African National Congress (ANC). South African President F. W. de Klerk said a fundamental turning point had been reached: whites would help create a multiracial government. It was a historic time, and I thought about how the world was changing before my eyes: the Gulf War had ended, the Soviet Union had collapsed and South Africa was bringing apartheid to an end. Most amazing of all, I had had a ringside ticket to each event as it happened.

★

Eventually it was time to leave Zimbabwe for a few weeks, and we made our way to the wetlands of the Okavango Delta in Botswana. It was a chilly morning when we arrived on the floodplains, and the snaking river channels were blanketed with a fine layer of mist. Our guides took us out on the water in wooden *moroko* canoes. Jacob, the oarsman on the canoe I was in, brought us through tunnels of hanging papyrus reeds so densely packed that they blocked out the sunlight. Suddenly, we heard the shrill warning call of a coppery-tailed coucal, as a magnificent crocodile slid from the bank into the water.

'*Ngwenya!*' the oarsmen cried, as he pushed us smoothly upstream and pointed at some crocodiles resting on the nearby riverbanks. He was Bayeyi, and his people had faced these dangers in the wetlands for hundreds of years.

As the midday sun was rising high in the sky, we found a small island, where we disembarked and waited for the others to catch up. It appeared to have been used by poachers in the past: all the vegetation seemed to be strewn with elephant bones. It could have been an elephant graveyard, but it seemed like an unusual place for elders to come to die.

'We'll use these as goalposts,' said Richard irreverently, keen to play some rugby.

Alex produced a rugby ball and we began to throw it around. Jacob played too, even though he had never held an oval ball in his life. Midway through the second half, one of our team, an English journalist called Mark, came down rather heavily after leading a sprightly charge against the Aussie pack. He lay on the ground, clutching his right arm and screaming with pain. It was apparent that he had either dislocated or broken his shoulder.

I felt the absence of a humeral head in its normal position and tried to reduce it by placing my foot in his armpit, but received only screams of distress from the patient. With no painkillers to relieve his suffering, I got him onto a higher surface and hung a weight from his arm for about twenty minutes. Much to my relief, the traction brought the shoulder back into position. Against my advice, the patient got up and moved his arm in a clockwise circle, demonstrating his regained function.

'Never worked better,' he said.

From the wetlands of Botswana, we made our way back again to Zimbabwe, to a campsite on the outskirts of Harare, from where we would finish the journey to South Africa. Life there was strained, as the Zimbabwean police kept a watchful eye on travellers, eager to catch them exchanging money on the black market. April was approaching and my window for working as a doctor in South Africa was diminishing, so I took a minibus south to Johannesburg. From a distance, it looked like a mini-Manhattan rising from the African skyline. The bustling metropolis had developed as a consequence of gold being found in the flat hills of the Witwatersrand; it had no natural water supply. This gave it the distinction of being the largest city in the world not situated on a river, lake or coastline.

Johannesburg appeared to represent the free spirit of South Africa, but one had only to enter the city to encounter a different world, where streets patrolled by armed security men were clogged with poverty-stricken urban Africans, begging and hustling. The glass skyscrapers were surrounded by dilapidated Victorian buildings, which housed Indian bazaars and shops for traditional African herbal medicine. For the first time in Africa, we felt uncomfortable as we looked for accommodation in this chaotic mixture of different cultures, all competing to survive in the crowded, modern metropolis.

I awoke early the next day and took a taxi to visit Soweto, as I was keen to do a travel article for the *Fermanagh Herald*. The hostels there reminded me of the squalid conditions of the Moroccan workforce in Gibraltar, where one toilet was shared by a few hundred men. These were ordinary people, trying to eke out a living, often working long hours in the mines for somebody from another country. My visit to Soweto was a harrowing experience, and one that I have never forgotten.

The next evening, I visited a friend from Fermanagh who lived in a middle-class white suburb in western Johannesburg called Melville. The beautiful purple hues of jacaranda trees surrounding his house did little to hide the fact that his family were virtual prisoners in a residence surrounded by perimeter walls with razor-wire electric fences. As we sat drinking wine amongst the blooming red bougainvillea creepers, I listened to the hardened attitudes of his Afrikaans friends and felt uncomfortable in their presence. I didn't think they would appreciate learning that I had joined the 'Free Nelson Mandela' campaigns of the '80s.

My next stop was Cape Town. I wanted to check out the possibility of finding some locum work at the Groote Schuur Hospital, where Marcel, my friend from Gibraltar, was working. It was a thousand-mile, overnight journey across the barren scrubland of the Great Karoo. The train arrived the next afternoon, and I found accommodation at the Cape Town English Guest House in Long Street. It was quite basic, really, but seemed like heaven to a hardened traveller who had been sleeping on the carpet of the African earth for most of the previous four months. In the room next to me was a tall, blonde-bearded Welsh university student called Simon. We shared some pints in the pubs around Long Street, discovered we had similar tastes in music and, within a short time, had become good friends.

At the Groote Schuur Hospital, I was surprised to find an Irish colleague from Our Lady of Lourdes Hospital in Drogheda.

'You can get a job as a locum working here, but everything has really changed,' Marcel said. 'It's now more gunshots than gallbladders. They've lost most of the better staff, and it's just like any other big African hospital now.'

He told me that there was a nice SHO locum job in cardiothoracic surgery going in a private hospital in Long Street. It seemed the better option. It was near the hotel, and I only had a short time to spend in South Africa before leaving to work as a doctor for Carnival Cruise lines in the United States.

★

Cape Town was beautiful: a scintillating jewel set in an amphitheatre of mountains at the southern tip of the African continent. I loved everything about the city. I somehow felt I'd lived there before, and on occasion I felt I could one day make it my home. At evening time, when a thin layer of grey clouds draped Table Mountain, Simon and I would take the cable car up to where the trails of mist blurred the edges of the peaks and watch the sun setting over the shimmering city below. There, on that gigantic rock, poised between the heavens and the earth, we would sit and wait as the evening light descended over the southern tip of Africa.

Then, as the reds of sunset deepened into purples, and a sliver of white moon rose above the horizon, we would watch as the lights of the suburbs below twinkled to life in an orderly fashion. First to light up were the outdoor cafés along the Victoria and Albert Wharf. Five minutes later, the houses lit up on Robben Island, where Nelson Mandela had been imprisoned for so many years. Lastly, the yellow glimmers of the Primus stoves and the dancing bulbs lit by a thousand generators in the Cape Flat townships would brighten the wastelands to the east.

At weekends, we took turns in driving to the greenish-blue hillsides of Stellenbosch and Paarl, visiting the nearby Cape wineries. There are fewer things on earth more pleasurable than to spend a Saturday morning sipping some pinotage wine amid those transplanted oak and pine trees. The landscapes of the wineries were breathtaking. Small turreted castles were set into undulating green hills smothered with vines nurtured from cuttings taken from France almost three centuries before. My favourite place was Constantia, known as 'the Beverly Hills of Cape Town', because of its lush green vineyards and sprawling mansions decorated with magnificent art works and old Cape Dutch furniture.

Despite the idyllic setting, the older problems of Africa were always close at hand. One night, while we were watching a Pink Floyd tribute band in one of the bars off Long Street, a commotion started at the door. We learned that a couple of black clients wanted to enter and the owner of the bar had set his dogs on them. One of the black men was bleeding from a dog bite on his arm, and the dogs were jumping excitedly as a crowd of onlookers gathered. Such was the power of apartheid that, at first, none of the customers wanted to stand up against this blatant discrimination – this was their bar, and no black had ever had a beer at the counter. We watched in horror as the owner unleashed the dogs on the other man. The band were playing 'Us and Them' when Simon left my side to face down the owner and the rest of his thugs. Africa was changing, and they would have to accept the winds of change. A fight started and, of course, I rowed in and ended up getting in one or two punches before we were asked to leave.

Although racism, at least superficially, appeared to be less prevalent in the Cape than the Transvaal, problems with the rising crime rate were everywhere. One morning, when I went out to my car, I found a young African man trying to break into it. The object of his desire appeared to be the cassette player. He told me that he had two small children and no way to feed them. I didn't know whether to hand him over to the authorities. I decided not to.

Instead, impressed with his honesty and tempted by curiosity, I offered to drive him back to the shanty townships of the Cape Flats, where I could elaborate on an article I had written for the *Fermanagh Herald* about the townships in Soweto. His eldest daughter, Danile, was a slender girl with coffee-coloured eyes, whose mischievous smile reminded me of a child, about the same age, who I had treated in Baghdad some years before. In later years, I often thought of them. What would be the little girl's destiny? Would she take the cable car to the top of Table Mountain and sit there watching as the lights twinkled to life or would she wander through the slums with a Persil box balanced on her head, rearing her young family in a tin shanty wallpapered with as-yet-unprinted editions of the *Cape Times*?

★

One day, amidst my post, I found a letter from my sister, Anne, which had arrived at her London home. It offered me a position as a ship's physician, and asked me to travel to Miami on 21 May 1992.

In some ways, I was sorry to be leaving sub-Saharan Africa, abandoning the people there to the plague of HIV/AIDS. However, I also knew the enormity of the problem that faced these nations, and that there was little I could do from my position in a private hospital in Cape Town. What I could do, however, was highlight the problem, by writing about what I had witnessed.

The countries of sub-Saharan Africa needed to commence HIV-prevention and HIV-treatment programmes immediately, as a matter of urgency, and the Catholic Church had to rethink its position on the use of condoms. I sent a report on conditions in the townships to the *Fermanagh Herald* and a letter to Dr John O'Connell, owner of the *Irish Medical Times*, about the possibility of a me writing a column in his publication.

For the time being, I was on my way to the United States.

20.
LIFE AT SEA

In late May 1992, I flew from Cape Town to Miami to meet Dr Moses Herzenhorn, medical director of Carnival Cruise Lines. He was Bolivian and had worked for many years as a doctor at sea before assuming medical command of the whole Carnival operation. He had ten ships under his control and was responsible for all medical operations aboard them. We shared a pleasant lunch in Bayside, a waterfront shopping area near Biscayne Boulevard. It was a beautiful spring afternoon, and as the sun glinted from the clear water on the bay, it made me feel a little better about leaving Cape Town and coming to America.

'I don't normally put new British doctors on the bigger ships, but I really like the fact you have Advanced Trauma Cardiac and Life Support,' he said. 'I'm going to put you on the *Jubilee* over in California. It has a six-bed hospital and a coronary care unit.'

Moses told me that being a doctor at sea is different to being a doctor in any other environment. By way of explanation, he told me that the previous evening, one of his doctors had seen a twenty-seven-year-old galley steward with a painful, swollen testis. It could have been a torsion (a twisted spermatic cord), requiring emergency surgery, or simple viral epididymitis, requiring only painkillers. The doctor had no ultrasound on board to confirm a diagnosis, and decided to evacuate the patient by helicopter. Everybody on board saw the dramatic evacuation. Imagine his embarrassment when the smiling patient was waiting on the quayside in Mexico the next morning when the ship docked.

'What would you have done?' Moses asked me.

'I'd have evacuated him and taken no chances,' I told him.

Moses drove me back to my hotel by way of the palm-lined MacArthur Causeway, where rows of cruise ships with Carnival's coloured funnels emerged on the skyline like a pack of giant whales' tails. There were also ships there bearing the markings of Royal Caribbean and Norwegian Cruise Lines.

'Welcome to the cruise-ship capital of the world,' Moses said. 'You see that big ship up ahead in the distance – that's the *Ecstasy* – Carnival's newest ship. When you've spent some time in California, I'll bring you back here and put you on that ship. It's the biggest in the fleet and, being in port in Miami, you'll be closer to Ireland.'

I flew to Los Angeles and boarded the *Jubilee*. Once aboard, I changed into my new uniform and made my way to the bridge to introduce myself to the master of the vessel, Captain Giampaolo Casula. Judy, one of the nurses, dropped by to say hello and to give me a beeper. The bridge was mostly staffed by Italian officers. They were chatting together, preoccupied with getting the large ship out of port. I wandered amongst them. The captain, whom I recognised by the four gold bars on his epaulets, lifted his head from one of the maps and glanced at me.

'Ah, Patrick, the new doctor! I've seen your CV, it's very good,' he said. 'However, I don't want a good doctor on board my ship – I want a lucky one.'

The captain explained that he didn't want to have to turn the ship back to port with a medical emergency and be late to the next port. He'd have to listen to Miami saying they would have to pay a lot of money to the tour busses and the stores for business losses.

'Try also not to get any "notifiable" diseases,' he continued.

I could see why the captain wanted a lucky doctor. For the first time in my medical career, I would be serving two masters: the Hippocratic Oath and Carnival Cruise Lines. This conflict would later become problematic, when I had to decide whether to treat seriously ill foreign staff in the United States or send them back home with a monetary payoff.

The captain took me to his office and gave me a small blue book with the gold-embossed words 'Seaman's Identification and Record Book Republic of Liberia'. He opened a page and stamped it with the company seal, recording my first day at sea: 24 May 1992.

On the way back to my cabin, I listened to the clipped English accent of the cruise director on the tannoy: 'Welcome aboard and bon voyage! We're on board the superliner *Jubilee* sailing to Mexico on a seven-day cruise to Puerto Vallarta, Mazatlan and Cabo San Lucas. We hope you have a good cruise – happy sailing.'

★

The evening clinic started at six o'clock. Nurse Judy told me that the infirmary was always busy, and we had a separate crew and passenger clinics daily, each serving about ten to fifteen patients.

'The first patient has lost his T-tube – from his gall bladder!' she said.

She introduced me to a pleasant septuagenarian called Stanley, from Las Vegas, who had recently been in hospital for the removal of his gallstones. It appeared that his surgeon removed the stones but left a T-shaped rubber drainage tube behind to allow the bile juices to drain into a small bag. The tube was to be left in place for three weeks and then removed when everything had healed. Unfortunately, the tube was now missing, and the patient didn't know what had happened to it. It had disappeared while he was crossing the Mojave Desert, and the hole in his abdomen was now leaking bile fluid onto his clothes.

'What are we going to do?' said Judy. 'We'll be at sea for the next three days – we could get him seen by one of the surgeons in Mazatlan, but he'll pour off his bile juices onto his clothes, and he's bound to get an infection through that opening.'

I pondered the problem and decided that the tube couldn't have gone back inside. In the end, I decided to manufacture a new tube from a urinary catheter bag. Thankfully, the device started to work almost immediately. I fastened it to the patient with superglue. The tubing was still working the next morning, and the superglue held until we returned to Los Angeles at the end of the cruise. I took great pleasure in reading his letter to me later:

> The following day we drove 290 miles back to Las Vegas, Nevada and home. I went to the hospital and had a new tube inserted to drain my biliary tract. The 'crazy glue' let loose fairly easily and the hospital personnel had little trouble getting the bag off my side. The surgeon told me you did a great job and you are a great credit to the medical profession.

At the end of the clinic the nurse told me there was a woman in one of the cabins who kept telling staff she was seeing bees in her room.

'But they've checked and there's nothing there,' the nurse said. 'She even points to them. They think she's mad!'

She told me that it was difficult to deal with a psychiatric emergency at sea. This type of patient often required constant monitoring in the infirmary in case they jumped overboard.

We went to her suite together. It had a large balcony overlooking the sea. The lady was an elderly German, who spoke little English and was travelling alone. She was dressed in a bathrobe, hugging the bathroom door and trying to breathe through the clouds of insect spray provided by her diligent galley steward.

'Look at them everywhere!' she said, pointing to her sparkling jewellery on the table.

I lifted the jewellery and carried it over to her. Her panicked reaction assured me that she thought I would be stung. When I threw some of the glittering earrings into the air, her reaction confirmed my suspicions – she was having a visual hallucination! Her medical history revealed that her doctor in Hamburg had recently put her on Tryptizol for trigeminal neuralgia. It was better known to me as amitriptyline, a well-known cause of visual hallucinations.

The remainder of the first few days provided the usual plethora of passengers with ear barotrauma after flying, crew members with gastroenteritis, falls and injuries. These took a lot of time to properly document, in order to guard against the risk of an insurance claim.

After three days of sailing, we reached the coastal town of Puerto Vallarta, nestled in the foothills of the Sierra Madre Mountains and beside the tranquil waters of Banderas Bay. I wandered along the cobblestone streets of the esplanade, eyeing the far-off white *casitas* snuggled into the hillsides as if they were suspended in space. The town retained an old-world charm, and donkey carts rattled along amongst the buses and taxis. Things moved slowly, the pace of life seemingly dictated more by the turning of the tides than the raising of tequila glasses. The town was famous, as Richard Burton and Elizabeth Taylor had arrived in 1963 to film *The Night of the Iguana*, and they had settled in the locality after filming ended.

I listened as the noon bell struck loudly from the Church of Our Lady of Guadalupe, and watched as old women blessed themselves and said prayers by the little sidewalk stalls. There was something familiar about Mexico. Maybe it was the Angelus bell, the Madonna icons or the rosaries that reminded me of an older Irish generation, my home in Garrison, and my parents preparing us for evening devotions.

A rising breeze carried the mournful chimes of the bell towards the Cuale River, where washerwomen gathered their clothes from the bougainvillea plants and made their way back home to prepare for lunch. Then came the sound of a wandering mariachi band, playing 'La Cucaracha' for some American tourists from the cruise ship. The driver of an old flatbed truck hooted loudly as he tried to clear a path round a broken donkey cart blocking his way. A group of workmen stood huddled together on the back of his gaily painted vehicle, uninterested in the altercation.

That evening, I caught the last tender back to the cruise ship, which made a magnificent sight as it lay anchored in the harbour.

★

A few days later, a galley steward named José came to see me.

'My mother has a problem that her own doctor cannot fix – she's very sick – *empacho*!' he said.

I knew from my experiences in Gibraltar that the word '*empacho*' can be a general term for stomach illness. I wondered why he thought I could do something other doctors couldn't, but my mind was made up when he told me that the family lived in one of the little white *casitas* on the hillsides surrounding the town: I would visit his mother and see if I could help.

The next time the ship docked in Puerto Vallarta, we took a taxi up the narrow, winding roads to the little houses in the tropical vegetation on the hillside. The driver stopped outside a tin-roofed house, where an old grey donkey stood tethered to an outside wall. We entered the homestead, and José introduced me to his sister Maria, who, with typical Latin hospitality, gave me the best seat in the house and a small meal of *tortas fritas de maíz y salsa*. Then he took me to a dimly lit room where his mother was lying on a bed. She raised herself on one elbow to look at me.

'*Tengo empacho*,' she said weakly reaching out to hold my hand. '*Tengo empacho*.'

I bent down and put my stethoscope on her abdomen, thankful to discover that her bowel sounds were present. In the poor light, it was difficult to know exactly what was happening, but her pulse was quite rapid, and I thought she felt feverish. Just as I was going to request a urine sample, José put something furry into my left hand.

It was a small ball of hair.

I looked at him, unsure of what to do. He whispered to me that he wanted me make it appear that it came from her tummy. I bent over the old woman again, cupping my hands, first concealing the hairball and then producing it for inspection. The old lady gripped my hand and started shouting praises to the Lady of Guadeloupe.

'Thank you, Doctor Patrick,' José said. 'She believes in the old Mexican ways, and thinks an evil spirit or a witch put the hairball in her.'

Although I had been taken advantage of by José, in those few minutes I learned more about healing than six years of college had taught me. In an attempt to make some sense of disease, societies had established their own ritualistic behaviours, hoping to gain some kind of control. This is how bloodletting and exorcism had gained popularity. It was still quite normal also to see scars on the bodies of South American crew members from 'cupping', that ancient form of alternative medicine in which a local suction is created on the skin. Practitioners believe that this mobilises blood-flow in order to promote healing.

★

Some weeks later, we got a new Italian captain, Leonardo Francolla, who was in charge on a September night when we shared an emergency at sea. It was almost five in the morning when the beeper went off. We were on the second day of our journey, heading along the Baja peninsula with the coast of Mexico on our port side. This meant that we were outside US territorial waters, without the US Coast Guard to help evacuate patients in case of emergencies.

I wandered sleepily down the corridor, wondering what interesting ailment lay ahead of me. Vicki, one of the nurses, met me at the door of the infirmary. She looked distressed.

'I have a young woman from New York with severe abdominal pain, probably a bout of gastroenteritis,' she said. 'She has no fever or diarrhoea and her husband is here with her.'

I knew by the look on the nurse's face that all was not well. Walking into the isolation ward, I saw a young girl in her early twenties wearing a light green negligee. She appeared to be in agony, screaming in a New York accent. Her husband stood beside her, holding her hand. I asked him to leave while I examined his wife.

The cause of her pain quickly became apparent. She was in the final stages of labour.

'When did you have your last period?' I asked.

'Four weeks ago,' she said. 'I'm regular as clockwork,' she continued, gyrating in pain to the rhythm of another contraction.

On completion of a pelvic examination, I was shocked to feel that the baby's head was already crowning. Our patient was going to deliver much sooner than we expected. Vicki was a good nurse, with obstetric experience, but neither of us was prepared for a birth at sea. Despite my best efforts to gain control of the situation, the baby's head started to appear. I tried to rotate it as I pulled down to get a shoulder out, but there was a spiral of cord loosely wound around the baby's neck, preventing it from moving another inch.

We were at least two hundred miles from the nearest American port. The cord simply wouldn't unwind, and the infant's colour was a light shade of blue. If I cut it, I might deprive the baby of oxygen – if I didn't, the baby could die. Vicki gave the mother some Entonox gas, and found me an obstetric kit.

'Vicki, do I cut the cord or not?' I whispered above the wails of a patient who was going through the full pain of labour.

After some tense minutes and a small tear, the baby slowly emerged from the birth canal and started to cry. I cut the cord and the mother took over. The cries of the slippery mass in the nurse's arms brought the father running back into the improvised delivery suite.

'We have a *baby*?' he said, almost crying with delight.

'Yes, a beautiful little girl,' the mother said, smiling adoringly at the baby.

'Oh, she's beautiful!' the father replied. 'Now what will we call her?'

Just then, I realised that I still hadn't informed Captain Francolla, as everything had happened so quickly. I went up to the bridge, and together we put a statement of birth at sea into the log. Then I returned to the hospital, where I learned that the couple had decided to name their daughter Julianne, after the ship, *Jubilee*. And with that, little Julianne became the newest passenger on board.

The new parents, Scott and Elizabeth, sent me a lovely letter a few weeks after they disembarked. It said Julianne was twenty-four inches long and weighed eleven pounds. She is allowed to travel free for the rest of her life on the *Jubilee*. We remain good Facebook friends to this day, as I follow her progress through journalism school in New York.

★

The *Jubilee* went into dry dock for that Christmas period of 1992, and I returned to Ireland. The problems in Northern Ireland had not abated, and I read that twenty-nine-year-old Sheena Campbell, a law student at Queen's, recently had been shot dead by the Ulster Volunteer Force (UVF) while in the York Hotel on Botanic Avenue in Belfast. Her only crime was that she had been a Sinn Féin candidate in the Upper Bann bye-election in 1990. The IRA had attempted to plant a large bomb at Canary Wharf in London, and had exploded two bombs in Manchester, injuring more than sixty people.

Against this background, my mother's reasons for me leaving Northern Ireland had never seemed more sensible, and it was with her goodbye smile that I left that February to take up a position on the *Ecstasy*, sailing from Miami. I was glad to learn that Franklin, the chief steward, and Tom, the head of food and beverage, from the *Jubilee*, would also be sailing. It was nice to have familiar faces on board, and it made life much easier when trying to get favours done, like getting spills cleaned up or meals sent down to patients and staff.

One night, Tom phoned to say that a Haitian cook was deeply disturbed and believed he was under a voodoo spell. He thought he would die unless he got off the ship immediately. The situation instantly reminded me of the soldier who had felt he could see the apparition of St John the Baptist and had died in my arms at the Ibn al-Bitar Hospital in Baghdad. Cultural religious beliefs, often promoted by guilt, fear and shame, can have deep mental effects on a patient, so I didn't take the situation lightly.

We transferred the hallucinating patient to the ship's infirmary. Before long, some of his work colleagues gathered outside the door, holding lighted candles and chanting monotonously. They didn't try to gain entry, but the patient became more and more agitated. The nurses were scared that unless we sedated him he could easily jump overboard. The head of security, David Kelleher, arrived and told me that the group outside were chanting to a voodoo spirit, and they apparently wanted to get a Haitian priest on board to exorcise the patient. The drugs we were using could only sedate the patient for short periods, and he showed no evidence of any pathology, infection or other cause of his almost delusional state.

Franklin visited the infirmary and told me about some of the voodoo beliefs that he had encountered as a child in Jamaica. What little I knew about voodoo I had learned from Hollywood films, but I did not fear it. Eventually, as a last resort, I tried some hypnosis, which I had been medically trained to use in Scotland. The patient appeared to respond, and the nurses asked me to continue. Within about fifteen minutes, he had almost become manageable, but I asked the nurses and security to monitor him overnight until he could safely disembark the next morning and be taken to a hospital in San Juan, Puerto Rico.

★

Working on the *Ecstasy* was a wonderful experience. I had grown comfortable with the various aspects of my new nautical career, and felt confident that I could handle any emergency at sea. It is well known that if the crew trust their doctor, staff morale increases. The new ports we visited with the *Ecstasy* included a route known as 'The Western and Eastern Caribbean'. The western Caribbean cruise visited Cozumel, Mexico, the Cayman Islands and Jamaica; it was followed the next week by the eastern Caribbean cruise to the eastern Bahamas, San Juan, Puerto Rico and the Virgin Islands. Most of the crew looked forward to the western route, especially the white sandy beaches of Ocho Rios and the party atmosphere of a pub called Carlos and Charlie's in Cozumel.

The western route also brought us to the lush green foothills of St Anne Parish, Jamaica, where Bob Marley was buried. Bob's mausoleum was located in the hilltop hamlet of Nine Mile, about ninety minutes from where the cruise ship docked. These were the same hills where the spirits of runaway African slaves lingered and people believed in Rastafarianism, a religion based on Ethiopian culture. The belief developed in Jamaica during the 1930s, when labour unrest on the island led to the deaths of striking sugar-cane workers. They believed that their salvation lay not in a white man's heaven, but back in their homeland of Africa.

One of the Carnival pursers, Richard Lloyd, jokingly read some Rastafarian literature he had found in Ocho Rios to me as we made our way up the hillsides to the grave. The brochure quoted from Leviticus 21:5: 'They shall not make baldness upon their head, neither shall they shave off the corner of their beard, nor make any cuttings in their flesh.'

'Ah, so this is why Rastafarians like dreadlocks,' Richard said.

The Rastafari also used other biblical quotations to support their practices, such as Psalms 104:14, which they used to sanctify their use of cannabis: 'He causeth the grass to grow for the cattle, and herb for the service of man, that he may bring forth food out of the earth.' It reminded me of some of the Christian religious zealots in Northern Ireland, who also quoted Leviticus 18:22: 'Thou shalt not lie with mankind, as with womankind: it is *toevah*.' Using the old text as a moral guidance has its limitations, as the word *toevah* apparently does not even mean 'abomination'.

The use of cannabis was not only legal, but encouraged at the mausoleum. Some children even sold 'spliffs' near the entrance. Respectfully, we took off our shoes and joined some believers sitting on rocks near a small hut. Overhead hung a picture of the former Ethiopian ruler, Emperor Haile Selassie, who visited the island in 1966. One of the men offered me a smoke from a long pipe.

'Ya know mon,' he said, 'Bob himself wrote da song "Three Little Birds" restin' on dat very rock you are sittin' on.'

For a while, he looked at me, calculating, measuring me up as he slowly inhaled again. Silence descended as his eyes glazed over, his speech slowed and the perfumes of the nearby flowering plants mixed with the sweet aroma of ganja.

'It's all about respect mon,' he said.

Richard and I took the taxi back along the road, up to the tiny hamlet, where we stopped for a while. I looked down over the tin shacks and wondered how a man born into such abject poverty could have been so influential in my life. Religions are often known to reflect the environments from which they emerge, and many of the Caribbean islands – especially Haiti – had developed new religions or maintained their old ones in hybrid forms.

★

Later in 1993, I joined the *Fantasy* leaving Port Canaveral, close to the famous rocket-launch site from which *Apollo 11* had blasted off on its mission to the moon in 1969. I still remember the pictures of the moon landing on our black-and-white television at home. One morning, I was privileged to watch the spectacular dawn lift-off of the space shuttle *Columbia* on its five-million-mile, fourteen-day journey into space. It was a humid morning and we stood together by the rail of the ship.

It started quietly, a startled bird on the wing, a change in the wind, a faint yellow light at the edge of the far horizon. The light continued to grow as a pillar of fire detached itself from its umbilical tower and started its journey heavenward. I watched in silence, feeling privileged to witness man's challenge to the gods. Enthralled, we watched *Columbia* climb as the bright golden glow softened into saffron and swirled into a canvas of reds and greys that melted back into the light of the coming dawn. The air around us became thin and heady and as everybody started clapping, I thought about the men inside, those special people who regarded the challenge of space travel as part of their daily existence.

★

I continued as a doctor on Carnival's cruise ships until 1995. That year, I returned to Dublin and worked in the accident and emergency departments of St Vincent's University Hospital and the Meath Hospital. During that time, I became friendly with Dr Oliver Keenan, who helped me to cope with the fact that Trish was marrying someone else that year. On that day, I sent her a large bouquet of flowers and wished her luck. My mother hugged me and said, 'That's the hardest thing you've ever had to do – now let's put it to bed and get on with the rest of your life.'

One day, I saw an advertisement in the *Irish Medical Times* offering work for after-hours deputising doctors in Australia. The thought of sunny days living in Melbourne appealed to me. My application was successful and the medical group wanted me to start straight away.

21.
THE FLYING DOCTOR

I arrived in Melbourne, Australia's second-largest city, in February 1996. It was a nice city, with old green-and-yellow trams that clinked their way through tree-lined avenues, giving the city a feeling of tranquillity and ease of pace. In some ways, it reminded me of Cape Town, as wineries – with exotic-sounding names like the Macedon Ranges, the Yarra Valley and the Mornington Peninsula – enclosed the city on all sides. I rented a house in Toorak, an expensive suburb filled with art galleries, elegant shops and picturesque red-tiled period buildings. Nearby was bohemian St Kilda, where houses with white fretwork handrails and ornate wooden windows, once favoured by the gentry, had long been abandoned to students. It was also the centre of the city's red-light district.

One day, over breakfast, I read an article about Men at Work, a Scottish-Australian rock band who were reuniting in an old hotel in St Kilda after a ten-year absence from playing together. They had achieved international success in the 1980s with their hit single 'Down Under'. Their farewell concert was within walking distance of my lodgings, and I decided to go and see them. After the concert, as I was making my way back home along Grey Street, I noticed two street walkers on one the corners up ahead of me. One was bent over the other, who appeared to be in difficulty on the ground, and she started shouting for someone to help them. I ran over and saw that the young woman on the ground was almost unconscious, and considered the possibility she was suffering from a drug overdose.

'Has she taken anything?' I asked, calling for an ambulance with my mobile phone and identifying myself to the switchboard as a Victoria state-registered practitioner.

Within a short time, the ambulance arrived, lights flashing.

'So, Doc, what do you think is happening here?' asked the emergency medical technician (EMT). 'Is she a heroin overdose?'

There was something about her deteriorating condition that made me doubt that. Maybe it was the dilated pupils, the stridor in her breathing, or my sixth sense, but I was unwilling to go along with the obvious diagnosis.

'Has she taken heroin?' the EMT asked her friend.

'Yes, she had some earlier in the evening.'

'I thought so,' the EMT said, rifling through the ambulance emergency bag for some Naloxone, a powerful drug that specifically acts on the brain to counter the effects of a heroin or morphine overdose.

'Do you want me to give the Naloxone, Doc? Will I draw up 0.4 milligrams?'

'No,' I said, still trying to establish the cause of her difficulty.

Her case was baffling. Normally, a heroin overdose would have tiny fixed pupils, but this patient had the exact opposite. The patient was deteriorating before our eyes and had turned blue, but I remained calm and tried to establish the correct diagnosis. Medicine has to be exact, as the consequence of a mistake can be the loss of someone's life.

'Doc, you have to decide. We're gonna lose her, and the IV Naloxone won't do her much harm,' the EMT said.

That was not true, as the drug had a lot of side effects, including heart-rhythm changes, seizures and sudden chest pain, and I knew that it should not be used if the diagnosis was in doubt.

'No, give her adrenaline,' I said. 'Half a mig of one in a thousand IM.'

'Adrenaline? Are you sure?' he said, reluctantly handing me the pre-filled syringe. I thrust it into her leg and, almost immediately, the patient started to recover.

Her first words to her friend were, 'Fruit and nut chocolate? I told you I was fucking allergic to nuts!'

As the ambulance team shepherded the two women away, their leader turned to shake my hand.

'You certainly made the right decision there. Who'd have believed it – a bloody allergy to hazelnuts? Fair dinkum to you, Doc.'

★

The work at the deputising agency proved to be rewarding. On any given night, I would see a diverse range of conditions, from a woman going into labour, preparing to bring a new life into the world, to the other end of the spectrum – an older patient who had reached the end and was dying at home. The Australian medical authorities recognised the problems doctors had working late at night and limited the amount of opiates that we could dispense to patients in a month. One had to be resistant to the charms of the chronically migrainous and the pancreatic patient looking for shots of pethidine. It was difficult for me to turn them away, but if I didn't, I would just be seen as a soft touch and they would make a habit of phoning up when I was on duty. I'd seen it happen to one or two less-experienced colleagues.

As the weeks passed, I gradually got to know the other doctors working for the deputising company. Most came from English-speaking countries, especially the United Kingdom, South Africa and Canada. Initially, we met only when we passed on the stairs or while handing in our reports.

One day, a doctor asked if I was from Ireland, and I nodded.

'I'm from Mayo,' he said. 'The name's Ray Brennan.'

Ray was a good-humoured sort who had been working with the deputising service for the previous six months. He had a large house in Box Hill, a more Asian part of the city, and was looking for some-one to share the rent. As I was living alone in Toorak I decided to take him up on the offer. We sometimes met up while on duty in the middle of the night and visited patients together. One of these patients, a crocodile hunter, lived fifty miles away in the

Mornington Peninsula. He suffered from phantom limb pain in a missing arm, which he had lost to one of the reptiles. It was difficult to drive so far just to give a patient pethidine for pain in an absent limb, but this was a recognised neurological illness and had to be treated accordingly.

Melbourne was a great city for sport, and Ray and I both went to see the Australian rules football, which had many similarities to Gaelic football in Ireland. I adopted the Carlton 'Blues' as my favourite, while Ray favoured the Collingwood 'Magpies'. Both of them used the Melbourne Cricket Ground as their headquarters, and we looked forward to dressing up in gear and going to the matches. Melbourne was also home to the opening round of the 1996 Formula One Grand Prix. I was lucky to be allowed to work as a medical doctor associated with the track.

In late spring, Ray's mother died and he went back to Ireland for the funeral. I was at a loose end when he left and decided to try for a position with the Royal Flying Doctor Service in Broken Hill. This was an ideal opportunity to combine work with pleasure and experience some of the Australian outback at the same time. I passed the interview process, no doubt helped by the fact that three of the interviewers had direct or familial connections to Ireland. The fact that I was a qualified GP, an advanced trauma life-support instructor and had many years of emergency-room medicine probably helped as well.

Broken Hill is a remote mining city in the far west outback of New South Wales. The station had been the location for the '80s television show *The Flying Doctors*. The town had received its name from an entry in the diary of explorer Charles Sturt, who mined silver ore there in 1883. The break in the hills that the explorer noted no longer existed, having long since been mined away. The Royal Flying Doctor Service (RFDS) was started by Rev John Flynn, superintendent of the Australian Inland Mission about forty-five years later. In the early days it was called the Aerial Medical Service and it provided emergency and primary healthcare for people living in remote areas of Australia.

I was excited about my new position, and my colleagues in Melbourne started to tell me stories they had heard about the RFDS. One of them referred to the medical chests that everybody in outback properties had, for treating different conditions. The chests contained prescription-only medication, and the drugs inside could only be used by licence on the telephone advice of an RFDS medical practitioner. To help prevent abuse, the drugs in the chests were coded using a simple numbering system known only to RFDS medical officers. The story concerned an old stockman who called the Flying Doctors one day about his sick wife who had a pain going down her left arm.

'Has she any history of angina or heart trouble?' the Flying Doctor asked.

'Yes Doc, what am I going to do?'

'Open the chest and take two tablets from tray number six; this is Angised – a heart medicine. Put them under her tongue and we'll get a plane out to you immediately.'

The plane landed on the old man's property some time later, and the old man came running up, shouting, 'I think we saved her Doc!'

However, he proceeded to tell the doctor that when he had gone to tray six, it had been empty.

'So, what did you do?'

'I gave her a number four and a number two and she came up fine!'

★

There were three doctors in our team: John from New Zealand, Tim from Cornwall and me. We shared the RFDS house in the town and got on extremely well. On occasion, we had to drive to the hospital in Wilcannia, a small town two hundred kilometres east of Broken Hill. The town had once been one of the biggest inland ports in Australia, on the Darling River, which snaked through, carrying bales of merino wool under the coolabah trees and out to the harbours on the south coast. With the advent of the railroad, the town lost its significance and many people drifted away.

The hospital was staffed by older nurses, experienced in doing X-rays and stitching whatever lacerations came their way. One of our duties was to do a weekly ward round in the hospital, which was mainly filled with local Barkindji people, eager to be discharged.

'This is George, a forty-three-year-old Aboriginal male with haematemesis for two days,' a nurse told me on one of my visits.

Haematemesis was the medical term for vomiting blood, and it could be very serious in some circumstances, especially if the patient had ripped the lining of the stomach. It was usually associated with excessive alcohol intake, although one had to be careful that there was not a gastric tumour on board. He had been 'scoped' a few times at the Broken Hill base hospital, and the nurses usually discharged him with medication after he had settled.

'Well George, what happened to you?' I asked.

'I fell out with the lady from the lake,' he replied.

I was amused by his reply, but thought little more about it and went to see the patient in the next bed. My next patient was something of a surprise: a one-hundred-and-fifty-kilogramme male victim of domestic violence. I was intrigued when he also told me that he 'fell out with the lady from the lake'.

'We've done a skull X-ray, Dr Treacy, and he had a small parietal fracture, but his neuro obs have been OK for the past two days, so we're just letting him home,' the nurse told me.

Next, we reviewed a fifty-four-year-old white female suffering from gallstones, awaiting transfer to the base hospital for removal of her gall bladder. This condition can be extremely painful and patients are often admitted for analgesia before they are operated on. These procedures had been done in Wilcannia hospital in the past, but the facility had been downgraded as the population had diminished.

After that was a below-the-knee amputee suffering from Type 1 diabetes. He had sustained some facial lacerations when he had fallen from his wheelchair and had been kept in for observation. His home circumstances weren't good, but he seemed to be a favourite with the nurses.

'So, what happened to you?' I said.

When the patient told me he had 'fallen out with the lady from the lake', I had to take the nurse aside and ask her what the saying meant.

'Well, the native Aboriginal population here likes to drink those cheap three-litre boxes of red wine,' the nurse explained. 'They can't pronounce "Cabernet Sauvignon", so they call it by the Renoir picture on the outside. It's of a gentleman rowing a lady in a boat on a lake. It's responsible for a lot of business around here.'

There was little doubt that the Aboriginal population, like many displaced populations everywhere, had a problem with alcohol. It was sad to see these indigenous people, who had lived on this land for nearly 45,000 years, fighting in the parks and letting their children run around unwashed because of this addiction.

On the way back home, I visited an outback pub. The bar was a blurry canvas of khaki Akubra hats, Coopers Brewery beer mats and blue NSW Waratahs rugby shirts. As at most outback pubs, the only women present were those serving behind the bar.

'Where are you from mate?" said an overindulged Aboriginal jackaroo standing at the corner of the bar. He was a squat man with large shoulders and a muscular body, and it was obvious that many hard years of drinking grog had made him look older than his years.

'Ireland,' he said.

'Ireland? My second name is O'Brien!' he said, taking out his driving licence and throwing it on the bar counter.

During the evening, he became boisterous and got a warning from the barman. Before long, he started shouting at another customer and, when he started fighting, staff intervened and showed him to the door. I watched him as he left; a mischievous grin lit up his craggy face as he came back up to me.

'You know, mate,' he said, 'that's the bloody problem with us Irish – everywhere we go, we just can't hold our drink!'

★

About twenty-five kilometres north-west of Broken Hill lay the

iconic outback town of Silverton. The town had a brief but spectacular career during the silver-mining era of the 1880s, but fell into
decline as the larger, wealthier mines in nearby Broken Hill became
more successful. Silverton was not quite a ghost town, but there
were only around fifty people living there. It had appeared in over
one hundred films and commercials, including Bryan Brown's *Dirty
Deeds*, *Mad Max 2* and *The Adventures of Priscilla, Queen of the
Desert*. On weekends, I loved to visit Peter Browne's gallery there,
with his collection of VW Beetles painted as emus. It never ceased
to amaze me how people there could eke out a living in such a hostile environment.

My favourite hour in the outback was just before dawn, when
everything was covered in a blanket of darkness and no wind blew.
There was a feeling of solitude in the air, a strange mixture of loneliness and expectation, and I often thought about life in Ireland.
There was magic in the wakening morning, as the colours of the
sandy environment began to change, and daylight spilled across the
plains, washing away the night. On one such morning, I watched an
old Aboriginal woman approaching along the dirt track that snaked
through the back of the town. She walked with slow shuffling steps,
dragging over-sized shoes through the red dust, which rose in
plumes about her. The dust settled on her ragged clothing, coating
her unkempt hair and rounded face, filling in each craggy line.

The old lady was Barkindji, a people supposedly charged with the
custodianship of the land and all living things upon it. Her people
lived in a collection of dirty tin shacks that nestled around the bank
of the Darling River, a sleepy place where children ran naked
through the paprika sand and lethargic dogs stretched and scratched
in the midday sun. She carried a small stick, possibly to poke for
roots or catch one of the lizards that darted across the desert floor.
Eventually she stopped just beneath my patio, and began looking at
some old stones, which littered the edge of the roadside. For a while,
we stared at each other as her unwavering eyes looked deep inside
me, and told me tales about her people's lost dignity. For a brief
moment, mine replied, before I had to turn away, embarrassed by

the intimacy. The irreverent cackle of a blue-winged kookaburra called out loudly from a nearby tree, as if he recognised my shame.

Suddenly, the old woman got up and left, wandering further out into the bush, turning every now and then in the desert landscape as if the scrubland came complete with traffic lights. In the distance, I watched her continue this ritual, pausing to sit on the ground at regular intervals, and wished to get closer to her, to understand all things in the Aboriginal culture that were denied to me.

Another morning, I was on the veranda with Tim, listening to the sounds of a distant thunderstorm brewing and the tinkling of some raindrops on our roof. The atmosphere was full of mystery and one could almost smell scorched rain in the morning sky. The phone rang and, as I was on call, I answered it. It was Maureen, a nurse at Tibooburra, calling to say they had a female patient with acute abdominal pain to be airlifted to the base hospital. Tibooburra was a gold-rush town in red-sand country up at the very corner of New South Wales.

'What's the landing strip like?' I asked.

'Oh, there's no landing strip. You'll have to land on the road.'

The King Air took off and, as we rose high into the sky, daylight began streaming through the aircraft. From my small, circular window, I watched the streetlights of Broken Hill grow smaller and smaller. Soon the plane was alone in the morning sky, with only the drone of its engines to keep it company. The pilot contacted the base station in Tibooburra and requested landing flares to be put in position on the roadway. The desert below us was starting to come to life, and in the faint light I watched as a group of kangaroos bounced across the saltbush, no doubt startled by the sound of the aircraft.

'I hope they steer well clear of the plane when we're landing,' said Magnus, the pilot. 'I don't want to damage another nose cone!'

The pilot lined up the plane to make his approach, preparing to land due south. There was a roar of engines. The plane flitted on the crosswinds as it approached the bitumen roadway, and then landed with a bump.

'Glad to see you fellas,' said Maureen. 'If you confirm a diagnosis of her gall-bladder problem, I'll give her some pethidine for the flight.'

I examined the patient and concurred with the nurse's diagnosis. It seemed cruel that a patient could be left in pain awaiting a diagnosis, but it was vitally important to prevent a situation in which a patient with acute appendicitis, or even an ectopic pregnancy, could deteriorate on board the plane, their symptoms masked by pethidine. As we ascended, I looked across at my patient. She was sleeping, and I considered that without the Flying Doctor service much of Australia would be completely uninhabitable.

★

While I was working in Broken Hill, a position for a GP with specialist knowledge of dermatology came up in Toowoomba, about eighty miles west of Queensland's capital, Brisbane, and I took it. It would mean leaving the Flying Doctors, but I had done six months and knew a position like this did not appear every day for a doctor trained overseas.

Toowoomba was a university town of about 150,000 people, situated in the Darling Downs. The job was mostly general practice and skin-cancer management, initially with Dr Cormac Carey and Dr Peter Beeston at the Wilsonton Shopping Centre; I later worked with Dr Neville Lutton and Dr Jim McConaghie at the James Neil Medical Plaza. It was greatly facilitated by easy access to radiology facilities on the premises.

One morning, Dr McConaghie asked me to see a patient who had had a persistent cough for some time. He had started off with a flu-like illness, but soon progressed to fever and chills. Jim knew that I had worked as a respiratory registrar with Malcolm Sear in New Zealand, and wanted an opinion, as his X-ray showed a small basal pneumonia. The patient was a singer by profession, who performed in the local hotels and had been off work for nearly three weeks. He gave a history of severe headaches, lethargy and joint pain, and I noticed he had a small rash. He had already had numerous courses of antibiotics, which had done little to alleviate the symptoms. Of more concern was the fact that, on abdominal examination, he also had a large spleen.

Dr McConaghie was a seasoned middle-aged physician who had worked out towards the bush, in the isolated towns of Dalby and Goondiwindi. I respected colleagues who based in these environments, as they worked in the absence of radiology and laboratory backup, diagnosing ruptured ovarian cysts and appendixes, possibly delivering babies late at night and allowing God to take away the aged by dawn.

'His Q-fever test is negative,' he said, holding the results in his hand.

Q fever is a disease that was first described by an Australian pathologist called Edward Holbrook Derrick after an outbreak of the illness in abattoir workers in Brisbane. It is caused by an unusual bacterium called *Coxiella burnetii*, which is found in ticks, cattle, sheep, goats and other domestic animals. It causes severe headache, respiratory distress and joint pain.

'I think I know what it is,' I said. 'Do you keep budgies?'

'I do,' he said. 'Why?'

'Because you need to give them the antibiotics as well as yourself. I think they're infected with chlamydia.'

Dr McConaghie looked at me with profound interest. He knew *Chlamydia trachomatis* was the cause of the well-known sexually transmitted variant, but I was referring instead to its biological relative, *Chlamydia psittacosis*.

'How did you work that out?' he inquired.

I agreed that the patient had the signs of Q fever, but he had an enlarged spleen on the left rather than an enlarged liver on the right. Although it was a rare condition, I had seen some *psittacosis* cases in respiratory medicine in New Zealand and, once seen, they are never forgotten. This patient presented with a raised pink facial rash called Horder's spots, seen almost exclusively in this condition.

Needless to say, the sputum results returned *Chlamydophila psittaci* and the patient returned to full health with a double dose of doxycycline. When I went to see him perform at the Spotted Cow, a historic hotel on the corner of Ruthven and Campbell streets, he invited me up to the stage and we shared a microphone for Van Morrison's 'Brown Eyed Girl'. It was a duet that we went on to perform together on many other occasions during my time in Toowoomba.

Within a few days, Dr McConaghie returned the favour of the difficult diagnosis. The patient was a thirty-three-year-old farmer, suffering from similar flu-like symptoms. Some of his joints were quite stiff and swollen, especially in the mornings. It was evident that the illness was more debilitating than life-threatening, but I didn't recognise it.

'He's even got a little rash, but I don't think it's Horder's,' Jim said sarcastically.

The patient was unwell, but wanted to return to his duties on the farm. I felt it had to be something transmitted from an animal; my sixth sense told me it had to be a local or tropical illness.

'I get the feeling it is a transmitted infection,' I replied.

'Good guess,' he said. 'We'll hold on to you – it's Ross River virus!'

Dr McConaghie explained that this was a debilitating disease transmitted by saltwater *Aedes vigilax* mosquitoes, endemic to Queensland. The virus was not contagious, but it used kangaroos as reservoir hosts. There was no cure, and the patient often remained debilitated for many months.

'The Ross River is very close to here,' he explained. 'It's up in northern Queensland.'

★

Australia was a wonderful place to learn about dermatology, as Queensland has the highest rate of melanoma skin cancer in the world. I had had an interest in this aggressive cancer since I was a student in the Mayo Clinic in Rochester, Minnesota, in 1985, when I wrote my first paper on it.

Some of my Toowoomba patients were part of a melanoma vaccine study at the Princess Alexandra Hospital in Brisbane, and I was disappointed when the final result did not show as much benefit as we had hoped. I was chastened one day when one of my patients from my Flying Doctor days drove 700 kilometres with his family to see me. He was not part of the Brisbane study, but his condition had spread, and even with the administration of the vaccine, there was little that could be done for the poor man. Such was the nature of malignant melanoma: once the tumour cells start to move into the deeper dermal layers of the skin, their behaviour changes dramatically and the patient has an extremely poor prognosis.

On another occasion, I was examining a truck driver, when I noticed what at first appeared like a recent blood blister under one of his thumbnails. Despite his protestation that it was a jacking injury, I took off part of his nail to have a closer look. There was no blood, just dark pigment. As I had suspected, it was a subungual malignant melanoma; my perseverance in obtaining a diagnosis probably saved his life. He left the hospital later that week dressed in bandages. They had taken no chances and removed the last part of his thumb above the joint.

At the end of six months, I found it more tax-effective to leave Australia and go to live in South Africa or California for a while. During this period, I would also work for a few months as an Emergency Room senior registrar in St Vincent's University Hospital in Dublin.

★

When I returned to Toowoomba from Ireland in the summer of 1997, I rented a new apartment on the southern slopes of the Great Dividing Range, overlooking the hills of the Darling Downs. It was a short distance from the new Grand Central Shopping Centre, where another colleague, Dr Michael Kornfield, had his medical practice. Michael was different from the other physicians in Toowoomba: he had a melanoma scanner and a computerised cosmetic dermatology practice. He also had an old red post-war Cessna aeroplane and often promised to take me flying in the outback.

One day, Michael asked me to come over to the Darling Downs Aero Club at Wilsonton, where he kept his aeroplane. I noticed it had the licence number 'VH-HRH' on the tail wing, and joked with him about flying the 'royal' plane.

'At least it's better than the one I had in the Flying Doctors – it was 'VH-MSU!' I said, referring to the medical acronym for 'mid-stream urine'.

We plotted a journey that would take us out over the cattle stations and the properties of the Darling Downs, to an air show in Bundaberg. With a wobble or two, we were airborne and looking down on the fertile, green fields of Toowoomba. It was exhilarating to fly by the seat of our pants, without the aid of GPS navigation.

We were flying somewhere over the town of Nanango when Michael turned to me and said, 'Patrick, you really should try and bring Botox into your practice.'

'Botox?'

'Yes, whether you're staying here or considering going back to Ireland,' he said, 'it's the future and will be used to treat pain, spasms in children, as well as wrinkles.'

'OK, why don't I come over to your practice and you can teach me how to do it?' I suggested.

When we returned to Toowoomba, I made arrangements for some formal Botox training in Brisbane. Over the next few weeks, I began practising on some of my friends and, as my experience improved, I started treating a few willing patients. After a few months, working sometimes at home, I began experimenting with other medical conditions, including sweating, flushing, tinnitus and even teeth grinding. These studies were performed on very small numbers, and my early trials showed that it was very effective in sweating and teeth grinding, but less so in tinnitus and facial flushing. I also learned that a patient's facial appearance after a procedure was dependent on the amount and location of Botox used, and any complications were nearly always related to the physician.

Public interest in Botox had started a few years earlier, when a Canadian ophthalmologist, Dr Jean Carruthers, wrote an article in the *Journal of Dermatological Surgery*, suggesting that a biological bacterial toxin could be injected into somebody's face in order to take away wrinkles. An ophthalmologist from Vancouver, she had been using Botox to treat some patients for blepharospasm when one of her older patients asked her for an injection in her forehead for some wrinkles there. The treatment was successful and the genie was out of the bottle. Within a short time, news had spread like wildfire of this new wonder treatment that could melt away wrinkles.

I had watched Jean inject and had learned some new techniques from her. As I started to become more experienced in the use of Botox, I quickly realised that this pharmaceutical could have far-reaching applications, especially when used in conjunction with the new hyaluronic-acid dermal filler, Restylane, as both could change a patient's appearance for relatively little money, and with minimal downtime.

22.
MY MOTHER BECOMES ILL

During the Irish summer, I took some time off from my job in Australia and went to work for a while with Dr Rita Doyle in Bray, a seaside resort about twelve miles south of Dublin. The town straddled the Dublin-Wicklow border and was home to Ireland's fledgling film industry. It was there that parts of Oscar-winning films such as *My Left Foot* and *Braveheart* had been shot.

Rita and I had a similar approach to medicine and got on well together. One evening, while sipping wine in her kitchen, she asked me to mull over the idea of becoming partners, as she was considering setting up a new medical enterprise, which she wanted to call the Bray Family Practice. It would use my experience to provide dermatology, skin-cancer screening and minor surgical procedures within primary care. In many ways I liked the idea, but didn't commit to an immediate answer as Rita had been in bad health for some time, and I wasn't sure if she would be up to the task. In the end, we decided it would be preferable to consider asking one of the other locums, Dr Emma Nelson, if she would also like to become a partner.

I had been working as a doctor outside Ireland for over ten years and the thought of returning home was certainly exciting, but I had already established a sizeable patient list in Australia. In the end, I promised to keep in close contact with both Rita and Emma and to make a final decision about the partnership when I went back to Toowoomba. Over the next few months, I toyed with the idea of returning to Ireland many times, but I was settled in Queensland

and had a lot of good friends there, many of whom pleaded with me to stay in Australia. Near the beginning of November, Emma contacted me and asked if we could meet in South Africa if I was going back through there on my way home to Ireland that Christmas.

Emma and I met in Cape Town and spent some wonderful days together, visiting the Cape wineries and discussing the merits of sharing a possible future as business partners. We had very different personalities, and I knew this would be reflected in the way we treated our patients. I tended to be less of a talker, much more interactive and hands-on. That didn't cause me any concern because patients tend to gravitate towards the doctor they feel most comfortable with, and we could always swop our dermatology and psychiatric patients.

One afternoon, we visited the bar in Long Street where I'd had difficulties so many years before. It was under new management, and Emma laughed when I related the story of my apartheid experience there – her heart was with the African people too. We wanted to visit Robben Island, where Nelson Mandela's cell block had just been turned into a museum. There were rumours that it would be declared a UNESCO World Heritage Site.

Despite the new freedoms, it was quickly apparent to me that South Africa had a lot of problems: street children huddled together and slept openly on Long Street at night, beggars flooded the streets of Stellenbosch, and there was evidence of a rising tide of crime everywhere. It seemed like there was no control over the generation who had been freed from the shackles of apartheid. Worse still, before we arrived, a pipe bomb had exploded at the Planet Hollywood restaurant on the Victoria & Alfred Wharf, seriously injuring twenty-six people, two of whom later died in hospital.

After some restful days in the Cape, I returned to Dublin, looking forward to spending Christmas at home with my mother. I was still feeling good when I arrived, and hired a car to go to Garrison. Raindrops lashed against the windscreen like bullets, the wipers barely able to cope with the onslaught. Such wet conditions made the road feel oily, and I had just about reached County Cavan when the car aquaplaned across the road on the slippery surface and skated towards the metal rail of a bridge that spanned the River Blackwater. I watched as a large articulated lorry sped towards me.

There was nothing I could do except turn into the skid, and hope to regain control before the lorry reached me. As the car spun, the lorry clipped the back of it: a slight bump, but enough to send me skating into the rail. I heard the sound of metal straining as the car slammed into it and came to a halt. The rail held, and I vacated the vehicle quickly in case my luck ran out. I shuddered when I looked at the river below, realising I would have had little chance of survival if the car had plummeted. Torrential rain soaked me to the skin within minutes. The lorry driver ran up and hugged me. 'God, I thought I had killed you!' he said.

I put a call through to a good friend, Michael Brady, and went to stay at his house for the night. As soon as I arrived, I rang my mother to let her know what had happened and to tell her I'd be home the next day. The gods were conspiring against us it seemed – she'd had her own mishap with a lorry only a week before. A slurry tanker, leaking its foul-smelling cargo, had sprayed the walls, path and roadway as it whizzed past our shop. The thick viscous liquid covered everything, and as she was cleaning up the mess, she had slipped, hurting her arm and banging the side of her head. She had attended the local doctor, who had diagnosed a Colles fracture and sent her to the hospital – her arm would be in plaster for six weeks. She also said that her face was badly bruised and that she was sore all over. We chatted for a while and she seemed much happier for me to drive up the next morning, Christmas morning, rather than risking it that night.

My mother was a robust outgoing kind of woman when we were growing up. She was a plain speaker: she said what she thought and meant what she said. There were no 'sides' to her. When she was happy, she shared it with us, and when she was annoyed, we knew all about it, in no uncertain terms. As a result, I always knew where I stood with her. That Christmas morning, she seemed much frailer than I remembered, but that was understandable – a fall of that nature can be hard on the young, so a woman of her age couldn't be expected to cope with it that easily. Her bruises had changed from a dark purple to that mottled yellow which means the body is recovering. I took another look at her and noticed that she had bruising to both sides of her face.

'You fell on the left side,' I said. 'Why are you bruised in your right eye?'

'The doctor said the bruises spread there.'

To me, this was anatomically impossible. How could a person bang one side of the face and end up bruised on the other eye? My mother was jaundiced!

I told her I'd be happier if she had a few more tests, just to be on the safe side. She agreed, but I suppose she wasn't expecting to have them during the Christmas period. My biggest fear was that she had pancreatic cancer. From observing her and from what she had told me, all the signs pointed to it, but I wanted to be sure. I phoned her doctor and told him my suspicions. He remembered the events surrounding my father's death and was much more courteous this time and willing to listen. In fairness to him, he organised an MRI scan at the hospital on St Stephen's Day, bringing in a radiologist over the holiday period and doing everything in his power to help.

My worst fears were confirmed the following day. I knew my mother would not have much longer to live. My brother Brian and I were standing outside the hospital when I broke the news, and he smashed his fist into the wall, damaging his hand in the process. I was trying to cope with my own emotions, and seeing his distress added to the rising tension and sorrow within me. My mother would have to be told, and I couldn't leave it to a stranger to do so.

She was very upset when I told her that my suspicions regarding a pancreatic cause to her illness was now confirmed by the MRI. I told her that I would take her to see Professor John Hegarty, an excellent hepatologist in St Vincent's University Hospital in Dublin, where I had previously worked. We made the journey to Dublin together, and when she asked him straight out if she had cancer, he told her that she did.

'How long have I got to live?' she asked.

'Well, Mrs Treacy, nobody knows for sure, but we're looking at years rather than decades,' he said.

When my mother left the room to get dressed, he turned to me gravely.

'I'd give her nine or ten months,' he said. 'But we can put in a stent, Patrick, and buy her some time . . .'

★

My mother's illness came as a shock, and it left me determined to move home from Australia to Ireland and be with her while she still had some quality of life, and share her last days on earth. We had been very close, and she had helped me through troubled days as only a mother can. I decided to formalise the GP partnership in Bray.

At the end of January, I went back to Toowoomba to let my colleagues and patients know that I was leaving. My patients accepted my decision, and we arranged a farewell party in town. It was difficult to leave Australia, where I had built up a good practice.

The days passed quickly when I returned to Ireland, and I spent most of the evenings with my mother in hospital. Once the stent had been placed in her pancreatic duct, her quality of life improved noticeably. She started to regain her energy, getting out and about and enjoying herself as she had done years before. As she regained her strength and her colour returned to normal, she started to talk about doing things she had always wanted to do, like obtaining a driving licence and possibly visiting her sister in California.

Unfortunately, she seemed to think that she could beat the odds, and it was very difficult for me to try to explain that she wasn't going to come out the other end of this illness. I was her son, a doctor, and I think, for a time, she placed her faith in me to make it go away. She was in denial. If there had been any hope of a cure, anywhere on this planet, I would have found it, but there simply wasn't. In a strange sense, I think she resented the fact that I couldn't make her better. I found it hard to cope with myself, and sometimes a black despair descended on me when I thought about it.

★

Bray Family Practice started to grow in leaps and bounds and, within a short time, we were turning people away, as we had too many patients on our books. While I was in Australia, Rita had converted the garage at her house, and I moved my office in there and began performing minor surgical procedures. Within a short time, patients began attending from all over Ireland for the removal of sebaceous cysts, ingrown toenails and screening for malignant melanomas and other skin cancers.

The Loreto nuns in Bray kept me entertained with their stories about Africa, and they also kept me up to date with all the gossip from Gibraltar, where they had a sister convent. One day, during a physical examination of one of the sisters, I discovered a small pouch stuffed with thousands of pounds strapped to her body.

'We've just been out to see Bono,' she said quietly, knowing that I would be well aware of the problems involved in carrying money through customs in East Africa.

★

Over that year, Rita's health continued to deteriorate, and my worst fears materialised: an ever-increasing workload. After spending many months working every weekend, I knew I had to start looking for a practice of my own. I would be sorry to leave Bray, but knew that most of my patients could see what was happening and would follow me back to Dublin.

My mother remained relatively well for about ten months or so, and then her body began to slowly give out. As the cancer spread, it caused some gastric bleeding and she had to be hospitalised for prolonged periods. Between hospital visits, she stayed with me in Dublin and often asked me to marry before she died, wanting to see me settled with a family of my own. It was heartbreaking to see such a strong woman, who had never taken a holiday and had given her whole life to her family, waste away before my eyes. Towards the end, we decided to take her home to Garrison to die in her own bed. My sisters attended her at all times until she passed away.

The months following my mother's death were difficult for me, emotionally. I had spent so much time looking out for her health that the loss of her as a parent didn't really hit me until she was actually gone.

23.
SETTING UP THE AILESBURY CLINIC

Although I had a great relationship with the patients in Bray, things were becoming more difficult for me there by the day. In the end, I decided to move my medical equipment back up to my house in Enniskillen, with the help of my good friend, Peter Hanley. We rented a van and left Dublin. But sometimes life has a way of throwing a curveball right into one's path: we were about halfway there when a classmate phoned to tell me about a medical practice for sale on Ailesbury Road in Ballsbridge.

I went to see the practice the next morning. The clinic was located on the ground floor of an apartment complex on Ailesbury Road, long considered the best address in Ireland. It was in the embassy belt, between the Spanish ambassador's residence and St Michael's College, one of the best private secondary schools in Ireland. There were other, well-established, second-generation dental, psychiatric and physiotherapy businesses operating in the complex. Initially, it had been owned by an orthopaedic surgeon, Jimmy Sheehan, who had left to co-partner the opening of Ireland's first high-class private medical facility, the Blackrock Clinic, in Dublin in 1984. Since that time, it had been owned and operated by a plastic surgeon, Dr Gerry Edwards, until he had tragically died before his time.

The Ailesbury Road clinic was within walking distance of my apartment and seemed the perfect place to establish a new practice.

'Well, what do you think?' asked Peter.

'It's absolutely perfect!' I replied.

Looking around the adjoining rooms, I knew this was an opportunity to design a clinic to my own exacting standards. I would put in glass doors between the marble columns and paint the stucco with gold-leaf paint. It would require a three-phase electrical system to carry the increased load of my lasers, and the telephone system would have to be upgraded to handle an Internet connection. I would make the whole office paperless, and we would use scanners to update the patients' records.

I completed the purchase before the end of the week, and then went down to the Companies Registration Office and registered 'Ailesbury Clinic' as a business name. It was from humble origins in that two-room apartment that the Ailesbury Clinic brand was born. The early days were tough, mainly because the banks could not understand the model I was trying to create and were unwilling to invest in the overall project. I was turned down by Anglo Irish and Sean Quinn, both of whom had filed for bankruptcy before the end of the decade. Within ten years, the Ailesbury Clinic would employ over twenty-five staff and have offices in London, Istanbul and Dubai.

As we approached the end of the twentieth century, many technical innovations emerged all at once to address the effects of facial ageing. These included Botox, hyaluronic-acid dermal fillers and the invention of the IPL laser for hair removal. The new century ushered in a new era of thinking in medicine, in which stem cells and cloning might revolutionise the treatment of chronic disease. Many felt that if we could harness the power of stem cells or fibroblasts, we could repair damaged skin, burns, acne scarring and even, potentially, eradicate wrinkles.

While the clinic was being fitted out, Patsy Keenan, a childhood friend from Garrison, called from Atlanta and asked if I would come over and watch the United States Grand Prix with him. It was being staged for the first time at the iconic Indianapolis Motor Speedway. He had known my mother well and was aware of how difficult it was for me at that time. We hired a large Winnebago and took it on the ten-hour journey from Atlanta, through the historic towns of

Chattanooga and Nashville to the Midwest state of Indiana. It was just the break I needed.

★

During 2001, I continued to work in the accident and emergency department of St Vincent's University Hospital while my Ailesbury Clinic client base was growing. That spring, I introduced the concept of a Dublin walk-in clinic for minor surgery and, as business increased, I decided to stop seeing general-practice patients altogether and focus on practising cosmetic dermatology.

The new field of aesthetic medicine was in its infancy, and had yet to evolve in any specific direction. I found myself at the cutting edge of it, both medically and politically, and knew that although Ireland was rushing headlong into a new century, there was a general antipathy amongst my colleagues towards the use of Botox, especially when used for cosmetic reasons. Aindreas McEntee, the editor of the *Irish Medical Times,* was also aware of this and asked me to write a four-part series of articles relating to its conventional use in dermatology and other aspects of medicine.

'Patrick, you're going to have to first educate them about the medical uses of Botox,' he said.

We titled the first article 'Mapping the Long Journey from Sausage Poison to Wonder Drug' and the last one 'Botulinum Toxin Will Revolutionise the Practice of Conventional Medicine'. The *Irish Medical Times* had just completed publication of my Botox series when the *Sunday Tribune* published a controversial front-page article about its cosmetic use, penned by one of my surgical colleagues. The poorly worded and rather misleading piece was entitled 'Botox Will Leave a Trail of Disaster for Many Years to Come'. It was accompanied by an image of a girl with extremely pouty lips. The article was actually written by the first plastic surgeon with whom I had ever worked, and I was sure he would have been horrified to think the article could send the wrong message to patients, who might associate the product with lip augmentation.

After some consideration, I took pen to paper to defend Botox, and the paper published my letter of complaint in the first few pages of the next Sunday edition, along with an apology. Soon afterwards, the manufacturers, Allergan, asked me to be their official spokesperson in Ireland. At the time, it was considered brave to take a medical stand on the issue, but it wasn't long until many other media people, who didn't subscribe to the scaremongering, came knocking on my door. The rebranding of the wrongly maligned pharmaceutical had begun.

Michael Ryan at RTÉ's *Nationwide* produced a colourful, edgy fifteen-minute television programme on the rising phenomenon of Botox in Ireland, which included video clips of patients treated at Ailesbury. After that, RTÉ's *The Afternoon Show* went one step further and showed a patient receiving Botox injections live in the RTÉ studio for the first time in Ireland. Over the course of the next six to eight months, I was invited back on a few more occasions to both RTÉ and TV3 to inject different dermal fillers on live television. Michael Brady, who was now CEO of 98FM, asked me to do an interview on the radio about rising trends in cosmetic medicine, focusing on Isolagen, the new fibroblast treatment for wrinkles. This was a seminal period for Irish aesthetic medicine, and many of the programmes were later shown on RTÉ's *Reeling in the Years*, a programme showcasing the news stories that changed the culture of Ireland over the decades.

Meanwhile, patients were voting with their feet: despite the apprehension of some of my colleagues, the new field of aesthetic medicine was here to stay.

★

That summer, I went back to Cape Town, eager to interview Health Minister Manto Tshabalala-Msimang and other government officials about HIV treatment there, for the *Irish Medical Times*. I wanted them to explain why they had decided to reject the use of AZT in all ANC-run provinces, despite the fact that the manufacturer was willing to cut the price of the drug. Thankfully, doctors in the Western Cape were not under ANC control and went ahead with providing the drug. This was a ridiculous position, as the number of people in South Africa with HIV was nearing five million, and it was obvious to one and all that the drug was preventing the spread of the disease in newborns.

While in Cape Town, I was invited to a bar on the waterfront for a social function that was attended by some senior ANC government officials. At first everything was fine, and the conversation centred on the political direction of the new South Africa. We chatted about how they should address the major social problems of housing and poverty. As the drinks flowed, I expressed my opinion that President Thabo Mbeki's belief that AIDS was caused by poverty, not HIV, was not based on science, and that it was lunacy to assume that the communist health minister's approved diet of beetroots and ginger could save their people from decimation.

The truth didn't go down well intellectually or socially. In their eyes, I had crossed the diplomatic line. The officials refused to talk any longer, and eventually asked the staff to remove me from the bar. What irony! Six years earlier, I had been asked to leave a bar in Cape Town because I had stood up for some poor blacks who had been refused a drink because of apartheid and white racial prejudice. Now, I was being ejected from another bar in the same city because I had stood up for them against their own new leaders' scientific ignorance.

As I walked away, past children sleeping beside Long Street, I thought about how the emperor might have changed his clothes in South Africa, but when it came to the future health of the nation, it certainly hadn't been for the better. I was so incensed about what was happening that I wrote an article for the *Irish Medical Times* entitled 'A Tragedy That Has Resulted in Countless Needless Deaths in Africa'.

★

That September, I was working at St Vincent's Hospital in Dublin when the news broke that a plane had crashed into the World Trade Center in New York. As concerned staff gathered around the waiting-room television, the Sky News reporter announced that an American Airlines flight had hit the burning North Tower. Almost immediately, I knew that it was a terrorist attack. This was confirmed when a second plane hit the South Tower about the time my shift was ending at two o'clock.

As I left the hospital, I knew that the world in which I was living would never be the same. I phoned Julie, my receptionist in Ailesbury, to cancel my patients and try to find me a flight to New York. It initially proved impossible to get a flight into JFK, but I felt a personal attachment to the city and wanted to help it in its hour of need. Things eased again after a few days, and I called my good friend Pasty Keenan in Atlanta and asked him if he would come to New York and join me at Fitzpatrick Manhattan Hotel for a few days. By the time I reached the city, most of the immediate crisis was over and things were already beginning to settle.

Many Irish members of the NYFD and NYPD had assembled in Fitzpatrick's hotel bar, sharing their horror with us about what had happened. One of them told me that most of the casualties had been brought to St Vincent's Hospital-Manhattan, and he could get us down near the site of the destruction, now called Ground Zero.

Patsy and I took a taxi that afternoon through the empty streets of Manhattan. It began to rain heavily as we passed along Broadway, where the shops had replaced their window displays with giant red, white and blue American flags. The driver left us at Canal Street, and we began slowly walking to the intersection with Fulton Street, where a large plume of greyish smoke rose in spirals, darkening the sky. An acrid smell of burning plastic, along with a putrefying smell, which I assumed was decaying flesh, filled the air. The white dust, which had been hanging in the air for days, had settled, blanketing the loft apartments and obscuring the wording on the police barricades.

We stood in silence as rows of demolition trucks lined up in formation, moving like soldier ants clearing up after their nest had been attacked. I paused for a while at an impromptu shrine of lighted candles and cards with heart-wrenching messages to the many who were missing, now presumed dead. My eye caught one about Dr Sneha Ann Philip from St Vincent's Hospital on Staten Island. Two people handing out prayer leaflets stopped to say a few words. They were eager to chat to us, and Patsy took their pamphlet and read it to me. It said, 'This is a struggle between God and Allah – and our God is the greatest.' I looked again at the pamphlet and told Patsy that America would go back to war soon . . . and maybe, as the pamphlet said, just to see whose God was the greatest after all.

★

The Ailesbury Clinic was flourishing during 2002, and I decided to introduce a new means of skin repair using a fibroblast transplant method called Isolagen. The process involved taking a small biopsy from behind the ear to harvest cells, which were then cultivated in a laboratory before being re-injected into the area to be treated. The US scientists behind the project were keen to get FDA approval, primarily to treat wrinkles but also to treat acne scars and burn victims. In this period, we were finding more uses for Botox and were having quite a lot of success treating excessive sweating and migraines.

In May, I decided to go to the Monaco Grand Prix. I had become acquainted with a young nurse, Julie, who also worked in St Vincent's University Hospital, so I asked if she would like to accompany me. That year, we celebrated the final night on Eddie Irvine's yacht. Eddie had finished ninth in the race and was now on the Jaguar team, having previously raced with Ferrari. We partied well into the night and left the boat just as a full moon rose over the Mediterranean. It was indeed a romantic setting but, as yet, romance hadn't really blossomed between us. As we looked out over the vast expanse of water, we began to share our dreams with each other, where we saw ourselves going in life, and Julie told me that she would like to work in the cosmetic medicine industry.

Following the trip to Monaco, Julie and I became closer. She resigned her position in St Vincent's and came to work for me at Ailesbury as an aesthetic nurse. The patients liked her and, within a short time, she was injecting dermal fillers and had become quite proficient in injecting Isolagen fibroblasts. Over the next few months, we started dating more regularly. It was nice to have someone close with whom I could share the experiences of building the clinic, someone who would accompany me on my travels to conferences around the world.

By 2002, there were over a hundred cases of 'mad cow disease' in Britain, and the disease had begun to spread to the United States and Canada. The fear of this new disease led to the destruction of 4.5 million cattle. Doctors became concerned that the collagen they were using to treat faces and lips could become contaminated with the virus, which until then had been sourced in the United States from calves' hooves. An alternative source, roosters' combs, was proving just as disastrous, as a new avian influenza virus had been detected that could potentially create a new subtype, lethal in humans.

US patients looked towards European clinics to provide safer alternatives, and many travelled from New York and Los Angeles to Ailesbury Dublin to get the safer hyaluronic-acid dermal filler Restylane, which had been invented by the Swedish company Q-Med six years before. FDA trials meant that US doctors would not be able to use these products commercially until at least 2005. My lectures regarding my experiences with these compounds became popular, especially among my American colleagues.

★

In the summer of 2003, Ireland hosted the Summer Special Olympic World Games. I felt privileged to be part of it all, from the extraordinary and unforgettable opening ceremony to presenting medals to the athletes in Morton Stadium on the last Saturday. The philanthropist Denis O'Brien made his private plane available to the Iraqi team so that they could travel from the bombed-out remnants of Baghdad to participate in the games. During those memorable days, Ireland also became a special place, defined, not by exclusion, but by inclusion, embracing togetherness, abhorring human barriers of any kind, striving to change negative stereotypes based on ignorance and prejudice.

Also in 2003, I published the uncovered story of AIDS in Africa in my 'Cutting Edge' column in the *Irish Medical Times*. The article focused on the willingness of the South African government, under the stewardship of Thabo Mbeki, to allow the pseudoscience of Peter Duesberg to masquerade as science. It highlighted the fact that the provision of antiretroviral drugs could save countless children from being orphaned. I was awarded the coveted GSK 'Irish Medical Professional Journalist of the Year' award for my columns.

In October, I was invited to New York to attend the 2003 United Nations Association of the USA Global Leadership Awards. That year, Bono presented the honours to Dr Alex Godwin Coutinho, Executive Director of the Infectious Disease Institute in Kampala and head of The AIDS Support Organisation (TASO), for his great work in combating HIV in Africa. The singer had long been an advocate of fighting preventable disease, especially in Africa, by raising public awareness and putting pressure on political leaders to make and keep responsible policies.

In 2004, Ailesbury trialled a new non-invasive cosmetic technique called 'radiofrequency'. The treatment promised a safer way of tightening and renewing the skin's collagen. In October, I presented my results to the British Association of Cosmetic Doctors (BACD) in the Mayfair Hotel in London and was interviewed by the BBC World Service about the new technology. Around that time, we also starting conducting clinical trials on a new form of fat-injection treatment, involving the chemical phosphatidylcholine known as 'Lipodissolve'. I wrote a paper on our findings, which was published in the *Journal of Cosmetic and Laser Therapy*. I continued my research by combining this compound and radiofrequency for the treatment of cellulite, and the results of my work earned me an invitation to Salzburg in Austria and, later, to the Grand Hyatt in New York to relate my experiences to the American Society of Mesotherapy.

I had grown accustomed to Julie travelling with me to conferences and, during the fall, we travelled together to the International Congress for Injection-Lipolysis in Dortmund, Germany, and later to Florence, Italy, to lecture at the European Academy of Dermatology and Venereology Congress. Those were the experimental days of cosmetic medicine, when everything seemed possible, and Dublin was often teaching new techniques to the rest of the world. In that period, we had doctors coming from the United States, Norway, New Zealand, Australia and the United Kingdom to the Ailesbury Clinic in Ballsbridge, and we forged many relationships that last to this day.

I went back to New York that winter, and Julie and I attended the wedding in Club 21 of my previous Ailesbury Clinic receptionist. We stayed in Lower Manhattan with Dr Ed Schulhafer, a New Jersey allergist whom I had recently trained in the use of Dysport, a European form of Botox, which was gaining popularity in the United States. We also indulged our love of French Impressionists by visiting many New York art galleries, and the Museum of Modern Art on 53rd Street, where we saw pieces by Claude Monet and Paul Cézanne.

In 2005, the requests for me to lecture at international conferences began to increase. I also continued my own education in cutting-edge techniques. In January, I went to Miami to learn about a new thread-lift technique and met the famous French plastic surgeon Pierre Fournier, considered by many to be the father of cosmetic surgery. Julie and I later met him again at his house in Paris, where he gave me an original copy of one of his older 1960 lectures, 'The Concept of Beauty', which I proudly hung back at Ailesbury. It always amazed me how true innovators of aesthetics never had to promote their wares. There was something humble about their approach to medicine, and they were always willing to help other doctors learn their techniques.

That year, I lectured about the application of radiosurgery in cosmetic medicine at IMCAS Paris. As usual, Julie accompanied me on the trip and, later, we flew to Monaco, where I delivered a speech to the Aesthetic and Anti-Ageing World Congress regarding the Polaris laser. Although she loved to travel, Julie never lost her fear of flying. The take-offs and landings terrified her, but not to the extent that she would opt to stay at home. In April, we travelled together to Moscow, where I spoke about Isolagen and fibroblast transplantation at the World International Symposium on Aesthetic Medicine. It was fascinating to see the city again after so many years. This was a different Moscow, where the new Russian state saw its glory in its saints and martyrs and in the splendour of its churches, arts, science and literature.

In September, I was invited to speak about radiosurgery in general practice to the European Society of General Practice on the island of Kos in Greece. The same month, I lectured to dermatologists at the World Congress of the International Society for Dermatological Surgery, which fortunately was held in Ireland that year. There followed a few whirlwind months during which I spoke about radiosurgery at a dermatology conference in Japan, about how to treat cellulitis with phosphatidylcholine at the International Lipolysis Convention in Salzburg.

While at the conference in Austria, I explained that it was preferable to inject Lipodissolve at a specific angle into somebody's thigh, in order to physically disrupt the fibrous tissue. One of my German colleagues asked me what that angle was. 'Forty-five degrees – the *Garrison* angle,' I jokingly replied. I was amazed when I heard him mention the 'Garrison angle' in a lecture in Paris about a year later. If only my fellow villagers could know they were being mentioned on the world stage.

That Christmas, Julie and I decided to spend the holiday in South Africa. We stayed at the Cape Milner Hotel, in Tamboerskloof, in the shadow of Table Mountain. When we arrived on Christmas Eve, fires set by arsonists were burning all over the mountain. The papers said that some British tourists had lost their lives. Julie was a fantastic travelling companion and we spent our time shark diving, going on safari and visiting wineries. During our visit to Robben Island, we chatted to Joseph Gumbi, who had been incarcerated with Mandela, and to a female ANC member. Both had been very appreciative of my dedication to Mandela's cause. They hugged me and thanked me with tears in their eyes – we had travelled a common road together.

That year ended on a high when Ailesbury Clinic was voted best medical practice in Ireland at the Irish Healthcare Pharmaceutical Awards.

★

In January 2006, Julie and I returned to Paris, where I spoke at the IMCAS conference about the use of Bio-Alcamid filler in patients who were suffering from HIV lipoatrophy. This condition caused devastating, sunken facial deformities in patients and created a social stigma almost as bad as the disease itself. In 2001, when I treated the first patient in Ireland for the condition, it was as yet unknown whether AIDS or the antiretroviral drugs used to keep him alive were causing it. My patient had flown to Ireland from Spain, and I had used a product called New-Fill to achieve the desired aesthetic effect. Although the compound eventually gave good results, it was very problematic in that it required three to five treatments one month apart, and the patient needed thirty to forty painful injections. The injections also bled profusely, increasing the risk of HIV transfer to the person carrying out the procedure.

When I used Bio-Alcamid on these HIV patients for the first time in 2004, it opened up a new, safer method of treatment, in which the person carrying out the procedure was less exposed to needle-stick injuries and the patient had a treatment that lasted for life rather than two and a half years. I published my findings in the *Journal of Dermatological Surgery* that year. Because of my growing experience with Lipodissolve, I also published another joint study, with a professor of dermatology at New York's Mount Sinai, about its use in the reduction of infraorbital fat pads. In New York, I treated three HIV lipoatrophy patients. It was the first time that patients had been treated using this method in the United States.

★

In the spring of that year, Julie told me she was getting restless and wanted to live in London for a while. I decided to put her in charge of the new Ailesbury Cork clinic as a change from Dublin, and I set her up in an apartment there. My time was split between Dublin and Cork, and Julie could travel back to Dublin with me at weekends. She remained restless, though, eager to find a job in London. I had thought that both of us were committed to seeing the Ailesbury brand grow, but such is life. In the end, I didn't stand in her way. The relationship didn't survive the move, and we decided to split up a couple of months later. Although I knew it was for the best, I also missed the great times we'd had together, even the odd argument at work, but more especially the romantic dinners in the evenings and dancing in the Dublin nightclubs until the early hours.

That summer, I decided to set up a hair-transplant unit at Ailesbury and flew to Athens to learn the technique from Kostas Giotas, who had founded a company called Direct Hair Implants. Greece was still special to me, and the new development gave me a reason to visit Athens a few times a year, to attend hair-transplant conferences and to lecture. The Dublin programme was very successful, as hair could now be transplanted without the need for surgery or scars. As the new method became more popular, I travelled with Kostas to India to open some more clinics in Mumbai. Lorraine Lambert and I later developed the Ailesbury Hair Implant brand on our own, and we set up clinics in Athens, Istanbul, Mumbai, Jeddah and Dubai.

24.
MEETING THE KING OF POP

In late June 2006, rumours circulated in the Irish media that Michael Jackson had been sighted near the village of Kinsale, in County Cork. Over the next few days, sightings of the singer gained some credence, especially when RTÉ interviewed Bert Hughes, of Hughes & Hughes bookshop in Dun Laoghaire, who confirmed a surprise visit from Michael and his children. Speculation became rife that Ireland might have become the land of choice for the singer and his family, as it was known that he didn't want to return to Neverland Valley Ranch in California. In the days that followed, there were other reported sightings of Jackson – in a bowling alley and in a chip shop – but I thought little about it.

When the singer failed to show up at a Bob Dylan concert in Kilkenny as rumoured, fans were disappointed, but the speculation about him remained. I wasn't a huge fan of Michael's music back then, much preferring bands such as U2, the Rolling Stones and Pink Floyd, but I certainly recognised his genius when he performed on stage. His creativity crossed not only musical genres but also ethnic lines, and made us believe that we could make this world a better place. Like many others, I had followed his recent child molestation court case in California and become acquainted, through the media, with most of the facts.

The problems for Jackson started in 2002, when he allowed a British documentary film crew, led by television personality Martin Bashir, to follow him around for six months. The programme was broadcast in February 2003 as *Living with Michael Jackson,* and it quickly became apparent that the reporter had gone out of his way to paint a very unflattering portrait of the singer. After the documentary aired, Jackson was arrested when a young cancer sufferer, Gavin Arvizo, accused the superstar of molestation. I think it's fair to say that within media circles, there was a general supposition of Jackson's guilt. He had been accused before, by a boy named Jordan Chandler, in 1993, and had reportedly paid him off. From what I had read, the FBI had already investigated the singer, and most people operated under the assumption that there was no smoke without fire. What the media failed to report was that the FBI investigation concluded that there was no case to answer.

As the Arviso trial continued, it became apparent that there was no substantial evidence against the superstar. His accusers were simply not believable witnesses, and the trial showed that the family had attempted extortion before, trying to elicit money from other stars, including Jay Leno. Arvizo's parents had allegedly used his illness for their own personal gain. On reflection, something that struck me as odd right from the beginning was the lack of further accusations. Normally, when a paedophile of some years' standing is finally apprehended, the floodgates open and numerous victims find the courage to step forward. This didn't happen, and, in fact, those who had spent time in Jackson's company as children categorically denied any wrongdoing on his part.

While half of the media in Ireland was trying to find out if Michael Jackson was really in the country, the other half quietly focused on our booming economy, including the recent phenomenal rise of cosmetic surgery. One morning in August, I did a radio interview with RTÉ presenter Ryan Tubridy about this trend. When I arrived back at Ailesbury, I was a little surprised to find that a smartly dressed woman without an appointment had been waiting for some time to see me. She was black, attractive, spoke with a soft African accent and had saffron-tinted hair that fell around her face in small ringlets. She introduced herself only as Grace, and politely asked if she could make an out-of-office-hours appointment for a very prestigious client.

The request was not unusual. Many celebrities send a representative to view the clinic before deciding to attend. Their greatest fear
is that they will find the media camped en masse on the doorstep,
awaiting their arrival, cameras in hand. I had witnessed this first-
hand when, some years earlier, I had been asked to treat a famous
New York female singer known for her material ways with a new
type of radiofrequency laser at a location in Harley Street, London.
I had done the trials of this new device in Ailesbury, and few people
had the skills yet to operate it to its best effect. Much to my annoyance, the proprietor had apparently tipped off the press, and she was
photographed entering the premises. He told me that celebrities
often expected to be treated at his establishment for free, seeing
their patronage – and the surrounding publicity – as a privilege for
the clinic. This never happened at Ailesbury.

It *was* a little unusual that, having met me and viewed the clinic,
Grace still refused to name the client, although she did say 'he' was
a very famous singer when referring to the star. I was curious,
intrigued even. Before she left, Grace said that the client wanted no
media attention about his medical consultation and that one of the
main reasons he had decided to attend Ailesbury, was my reputation
for maintaining patient confidentiality.

'The singer finds it very difficult to trust people,' she said. 'People
are always trying to get something from him, so please don't mention our meeting to anybody. The singer already knows your work
and he'd like to become your patient.'

She smiled in agreement when I asked if the singer was
American, but was unwilling to give any more information about
him. For the next few days, I wondered who the famous singer
might be, half-hoping it might be Jay-Z or Puff Daddy who would
grace my waiting room. At that time, the hyaluronic dermal fillers
that we were using were not available in America, and I presumed
this was probably the reason for the visit, because we regularly
treated patients from California and New York.

On the agreed night, my nurse Carmel and I returned to the
clinic at about nine o'clock. She had her suspicions that it might be

a black singer and joked with me about whether she could get his autograph if it was Jay-Z. We passed some time cleaning up the clinic and then, right on cue at ten o'clock, the buzzer sounded. Trying to maintain a level of professionalism, we looked at the black-and-white video screen, where we could make out the image of Grace and a taller, male figure. Carmel buzzed them both through to the clinic, and I waited by the reception desk to meet them. An instant later, the door opened and the visitors entered. Grace kissed me lightly and introduced the male figure behind her. Before she could talk, he extended his hand to shake mine.

'Hi Doctor Treacy,' he said. 'I'm Michael Jackson.'

It happened so quickly that I was totally unprepared. He was the last person I had expected to walk through the door. Startled for a moment, I wondered why he would even feel the need to introduce himself – there would be few people on the planet who wouldn't recognise him. Michael was slightly taller than I had expected: slim, but not too thin. He wore a black fedora, his curly hair was tied at the back and he had a smile so infectious that it was impossible not to warm to him. His jacket was made of velvety black suede and it covered a white V-necked jumper that stretched tightly over his light frame. He wore little leather bands on both wrists, the type one gets on the beach during holidays on Greek islands.

We gathered by the glass doors near the clinic's reception area. He turned back around to me.

'You've already met Grace,' he said, 'and she tells me you're very interested in Africa.'

'Yes, we met a few days ago,' I told him, and then, smiling at her, said: 'I thought you were from Africa. Which country do you come from?'

'I was born in Rwanda but grew up near Kampala in Uganda,' she said.

'Kampala . . . I've never been there but I recently met Dr Alex Coutinho and his wife,' I said. 'He's working with HIV research at Makerere University?'

'I know Makerere – it's very famous,' she replied. 'I left Uganda when things got bad after Idi Amin, and was educated in the United States.'

I'd met Alex at the 2003 UNA-USA Global Leadership Awards Dinner in New York, where he'd been rewarded for his pioneering efforts to expand access to life-sparing medicine for people infected with HIV. I told Michael that Bono had presented the doctor with a global leadership award, but this didn't seem to elicit any response.

'I know that you do some humanitarian work in Africa,' he said.

'How do you know that?' I asked, assuming that during his research he had seen some of my YouTube videos.

Of course, I was flattered, well aware that Jackson had co-written the single 'We Are the World' with Lionel Richie and had donated all of the proceeds to help the needy in Africa. It had sold nearly 20 million copies, raising millions for famine relief and becoming one of the best-selling singles of all time.

I was completely taken aback when Jackson then retrieved an old, curled-up *Health & Living* magazine from his inner jacket pocket and proceeded to read aloud from it. Slightly bewildered, we listened. It was an article that I had written some years earlier. I never expected to hear an excerpt read aloud by Michael Jackson while he was standing in the waiting room of my clinic! 'There is an unchanging magic in the landscape of Africa but later, we pass many empty villages and vacant huts that are a testament to the destructive power of the plague whose path we follow,' he read.

I turned to Carmel. Her mouth was agape and her eyes wide.

Jackson continued reading: 'I am haunted by these deserted hamlets and, in the restless winds that stir the blue savannah grasses, I listen expectantly to hear the noise of playing children or the sound of barking dogs, but no sound comes.'

He lowered the magazine.

'You know,' he said to me, 'I really cried when I read this article. It captures the devastation of HIV in Africa.'

For a moment, I wondered if he had got somebody to check into my background, but then I realised that Grace had probably picked up the article from a selection I kept in a book on the waiting-room table. I sometimes complained when patients 'lifted' things from the display book but, in this case, I made an exception.

'I'm thinking of doing a big concert in Rwanda for all the children suffering from HIV,' Jackson said. 'Maybe we should do something there together.'

I thanked Michael for his kind compliments about my article. It had already won some awards for bringing the issue of HIV to a wider audience but, for a moment, I was unsure if he wanted to become my patient or wanted us to do a charity concert together in Africa. Recognising that it was probably the former, Carmel steered Michael and Grace into the waiting room to fill out some preliminary medical-history forms.

Grace then came back over to me and said, 'Tonight, we're only going over what Michael needs done, and giving you a chance to get to know each other.'

Michael came to join us.

'Grace says that I could do a concert in a stadium in Kigali that holds forty or fifty thousand people and, if not there, they have a large abandoned airfield,' he said.

I told him that I would love to help out in any way that I could on an HIV charity concert in Africa, but I was unsure about staging it in Rwanda.

I then suggested that the concert might be better staged in Cape Town, South Africa. In saying so, I was careful not to offend Grace by querying her homeland as the choice of venue, and I didn't know how far the project had already progressed.

Before she could answer, Michael spoke.

'No, we'll do it in Rwanda and then fly down in my private plane and visit Nelson Mandela in South Africa.'

The prospect of doing something about HIV in Africa with Michael Jackson was deeply attractive to me. With his help, a lot of my dreams and aspirations could be turned into reality. I felt I had walked away from the problems of that continent many years before, even though I had been highlighting the issues in the media. The invitation to help one of the most famous people in the world organise a concert, and the thought of meeting Nelson Mandela, made me feel that everything I had done up to that point in my life was coming together. I tried to curb my enthusiasm. After all, I had only met him for thirty minutes, and I realised he could just as easily change his mind – but I hoped he wouldn't.

On a personal level, I knew very little about the singer, except that he had given away millions of dollars to charity, which I admired. He had done this from an early age, while still a member of the Jackson 5, donating his share of their concert fees. He did it without fanfare or publicity, which others in his position might have sought. He had organised African charity concerts with Luciano Pavarotti, and donated the proceeds to projects like the Nelson Mandela Children's Fund. He had been determined to see projects through to fulfilment, and so he had decided not to use the United States as his base any more. If he had been found guilty and imprisoned there, his philanthropy would have stopped, and charities all over the world, especially those helping HIV victims in Africa, would have felt the immediate effect.

In the clinic, it was time to get to the business in hand – the medical consultation – so Grace left with Carmel to look at some cosmetic products, and Michael entered my office. There was something fascinating about him. He removed his dark sunglasses, placed his hat on my desk and took a seat opposite me. It was a surreal moment – I knew it probably wasn't the same hat that I had seen the singer tilt forward on his head, or fling jubilantly into the air at the end of a concert, but that was how it felt.

I turned from my desk and took a moment to study the singer's face more closely. His lips appeared to have been tinted bright red, probably coloured in with semi-permanent make-up. It must have been done recently, as that kind of 'tattoo' usually fades to a more natural pink within a couple of weeks. His eyebrows and eyelashes were jet black; given his age, I assumed that they had been dyed. His most peculiar characteristic was his skin colour, which was an artificial-looking peach-white, heavily camouflaged with beige foundation and rouge, and populated with lots of unshaven black stubble.

There was a large flesh-coloured Steri-Strip stuck over the tip of his nose, which I presumed was there to hide some damage caused by previous surgery to the area.

The whole effect was a strange fusion of David Bowie's Ziggy Stardust and Michael Jackson, all wrapped up in Kabuki-style make-up, but somehow I doubt that Bowie's chief designer, Yamamoto, would have approved of the look. Although I am known for being honest about my opinion on any aesthetic look, I considered it more sensible not to pass any comment on Michael Jackson's particular look at that time. He interrupted my reverie by leaning forward in his chair and clearing his throat a few times.

'I've heard much about you and I'd like to become your patient,' he started, shyly.

His voice transmitted in a kind of stuttering falsetto that only served to complete the theatrical effect. It was one of those moments when you are alone with a patient, and you can hear their emotions subsiding into breathing. I got the distinct feeling that he wanted to talk about something, but was too shy to mention it.

For the next thirty minutes, Michael and I talked in detail about his previous illnesses. He was nervous and reticent about discussing certain aspects, but after I eased his anxieties, he was more forthcoming and relaxed. He mentioned various cosmetic procedures that he was considering undergoing and we discussed the suitability of each of them. After I gave him my medical advice, we decided to go ahead with a cosmetic procedure for his face.

'I'm going to meet the Queen soon and I want to look my best,' he said.

'Fantastic. When will you be meeting her?' I inquired.

'It's not for a few months yet, in London.'

Michael told me that the Queen and Prince Philip were attending the opening of the movie *Casino Royale* in Leicester Square, and that he had been invited to the premiere, where he would be presented to her. He seemed quite nervous about it. However, it was still a few months away, and I suspected he had other concerns, apart from trying to perfect his look.

'How do you think you look at the moment?' I asked.

'Terrible – that's why I'm here,' he joked.

His attention was drawn to a picture high on the upper part of my wall, which he studied intensely. It was an image of a young doctor, Sneha Ann Philip, who had gone missing during the World Trade Center terrorist attack. I had got her poster from amongst many others when I had visited New York, and I had framed it into a collage of the American flag and the twisted metal structure.

I was originally drawn to it because she had worked as an intern in St Vincent's in Manhattan, where most of the victims had been taken. While in New York, I had written two articles for the *Irish Medical Times* about the medical aspects of the terrorist attack, including how the hospital had coped during the emergency. I had also interviewed many of the staff there, who actually showed me to her room to confirm that she had never returned. Visiting her room and having the missing poster somehow connected me directly with the horrific events in a human way.

Much had happened to me in those intervening years, but nothing as remarkable as what was happening now. I thought again about New York and watched as Michael stood up, took the picture from the wall and studied it. His facial expression totally changed, and his eyes grew sad as he focused on the picture of the missing intern set against the twisted wreckage of the buildings. That the singer was a deeply empathetic person was now beyond doubt in my mind.

'That's so very sad,' he said in a mournful voice, his eyes fixed on the message. 'Were you there, helping in New York?'

I told him that I had gone there in the aftermath of the tragedy, believing in my heart that it was right to share in the suffering and help in whatever way I could. He gasped lightly when I told him about visiting her room at St Vincent's, where her colleagues confirmed that she had never returned, and I presumed she was one of the victims of the terrorist attack.

'It was a terrible thing – all those people . . . ' he said.

He shook his head silently for a moment, remembering the horror of 9/11, and then spoke.

'I was in New York. I thought terrorists groups were going to blow up the whole city.'

'That must have been a frightening experience for you,' I replied, taking away the picture, as it was disturbing him a little.

'It was, but we are all God's children, and we have to pray for a tomorrow where we'll all love each other again,' he said.

There was something in that moment that made me realise there was more to Michael Jackson than the surgically altered androgyne who stood before me, whom the tabloid media loved to ridicule as a freak.

'You did a special concert for 9/11, didn't you?' I asked.

'Yes, I did a concert in Washington DC, but that really doesn't bring anyone back, does it?' he replied, his voice barely a whisper.

'There was an African connection to that concert as well,' I said, trying to lighten the mood, and remembering that Grace was waiting outside for us.

'Was there?' he asked, as if he had missed an important part of the concert.

'Your song "What More Can I Give" was originally written for Nelson Mandela, wasn't it?'

'Right,' he said, smiling and pointing his finger at me. 'You certainly know your music.'

'No, I probably know my Nelson Mandela – I once protested for his release!' I said, smiling back.

'Ah, that's good. Nelson's a good friend of mine for many years,' he said, as if casually mentioning the name of a neighbour who lived down the street.

The links between us deepened, and I thought that now that he had opened up to me, he was going to quiz me further about what I thought about his music. Instead, he became very contemplative.

★

Outside the window of my office, a resident pulled into the car park and went to get something from their boot. I closed the venetian blinds more tightly, to make sure nobody could see in, and went to find Michael. The door of the library was slightly ajar, and I found him reading Anthony du Vivier's 630-page *Atlas of Clinical Dermatology*.

He sat silently, slowly fingering through the words. The graphics on the page he had opened were mostly of black African adults and children, some with leprosy but all in various stages of hypopigmentary conditions. One image, of a child who had a large white abdominal patch and several more on his legs, appeared to catch his attention. He gazed at it for a long time before he began to read from the book aloud.

'Vitiligo is usually symmetrical, but occasionally can be segmental. The patches are completely de-pigmented and appear white, but not always in the initial stages,' he read, and then stopped and turned to me.

'Nobody knows how devastated that child feels. These pictures only tell some of the story. They can never show the emotion that the child feels, in here,' he said, pressing a fist tightly to his chest.

He pulled up one of his trouser legs and said, 'You see, I too have vitiligo!'

I was rather shocked to see the extent of his disease. For a long time, neither of us spoke, not daring to give words to our thoughts. Could it be that the world had been wrong all along about Michael Jackson, accusing him of denying his race while he actually had a medical condition that made his skin appear to be white?

'How bad is it?' I asked.

He seemed to think about the answer for a moment and then sat back in the chair. Shyly, he framed his face with his hands, lifted his shirt to show the porcelain-white patches on his body, and said, 'It's very bad!'

Then Michael took off his trousers, and I could see that his legs were so badly affected that they looked like a white man's limbs with large black spots, some as large as six to eight centimetres in diameter. The condition covered most of his body, making me believe that he had had it for many years. The average age of onset of vitiligo is usually in the mid-twenties, but it can appear at any age. It tends to progress over time, with larger areas of the skin losing pigment. Some people with vitiligo also have patches of pigment-loss affecting the hair on their scalp or body. He told me that for the previous twenty years he had been attending a Californian dermatologist named Arnold Klein, who had treated his skin for acne and the hypopigmentation caused by vitiligo.

I looked at him standing there and thought about all the tabloid newspaper reports that had accused him of wanting to deny his colour. I felt really sorry for him. Someone coping with an illness like vitiligo has enough to contend with psychologically, as their life is disrupted in a myriad of small ways that most of us are not even aware of. The complete lack of melanin means that a sufferer is also susceptible to skin cancers and must shield themself from the sun at all times, even in winter. For years, Michael had worn hats, gloves and scarves and carried an umbrella, rain or shine. Apart from the risk of skin cancer, his disfigurement prevented him from wearing T-shirts, or jumping into a swimming pool without covering up. I had seen TV footage of him jumping into swimming pools fully clothed, but never in a swimsuit. He had lived with this illness since he was a young man.

We talked about the disease for a while. He told me that when he was younger, he had tried to hide the disease, as he felt that his fans wouldn't listen to his music if he appeared less than perfect. Initially, he tried to cover the white patches with black make-up, but as time went on, and the disease progressed, it became easier to bleach out the small black patches left on his face, neck and hands. Eccentricity began as the perfect cover; later it just became second nature.

I began to believe that the world had treated Michael cruelly. When he was in my library talking about the emotional impact of vitiligo on the African child in the photo, he understood the psychological aspects of the condition on a far deeper level than I had imagined. I tried to envisage what it must be like to be accused by the media of denying his people, while carrying such a burden alone, painting his skin with creams, trying to control a condition rather than change his race. When he eventually found the courage to tell the world of his illness, it was deemed untrue, an excuse for changing his skin colour.

He asked if he could keep Anthony du Vivier's book, but I refused, saying that it was the only one I had. When he said he liked reading about medical topics, I offered him a smaller book, which also had information about vitiligo, but he declined.

'Here's my private cell number so you can keep in touch with me. Don't let anybody else have it,' he said. 'Oh, and I'll also need an anaesthesiologist when we're doing the facial procedure. The area around my nose is very sensitive. Can you arrange that?'

I thought that it was a very unusual request, but he explained that he had developed facial hypersensitivity after a botched cosmetic procedure on his nose. A few of my patients preferred full sedation while having more invasive procedures, and we always had an anaes-thetist on standby. In the end, I decided to comply with his request. 'That shouldn't be a problem,' I said.

After he had left, I thought about how he seemed like such a sensitive person. We shared common interests, and it would be nice to get to know him better and help organise his concert for HIV relief in Africa.

I would have loved to tell someone about meeting the star, but, of course, I couldn't. The urge to call my brother Sean almost got the better of me, but good sense prevailed. A number of celebrities from Ireland and abroad have visited my clinic, but this was the first time I had felt like sharing the news. Instead, I trawled the Internet to find out as much as possible about my prestigious new client.

Much to my surprise, I received a phone call from Michael a few days later, asking to see me again, as there was something else he needed to discuss. It was already dark when he arrived in a small black VW transporter. His American driver, Frank, waited for him in the car park. We talked about his vitiligo while he skimmed through the titles on the shelves. Then he asked if I had anything on the treatment of children's burns. I was a little surprised and asked why he wanted to read about that.

Some hair rose on the nape of my neck as he took two centre pages from the *Irish Times* and placed them on the blue granite countertop. I was surprised that he would be reading this paper and had a feeling that I was about to learn something else about him. The article he highlighted was about two children who had been set alight in the back seat of a car, in Moyross, Limerick, in the west of Ireland. Their mother, while visiting a friend, had been approached by two youths, who had asked her for a lift to the county court. She had refused, and, after some abuse, the youths had left. But then they came back with a friend, armed with plastic lemonade bottles filled with petrol.

They stuck rags in the bottlenecks and set them alight before lobbing them at the car. The two children sitting in the back were quickly engulfed in a roaring inferno. Gavin, who was five, and Millie, who was seven, writhed in agony as their horrified mother looked on. Sheila Murray managed to pull her daughter, Millie, from the car, while neighbours – including one of the perpetrators, who had been posted as a lookout and hadn't realised the children were in the car – rescued Gavin. Both children had to be sedated before being transferred from the Mid-Western Regional Hospital to Our Lady's Children's Hospital in Crumlin, Dublin.

'Oh Patrick, I think about those poor children all the time,' Michael said. 'They must be in such pain. They'll give them morphine, right?'

'Yes, they'll probably be on a morphine drip. In fact, I used to work at that hospital, in the accident and emergency department, and in orthopaedics. They'll be well looked after.'

Michael became more agitated as the discussion went on. It was certainly a horrific story, and I could imagine how it had played on his mind, but this was different – it was almost as if he could actually feel their pain.

'Do you know the hospital? Will you please take me to visit them there so I can see they're all right?' he asked.

I hesitated, feeling that it would be foolish for him to visit these children so soon after he had been accused of child molestation, particularly as one of the young burns victims bore the same Christian name as his accuser.

'I don't think that's a very good idea Michael,' I said.

'Patrick, I know what kind of pain they're going through. It's horrible – just horrible. Maybe I could help them in some way,' he said.

'I'm sure the doctors are doing everything necessary to lessen their suffering,' I said, not quite sure how to broach what was really on my mind: the press would have a field day.

'Why do you think I shouldn't go there?' he asked quietly.

I realised he was trying to gauge how I felt about the outcome of the trial, and I thought carefully about how to respond.

'Why do you think I shouldn't go there?' he asked again.

'Because the media would think it inappropriate to see you visiting a children's hospital,' I said.

He was very quiet, and I felt that my answer had disappointed him. I shouldn't have said what I had, but I couldn't take it back. I was completely unaware at the time that he had visited children in many hospitals, especially paediatric burns victims, all around the world while he was on tour. He often spent time with them after concerts, when most artists would have been either exhausted and wanting to sleep, or high on the energy rush and searching for a party. Michael had donated a vital piece of expensive equipment to a hospital in every city that he had visited while on tour. I should have answered him differently, said that the media would find out where he lived and follow his children around. My answer suggested that I didn't really believe the outcome of the Santa Maria trial.

'Do you think I would offend children?' he said, tears in his eyes.

'No, I think you're more like a modern-day Jesus Christ,' I answered sincerely.

The bright light had now died in his eyes, and his shoulders seemed to collapse in on themselves as he hunched forward in the chair. His whole persona seemed to disintegrate, and the vibrant, powerful personality diminished in front of my eyes. He then took off his black wig and showed me his scalp, his natural hair tightly cropped, wispy in places, with bald patches and a large scar on the crown of his head.

'This is why I want to go there; this is why I wanted to talk to you today,' he said. 'I was once burned too and I know what it's like.'

I was at a loss for words, so I fell back on what I know best – medicine. I got up and asked him if I could look at his scalp. I placed my hand on his shoulder and could feel the tension that had set in. My mouth felt dry. I knew I was stalling. I simply didn't know what to say.

He told me that while filming a Pepsi-Cola advertisement in 1984, a pyrotechnic display had fallen from the set, landed on his head and set his hair alight. It was apparent that he had suffered second- to third-degree burns to his scalp. It was only later that I discovered that he had donated the $1.5 million in compensation that he had received for the injury to a children's burns unit in Los Angeles. The Brotman Medical Center in Culver City, California – which later renamed its burns unit in Michael's honour – used the money to buy the best available technology for treating burns victims.

When I had finished examining his scalp, we discussed the possibility of treating the area with hair implants. Michael told me that he had had balloon implants inserted in his scalp in an effort to stretch the area, cut out the scars and, hopefully, restore his hair. This had gone on for a number of years, and he confessed that he had given up hope of ever repairing it and instead chose to wear a wig.

The event was all the more traumatic for Michael, as he had – I later discovered – become addicted to painkillers during that time. This was understandable, as many ordinary people have terrible things happen to them for which they require pain medication, and then have difficulty weaning themselves off it. I feel that in Michael's case, this was even more difficult because of media intrusion. When he signed himself into rehab, an undercover reporter had paid more than $40,000 for rehab fees on the off-chance that he would get to sit in on group therapy sessions with Michael Jackson.

Given the amount of underlying scar tissue that had resulted from a failed repair attempt, I almost immediately decided that Michael was not a good candidate for hair implants. My needle-stick injury, sustained so many years before, sprang into my mind, and I considered how a single incident could change one's life forever. I felt sorry for him.

'Michael, I'll personally visit the hospital tomorrow and find out how those children are, but I still don't think it would be wise for you to go there,' I said.

'Is there anything I could get for them – to make them more comfortable, I mean?'

'Let me assess the situation first,' I said, thinking that I might be able to chat with the parents to establish if the children were old enough to appreciate Michael's music, and to see if they would actually welcome a visit.

Michael replaced his wig, adjusted it in a small mirror, and composed himself. I still felt awkward. For some strange reason, I felt as if I had let him down. Before he left, I assured him that I would go to the hospital the next morning and give him an update on the condition of the Murray children.

The next morning, as promised, I went to make enquiries about the children. Many of the consultants that I met in the corridors had been junior doctors with me back in the '80s, so it was like stepping back in time in some ways, except that we had all grown older. The boy, Gavin, had suffered horrific injuries. Millie, his older sister, had received burns to 30 percent of her body, including her face, right arm, right thigh and lower back.

I decided that it would be unwise for Michael to visit the hospital. There was no way that such a visit could be kept secret, and it was almost a certainty that the foreign press would be notified. They wouldn't rest until they discovered where he was living. The Murray children were being well looked after, were sedated, and had been made as comfortable as was humanly possible. I also thought that they deserved the opportunity to recover in peace, and should not be subjected to a media circus. The only thing that remained for me to do was to break this news to Michael.

I made the call and told him how the children were doing. He was horrified at the extent of their injuries and still wanted to visit, but he had given some thought to what I had said, and decided I was right – the media intrusion would be too much to bear. I was relieved, and told him that I thought that he had made the right decision for all concerned.

'As a parent, there's nothing worse than something bad happening to your child,' Michael said. 'I really wish that I could visit them.'

He went on to talk about how much he was enjoying the quality time he was now spending with his children.

'I really feel blessed that I can have this time in Ireland with my own children,' he said. 'You know, today we were out horse riding. I just love the solitude of the Irish countryside.'

He said they were sleeping like logs as soon as their heads hit the pillow because of all the fresh country air.

'Do you not miss the sunny Californian weather?' I asked.

'No, I actually like the rain and the mist, especially after living in Bahrain.'

'How was that then?'

'Well, we left and we're not going back there. I'd like to settle in Ireland.'

'Where would you live?'

'Wicklow is nice and we're now looking at other property.'

'Maybe you should look at Fermanagh, where I grew up,' I said. 'It's all castles and lakes.'

'Castles and magic – the kids would love that.'

Michael mentioned that he wanted his kids to have privacy while they were growing up. He said that Prince William and Prince Harry had been allowed to live their lives without press intrusion since their mother's death. He wondered if a similar arrangement could give his children that kind of freedom in Ireland. They were getting older, and he felt it was time they went to an ordinary school, somewhere they could socialise outside of their own family, and forge their own relationships. Apparently, they enjoyed playing with the local children where he was living, somewhere in the centre of Ireland.

After a while, the conversation came round to the World Music Awards, which Michael was due to attend in London in November. He was aware that the British tabloids were proclaiming that he was expected to make a triumphant comeback at the event.

'How long is it since you did a concert in London?' I asked.

'The last time I sang in London was at the 1996 Brit Awards,' he replied. 'It's not a good memory, because some British guy invaded the stage.'

Ten years had passed, and I had forgotten that his performance of 'Earth Song' had been disrupted by Jarvis Cocker, front man for the band Pulp, as a protest against the way Michael was portrayed as a kind of Christ-like figure suspended above the stage.

★

By the time the long days of summer had abated, Michael and I had fallen into a routine of chatting casually, often for an hour or more, before I would begin any treatments. He used to call me nearly every other day on the phone, and I looked forward to our conversations. They gave me great insights into his thoughts, as the bond of friendship between us grew deeper. From time to time he mentioned the HIV concert in Africa, but mostly his thoughts were focused on making a new album with the cooperation of the American singer will.i.am. He said he was happier than he had been in a long time and that he liked life in rural Ireland, wandering in the hills on horseback with his family.

'I must bring you down to the house – you'll love it there,' he said.

'Where are you living, Michael?' I asked.

'Close to a recording studio in Westmeath now.'

It suddenly occurred to me that during all of our telephone conversations and his visits to the clinic, I had never asked where he lived, and he had never offered up the information. Grace had told me that people he had trusted had betrayed him in the past, so he had probably learned, over time, not to be forthcoming with the information, particularly when it came to his personal circumstances.

'I live near the geographical centre of Ireland,' he said, 'where the high kings were crowned.'

I wasn't sure where he meant, but had heard him talk in the past about taking walks with his kids in the Wicklow Hills and along the banks of Whitecastle Creek in County Cork. I'd noticed that he hadn't given me a specific address on the medical history form, but had accepted that he probably hadn't wanted to give any details of his location that could have been used to disturb his privacy. I guessed he was living near Paddy Dunning's place, Grouse Lodge, but I didn't let on.

'Are you recording something new?' I asked.

'I'm trying out some new songs,' he said.

★

When Michael invited me to his house again, I said that it would be an honour to see the recording studios and joked that maybe I could play guitar with will.i.am and himself – on one of the backing tracks. We joked around for a while, and then he asked if I knew a good dentist, as Blanket was having a problem.

Michael had already attended a dentist in Dublin and was satisfied, but he wanted someone suitable to treat children, and, of course, someone who would be discreet. I recommended a dentist who worked in the clinic beside me, saying that his work was excellent and that his discretion could be relied upon.

The next evening, we rang his Californian dermatologist, Dr Klein. Michael chatted to him for a while and then he turned to me.

'Patrick, I'd like you to talk to Carrie Fisher,' he said. 'She's a very good friend of mine and she's with Arnie in the office.'

I was surprised at the informality of it all, and I didn't know much about Carrie, other than that she had acted in the George Lucas film *Star Wars*. I needn't have worried, as she was a pleasant woman who spoke with the warmth and ease of those used to dealing with strangers.

'Hi, Patrick. I hear you guys are taking real good care of Michael in Ireland,' she said.

'Yes indeed, he loves it here.'

'He told me that – he's told me about you too.'

'All good I hope?'

The actor laughed and spoke for a little longer until I excused myself and handed the phone back to Michael.

'She's a very special friend of mine. I'm glad the two of you got to talk,' he whispered. Such a small incident seemed to give him genuine pleasure. Throughout our time together, Michael had a habit of passing me his phone and sharing his acquaintances and friends with me.

Now Dr Klein got on the phone and Michael had a few words with him before passing him on to me.

'Hello, Dr Treacy?' Arnie Klein here.

Michael sat to my left, listening to our conversation. He kept his head bent most of the time, but appeared interested in every word. Once we had agreed what needed to be done, Dr Klein and I started chatting academically, and our conversation soon became more natural – two colleagues in the same industry sharing what we had achieved in our field.

'Did you see my article in the *Journal of Dermatological Surgery* a few months ago?' he asked. 'It was called "Minimally Invasive Esthetics: My Life's Journey".'

As luck would have it, I had read the complete article; the same edition had included a research paper of my own, about Bio-Alcamid facial implants in patients who suffered from HIV lipoatrophy. We chatted for a while about HIV, and I forgot about Michael, who was waiting patiently for me to end my conversation. I explained that Bio-Alcamid was a one-off, permanent procedure, which reduced the requirement for having to repeatedly put a doctor, or his staff, at risk of accidental injury through exposure to the virus.

'Do you get many HIV patients in Ireland?' he asked.

'I did, but I get fewer now, as the hospitals have begun to treat them aesthetically.'

Michael then stood up and began to pace, obviously tiring of the conversation, which was going on much longer than he had imagined it would. I knew he was nervous about the upcoming events in London, so I brought the telephone call to an end.

'What's HIV lipoatrophy?' Michael asked me. 'You know, I really like what you are doing for the patients with HIV with that new product you mentioned to Arnie. Is it a type of filler? Could it be used in Africa?'

I explained that lipoatrophy was a type of facial-fat wasting, probably a side effect of the antiretroviral medicines that we were using to keep people with AIDS alive. Because African patients, particularly those in the sub-Saharan area, were often deprived of these medicines by their own governments, there wasn't a lot of use for the filler there.

'And what about the HIV patients in Uganda?' he said, taking his mobile phone from his pocket.

'Actually, I've already put a call through to Dr Alex Coutinho in Kampala,' I said, 'and we've discussed doing a trial on patients there, but I've had previous problems with the Italian company that makes that product, and I wasn't very happy with their response.'

Michael's mobile rang, and he answered it. With feverish eyes, he handed the phone to me.

'Chat to him!' he said. 'Go on, it's my friend. He'll help us with the concert in Africa.'

I sighed and took the phone. It was hardly the time to start talking to someone who I presumed was a concert promoter. I heard a distinctive voice talking in the background, and thought the person was probably an Afrikaner.

'So, are you going to help Michael and me get this concert in Africa organised?' I asked.

'Yes, how are you? We can make everything possible here in South Africa,' the man on the phone said.

'I'm not sure, but I think the concert will be in Rwanda,' I replied, looking sharply across at Michael. This person didn't even seem to know where the concert would take place.

'Where are you speaking from?' I continued.

'I'm speaking from Cape Town.'

'Oh, I used to live in Cape Town!' I replied, giving up my annoyance and trying to make the person on the other end of the phone feel more at home.

Michael started to laugh. Feeling that a joke was being played on me, I asked the man on the phone who he was.

'It's Madiba,' he laughed back.

'Who's Madiba?' I replied, absentmindedly, trying to concentrate again on what I had been doing.

Michael took the phone back just as I realised that the distinctive voice on the other end of the phone was Nelson Mandela. I couldn't believe that the person I had supported, in my small way, in his struggle for freedom had just been talking to me and I had been so abrupt with him. Michael continued to speak to him, but no matter how many hand signals I made, he wouldn't hand the phone over again. Maybe it was just Michael's way of saying that he was annoyed that I had dallied on the other phone with Dr Klein, but he terminated the call and put the phone in his shirt pocket.

'I wanted to commiserate with him about the recent death of his son from AIDS,' I said.

'Don't worry,' he said, sensing my disappointment. 'He probably won't remember anything anyway. Not many people know it, but he's in the early stages of Alzheimer's disease. We'll have to deal with his son to help us organise the concert. But I promise we'll go to see him personally when we're in Africa.'

'On the subject of HIV, I saw there was a story going around a few years ago that you refused to kiss the Blarney Stone as you thought you could catch AIDS or something else,' I said.

'Most of that was nonsense,' Michael replied. 'It was a different time, when people thought you could catch AIDS from kissing, and there was no cure for it.'

'I know – I once got stuck with an HIV needle,' I said, pulling up my trouser leg to show him the scar where I had been accidentally injected.

He looked at the scar silently, time ticked away, and he just didn't know what to say.

'It's OK,' I said. 'I went to theatre and got the surgeon to cut a lump out of my leg. I never seroconverted – it was nearly twenty years ago.'

'Then the children with HIV in Africa are the same for you as the photographs in your book were for me,' Michael said.

It was a deep, philosophical statement, and we hugged each other close. For a while, neither of us spoke. There was no need to say anything. I had defeated my opponent at an emotional price, while Michael was still living his nightmare. Yet our fates were also intrinsically linked by the events themselves: without my needle-stick injury, I would have been less drawn to Africa, and without the HIV article, Michael Jackson may never have become my patient.

★

I was in my office when Carmel came to get me.

'You'll have to go up to the glass room,' she said. 'He's taking all our creams and putting them into his pockets.'

The glass room was an area in the clinic that is constructed almost entirely of glass, with backlit shelving, where we kept expensive cosmetic products on display. It was big enough to hold a consultation, and had a table, chairs and a skin-analysis device. I went up and saw Michael with his back to me, stretching up to the top shelves, removing the more expensive bottles and placing them into his jacket and pants pockets. When these were full, he took a chair to gather a selection of the medical-grade facial creams and put them into a plastic bag that he had found in one of the drawers.

'You realise there's going to have to be a charge for these, don't you?' I asked.

He turned his head and looked at me sheepishly, slowly withdrawing some lotions from his pocket and pretending to polish the glass shelving before carefully placing the products down. I was amazed at the fluidity of his movement, especially since he was in his late forties.

When he had decided which products he could part with and had returned them to their shelves, he turned to me, showed me what he had left in his hands, and said, 'I'm taking these with me.'

I was surprised at his impulsivity, but presumably he felt that he was allowed to take whatever he wanted when he visited a clinic because he was *the* Michael Jackson.

'There'll be nothing left for the Irish ladies,' I sternly replied.

Obviously I had read the reports in the newspapers which called Michael a 'child/man', but that couldn't have been further from the truth, which is that when he relaxed, he became childlike. There is a world of difference between the two phrases. The man I knew was an intelligent, articulate, artistic and incredibly focused human being who also happened to be very gentle and kind.

I was not really surprised when he phoned me again the next day, saying that he wanted me to visit him at Grouse Lodge.

'If I send a driver for you, could you come down to the house tonight?' he asked. 'I'd love you to see my home.'

The driver's name was Ray O'Hara. He had worked as a DJ with Phantom FM radio, so I had heard his voice before. Ray was Michael's main driver in Ireland, but there were others. We chatted for most of the journey, and he told me that he worked as a chauffeur for Paddy Dunning, the owner of Grouse Lodge recording studio. Over the years, he had carried various bands from the airport, delivering them safely to the Lodge. We weaved our way around the Irish countryside for a while and, once Ray was satisfied that no one was following, we made our way to the village of Rosemount in County Westmeath. Apparently, some people had been found wandering in the grounds a few nights before and were escorted off the property.

'Will.i.am is down there at the minute – I brought him in from the airport,' Ray said. 'They're trying to record an album together.'

Ray told me that Billy Bush from *Access Hollywood* had recently interviewed Michael in the recording studio, and had then told everybody he met where he was living. Many reporters had started to arrive in the village, asking villagers about reported sightings.

'The villagers are saying nothing,' he said. 'They're great!'

We arrived by the entrance to the estate. The sun was being slowly swallowed by the countryside, and the shadows were falling fast over the nearby hills. There were some winding roads surrounded by low stone walls, and every now and then the driver would point out security guards watching the property. We passed the studio where Michael was recording his new album and made our way towards Coolatore House. The seclusion of the property had already attracted poets and musicians such as Nobel Prize-winner Seamus Heaney. Its two world-class studios had been used by everyone from R.E.M. to Snow Patrol and Shirley Bassey.

Grace was waiting in the dimly lit entrance porch to welcome me. It was a fiercely cold November night, and we made small talk about the weather before she took my green overcoat to hang it up. It was the one that my mother had got for me before she died, and I treasured it. After a while, Michael arrived and took my medical bag inside. We chatted for a short while in one of the lower rooms, which was decorated with dated period furniture and high, newly painted ceilings. A short while later, quite unexpectedly, he got up, saying he had better put the children to bed. He told me to follow him into one of the lower bedrooms, where Prince Michael was already in bed. In the dim light, Michael bent over him and kissed him goodnight.

'I love you Daddy,' the child said.

'I love you too,' Michael replied.

There was something extraordinary about witnessing that moment in a dimly lit room in the centre of the Irish countryside. Had the whole world made an awful mistake about this person? And was I wrong by not bringing him into the hospital to see the Murray children? Michael's personality, warmth and compassion were clear to see in the loving bond between him and his children.

Michael and I then went into one of the downstairs living rooms, where Paris and Blanket were already asleep with a jacket over them. Michael took one in his arms to carry upstairs, and asked me to get the other. I carried the sleeping four-year-old up to bed in my arms. Not knowing the difference, and seeing the long hair, I thought that I was carrying a girl. We were halfway up the stairs when I turned to Michael and said, 'She's a lovely child.'

'Don't let *him* hear you say that,' he laughed. 'He's my youngest son!'

So, this was Blanket, the child that Michael had dangled over the balcony for the fans at the Hotel Adlon in Berlin that night. I still remembered the tabloid images of the nine-month-old child in a blue jumpsuit, with his head covered by a towel, and it started to erode my positive impression of Michael. Which was the truth? The loving father or the erratic individual represented in the British tabloids. Every inch of me screamed that it was the former, and for a moment, I thought about asking him what had really happened that night. However, it never seemed to be the right time to ask these delicate questions.

'Why did you call him Blanket?' I asked.

'That's his nickname – his real name is Prince Michael Joseph Jackson II. Blanket is his nickname, it means "blessing".'

We left the children in their beds. Paris shifted, snuggling into him, and he gently kissed the top of her head. I had always thought that Michael Jackson was in his element on stage, but *this* was his element. I was touched by the love and normality of the scene. He was very obviously a doting father, much loved by his children, someone far removed from the media's interpretation of him. More than once, they had intimated that he was damaging his children in some way by keeping their faces hidden behind veils and home-schooling them.

When he had made sure that the children were settled, he showed me into another room upstairs. We chatted for a while about how the Murray children were progressing, and how he had enjoyed his day with his children. Then we got back to talking about a procedure.

'How bad will the pain be?' he asked.

'It's a bit painful,' I said, 'but if you really think you need to be sedated, I can do it myself or I can organise a highly qualified anaesthetist from a local hospital to be on standby.'

I was quite comfortable doing this, as I had gained a lot of IV-sedation experience with the Royal Flying Doctor Service in Australia and while working in accident and emergency departments, resetting dislocated shoulders or broken bones.

He thought for a few moments before he spoke.

'I'll have it without,' he said. 'I wouldn't have sedation without an anaesthetist present.'

Even though it meant nothing much at the time, those words

would ring loud in my head on many occasions in the years after his premature death. During the trial of the person accused of causing his death, Dr Conrad Murray, defence lawyers produced a scientist called Dr Paul White as their final star witness. He gave an expert opinion accusing the legendary singer of causing his own death. He stated that Michael had injected himself with a dose of propofol after an initial dose by Dr Murray had worn off. This is totally at odds with what I witnessed that night. My patient openly stated to me that he wouldn't receive sedation unless an anaesthetist administered it. I never saw any drugs in Michael's house, and he never asked me to write him a script for anything stronger than diet pills. How a cardiologist could end up giving him IV doses of propofol in his own house, with his children present, is beyond me.

He asked if I was in a rush to get back to Dublin, and I said I wasn't. In fact, I wanted to talk to him about the not-so-small matter of his bill.

'I'm really sorry Patrick, but you'll have to wait until I get back from London to get paid. My money is all tied up, but I have people working on it,' he said.

I agreed to wait. I had little choice in the matter. Finding himself virtually penniless in real terms – after generating so much cash throughout his life – must have been difficult for Michael to cope with. Some celebrities took the attitude that I should be grateful that they allowed me to treat them, but they were of no value to me, as I couldn't speak about them. Michael was different; the situation was obviously alien to him.

'I have to get control of my finances,' he said. 'I don't want to die another penniless black man while others benefit from me.'

'Well, there's not much danger of that happening – you're as fit as a fiddle.'

'As fit as a fiddle,' he repeated, and then threw his head back and laughed. 'I like it!'

Michael then opened a bottle of wine and we had a few glasses.

'Do you miss Neverland?' I asked.

'No, Neverland is now over. The media are probably wondering how I'm surviving without a daily ride on the Ferris wheel. They're stupid!'

He went on to explain that Neverland had been his dream home, and he had loved it for a long time, but it had been turned into something sordid. His home had always been more than an amusement park. It had entertained thousands of children: not only those who were sick, but those from underprivileged areas, giving them a break from their daily, grinding poverty.

'I built a home where children could feel safe, a sort of sanctuary,' Michael said.

He flopped back into the chair and sighed. I couldn't help thinking that if he hadn't had vitiligo, a lot of the negative press would never have occurred. He looked odd, ergo, he must be odd – that seemed to be the idea, and once that was embedded in the public psyche, the media had to feed the frenzy they had created. Michael Jackson sold copy.

'There are a lot of crazy people in America,' Michael said. 'I put veils on my kids so that when they went out with the nanny they could have a *normal* time. If I could keep their pictures out of a newspaper, the risk of them becoming targets went down.'

'Do you think you'll make your home here?' I asked.

'Patrick, I love Ireland, and this would make a great place to raise children. We get to do a lot of things together here. I'm working on it. I just have to get myself back out there, sort out my finances, and I'll set up home here. I probably won't be able to live here all year round, but most of it, anyway.'

We talked a little about the World Music Awards. I told him that Andrea Bocelli was going to be there. I had seen both Bocelli and Pavarotti in one week a few years previously. I also told him that I had met Pavarotti backstage before the concert, and it was a special time for me because on the Monday of that week, I had also seen U2 in concert in Munich.

'Bono does a lot for Africa. Maybe if you came to live here, the two of you could team up?' I said, laughing.

'I don't think Bono likes me,' he replied.

I never went into the finer details of why he felt that this was the case.

'Where are you from? Have you always lived in Dublin?' he asked.

'No, I'm actually from Fermanagh, in Northern Ireland.'

'Oh, you said that before. And how many are in your family?'

'I've three brothers and three sisters.'

'Almost as many as my own. Where in Fermanagh?' he asked. 'I hear there are some beautiful properties up there.'

'I grew up in Garrison, a little village by the shores of Lough Melvin. You like Charlie Chaplin, don't you? He used to fish on that lake.

'I love Charlie Chaplin! That's amazing! We must go up and visit that lake.'

'You'd love it, it's really beautiful.'

I told him I had just loaded a video of Lough Melvin onto YouTube, and explained that we had a shop, a filling station and a garage near the lakeshore, and that we would go swimming there in the summer.

'Sounds like a wonderful childhood,' he said. 'Did you have a good relationship with your father?'

'Oh yes,' I said.

I explained that my father had died many years earlier, but that he had been a good man and everybody had loved him.

'I hope my children say that about me one day, Patrick.'

'I've seen you with them, and I'm sure they will, Michael.'

'Thank you, my friend.'

He had brought my father to mind, and I started reminiscing about the good times we'd shared and how he had always been there for all of us. I told him a story about my father, from when I was still at St Michael's College in Enniskillen. I had entered the Irish Aer Lingus Biochemist of the Year competition with a study on the effects of different sound waves on the growth of mung beans. The project required special wooden boxes with acoustic wadding, so that the growing plants could be isolated from contamination by other sound waves, and be influenced only by those that were generated by an audio frequency oscillator. The materials were expensive, and I went to bed one night, depressed that we didn't have the money to buy them, I told Michael.

'And what happened?' he asked.

'Well, the following morning, I woke up to find that my father had made the acoustic boxes during the night,' I said. 'Incredibly, he had taken down the large, wooden road display from outside our garage and worked for hours during the night to complete the task.'

I explained to him that the advertising display sign had been easily fifteen feet by ten feet, and that it had cost my dad a few hundred pounds to erect in the first place. Michael was absolutely absorbed by the story and clapped his hands as he asked me what had become of the project. He was fascinated when I told him that the plants grew to nearly four times their normal size, and that the project had won the competition.

'That's just incredible,' he said. 'Why do you think they did that? Did they respond to a special sound that they loved?'

Michael had a long history of producing environmentally conscious videos about the earth and saving Amazonian plants. He listened intently, nodding with naive enthusiasm, when I started talking about the acoustic wavelengths that I had used. I half-expected him to use them for some record to save the planet. I knew he wanted to hear that my plants had loved a particular sound, and that that was what had caused them to grow so tall.

The truth, however, wasn't at all romantic. The plants possibly didn't grow because of their love for a particular sound: they might as easily have responded to a negative growth inhibitor, ethylene gas, which was released from the soil when the sound waves from the audio frequency oscillator blasted them. This was actually the most plausible scientific explanation put forward by me at my level of research at the time of the experiment.

Michael seemed very disappointed with my unemotional scientific answer, and I got the feeling he thought I was joking with him. To be honest, I felt I knew him well enough at this stage to throw some humour into the conversation.

'Michael, if I'd known you back then, I would certainly have played them "Earth Song".'

He studied me for a while and then starting laughing.

'No,' he replied, 'it sounds like those plants needed to listen to "Beat It" played way up loud! With Eddie van Halen on a Marshall amp as well – that'd get them growing.'

We laughed together for a long while and poured some more wine.

'You don't have any more patients to see tonight?'

'No.'

Michael went quiet for a few moments.

'That was such a great thing your father did,' he said. 'I don't think Joe would have done that for me. Did your father ever beat you?'

'Oh God no, he never raised a hand to any of us, he wouldn't—'

'Joe did – all the time,' Michael interrupted. 'He once wanted to be a professional boxer you know, so when he hit you, you knew you'd been hit.'

In my mind, the man's aspiration to become a boxer made it all the more horrifying that he would beat his children. I realised it was a different era and corporal punishment was acceptable back then, but according to Michael, Joe seemed to have gone beyond the accepted norms, even for the time.

'I try to understand it,' Michael says. 'Sometimes I think he felt he was doing his best, with a lot of kids, in a bad neighbourhood.'

Michael paused, trying to choose his words carefully.

'He wanted to be a musician, but he had kids to feed. Maybe it was failed ambition, maybe he saw the talent, so he worked us and worked us and worked us . . . I was terrified of him. Sometimes I think we were just his meal ticket. Fatherhood can be difficult, but I hope my children will have better memories of me.'

'Of course they will,' I replied.

'My mother was different though,' Michael said. 'She's one special lady: kind, gentle and way too trusting. She's the matriarch of the family and I got my voice from her.'

When Michael spoke about his family he was defensive.

'I don't really like my family,' he would say. 'However, one day I'd like a proper relationship with my father.'

I knew that when he had been accused of child molestation, his sister La Toya had given a statement to the press saying she could no longer condone his behaviour with young boys. He was still bitter about it. He started to talk about his brothers, but then didn't want to talk about them any more.

When I thought about it later, I felt I understood Michael Jackson a little better. His mother, Katherine, had contracted polio when she was quite small, and walked with a limp. He had witnessed that disease on an almost daily basis as a child. He had been raised by an abusive man and thought that Jesus was a saviour. Destiny meant that he had achieved fame, but he still remained penniless and dependent on others. His humanity meant that he had given away millions and still couldn't afford to pay for a few skin creams. It really was no surprise that he tried to make everything better – tried to heal the world.

As we both got a little drunker, he started talking about the Santa Maria trial and strongly hinted, regarding the issue of child molestation, that he had been set up.

'I'd never harm a child – anyone who knows me, knows that. They told me to part with some of my catalogue or the case would be brought against me.'

'Who did? Your record company?' I asked.

In retrospect, I know that this conversation is of public importance, but he never really answered that question properly. He said that he had received a telephone call, and I got the eerie feeling that he was very afraid of someone.

'They're watching you, watching all of us,' he said.

I felt a cold shiver and slipped naturally into my doctor's 'bedside manner', allowing him to unburden himself some more. So many in America still believed he was guilty, despite the verdict, that he felt badly let down by his own people – even those he had worked so tirelessly to help. He talked about Martin Bashir, and then he became silent. I looked into his eyes and saw small tears collecting at the edges of his lower lids. He wiped the back of his right hand against them and said nothing for a long while.

I felt I was intruding on his personal space and decided not to push things any more.

'It's time for me to start getting back to Dublin,' I said.

'You've no more patients to see tonight, I hope. Thanks for the chat,' he said, shaking my hand.

'That's no problem,' I replied. 'Look, grab a mirror – the filler has disappeared already.'

He brought out a mirror and looked again at his face.

'Great!' he said. 'That's exactly how I wanted it.'

We got up together and I went to get my green overcoat, but it wasn't hanging in the hallway any longer. If it had been any other coat, I would have left it and simply asked Michael to bring it with him the next time he visited the clinic. Michael and I searched the lower rooms for it but couldn't find it. We even asked Ray to give the van a quick check in case I hadn't brought it in, although I was sure I had. Eventually we found it behind the sofa in the room where Blanket had been sleeping.

Michael tried not to laugh, but couldn't help himself as he handed it to me.

'Sure, he's a thief and takes after his father!' he said, in a dreadful Irish accent.

It wouldn't be the last time that Blanket took a shine to something belonging to me.

A few days later, Michael flew to London and performed at the World Music Awards. It was his first UK performance in nearly a decade, and he was given the Diamond Award for having sold more than 100 million albums in his career. He had already been given the Millennium Award some years earlier, as he had sold nearly three quarters of a billion albums in his career. Although the reception he received was incredible, things started to go wrong for him later on in the awards ceremony, possibly around the time the audience discovered he wouldn't be joining Chris Brown to sing 'Thriller'. They were not impressed when he finally came out on stage and performed a very feeble version of 'We Are the World' with a children's choir, which sang most of the song. In truth, he only sang the chorus of the charity hit before stopping to repeatedly tell the audience: 'I love you, I love you.' The crowd started booing him as Rihanna came onto the stage.

The British tabloids were relentless in their criticism. The *Daily Mirror* reported: 'When he stopped singing no one could understand why. But when he started rambling, a lot of people lost their patience with him. That's when the booing started and it got louder and louder until he left the stage.' The last line of the report summed up most people's feelings: 'This was supposed to be the great return of the King of Pop but it ended up a shambles.'

I felt very sorry for Michael when he returned to Ireland. After a few days, he opened up and said he didn't have the confidence to meet the Queen after what had happened at the World Music Awards. I knew how much he feared meeting the Queen and how shy he was beneath his exuberant exterior.

'I really messed that up,' he said. 'I'm not going to even read the papers. I know they hate me.'

There were times I felt like Michael was alone and needed a close friend to chat with. True, he was close to Grace, but there were other things pressing the life out of him. He was worried that his fans would turn against him and he would be isolated, away from his home, his friends and his work. He wanted to make a new album, but now his confidence in his music had been shattered. I felt I didn't know enough about his new album to be of any real help.

I was also somewhat annoyed when the London tabloids stated that his last-minute demand from the World Music Awards organisers allegedly was a fee of $500,000, including twenty first-class plane tickets. One paper stated that he had erected a twenty-foot wall around the Hempel Hotel in Bayswater, where he and his party had paid £50,000 per night. But he had yet to settle his account with Ailesbury Clinic.

★

Near the end of November, I scheduled another trip with Kostas Giotas, the CEO of Direct Hair Implants, to see about twenty patients in Abu Dhabi who were interested in the Follicular Unit Extraction (FUE) hair transplant. I flew via Manchester, where I had been asked to conduct a training session for some doctors in the use of Bio-Alcamid implants in HIV lipoatrophy patients, as the NHS was considering introducing the treatment to public hospitals in Britain. During the session, Michael phoned me to see how I was, and asked the stunned lady who was holding my phone while I was lecturing if he could speak to me. He wished me all the best and asked if I would be kind enough to bring him home a souvenir dinner menu from the Emirates Palace in Abu Dhabi.

'And when you return from Abu Dhabi, I want to discuss more cosmetic treatments with you. I hate growing old and will have to stay in Ireland forever for you to keep me young,' he said, and laughed.

When I got back to Ireland from the Emirates, Michael called me again and asked if I would take Blanket to see the dentist. He said that he was in the studio all day and couldn't accompany his son, but wanted to send him to Dublin with a driver. Michael's children were lovely, mannerly kids – a credit to him. Blanket was the quietest, in my view, but reminded me very much of Michael. Although he didn't say much, he always struck me as being very observant, taking in all that was going on around him. His father said he wasn't that quiet at home, but he took a while to loosen up with new people. He had already met me on a few occasions, so I was no stranger to him.

I met the car when it arrived and took Blanket's hand to bring him in to see the dentist. As usual, he looked squeaky-clean. He always gave the impression that he had just been freshly scrubbed, with his long shiny black hair tied back, framing his pale face and big, dark, intelligent eyes. Ailesbury was literally a few steps away from the dental clinic, so I went with him in my scrubs. He looked so small in the dentist's big chair; his eyes were glued to my face.

When the procedure was over, I took him back to my clinic and sat him on the sofa in the waiting room, where he was completely absorbed by the flashing lights on the Christmas tree. It was lunchtime, so I told him to watch television for a moment while I got changed to go out. I was only gone a couple of minutes and, on my way back to the waiting room, I was informed that his driver had arrived. Blanket was now over by the fireplace, standing side by side with a decorative wooden snowman, which was much bigger than him. His eyes seemed to be huge in his head, and his arm was thrown around the snowman's neck. I stood in the doorway and told him that his driver had arrived. He stayed where he was.

I stretched out my hand and wiggled my fingers, signalling him to come to me. He didn't move. His lips sealed in determination, he tightened his grip on the snowman and seemed to be holding his breath.

'Why don't you bring your friend with you?' I said.

He visibly exhaled and, for a moment, I was treated to a wonderful smile, which lit up his whole face and reminded me of his father. He began to walk towards me but was hampered by the weight of the snowman as he dragged it alongside him. I bent down to carry it for him but he whipped it away – no one was getting their hands on it but him!

Blanket struggled with it all the way out to the door, where the driver also tried to give him a hand – but he was having none of it. It was really funny to see the determined little character drag his new best friend all the way to the car. It's an image that I'll never forget.

★

I called Michael again about his bill and he said he would send a driver to Dublin with the cash. The driver arrived, as expected, with rolls of dollars.

As Christmas drew closer, he seemed happy again, especially about having his family around him and thinking about buying presents for them. He fretted about what to buy Paris, who was eight.

The early part of December was dominated by deep Atlantic depressions, bringing spells of heavy rain at times. Towards the end of the month, there was a lot of air frost, and Michael phoned to tell me he was going back to the United States to escape the worst of the Irish winter. I suspected that although he had grown up in Gary, Indiana, it had been some time since he had lived in a cold climate during the winter.

On Christmas Day, the soul icon James Brown died, and I texted Michael to send my commiserations. I never received a reply, and I assumed that Michael was no longer using his Irish phone. He later contacted me to say that he was living in Las Vegas and would try and get back to Ireland as soon as he could. The years passed and other events began to take over his life, though. He never returned to Ireland.

25.

THE DEATH OF THE KING OF POP

Beginning in the early 1990s, Ireland had experienced unprece-
dented economic growth, which had seen real GDP double in little
more than a decade. There were many reasons for this, including EU
membership and Ireland's low corporation tax rate. Many countries
praised the nation's investment in education and training and its
ability to reverse many years of economic emigration. I never
believed that this was real economic growth, as it was mostly seen in
the building and construction sector, generated by a property-mar-
ket bubble that left Ireland in a very precarious position by 2007. In
this period Ailesbury expanded its influence into London and the
Middle East, and an opportunity to open clinics in Saudi Arabia
appeared, which required me to engage more staff to formulate a
business plan.

In April 2007, I attended the DHI hair transplantation awards in
Athens. Ailesbury was by then the second-most-successful FUE
transplant clinic in Europe practising under the DHI licence. The
method did not require major surgery and was practically painless.
We were beginning to attract many celebrities to the clinic for it. In
May, I returned to the Greek capital to speak at the European
Society for Laser Aesthetic Surgery conference. Sharing the podium
was Dr Yves-Gerard Illouz, the French plastic surgeon recognised as
the father of modern liposuction. In June, I received a citation at the
Aegean Masters Hair Transplant meeting in Sounion, Greece.

Michael called from time to time to say how much he and the

children were missing Ireland, and that he hoped to make it back as soon as he could. There was talk about him opening a Michael Jackson Hotel and 'doing an Elvis' by having nightly shows there. In many ways it seemed like a good idea, considering his financial circumstances. He also asked how the Murray children were doing, but their case had by now receded from the media, and I presumed that they had returned to Limerick.

'What about the album that you were recording with will.i.am?' I asked.

'It's going good, we're going to finish it in New York,' he said.

★

In 2007, Ailesbury introduced the Active Fx, a new method of laser skin resurfacing. The technology was a marriage of the Fraxel laser and older CO_2 lasers. Lumenis, which made the device, asked me to lecture about it at both the Aesthetic Cosmetic Medicine Fair in London and the Aesthetic Dentist Show in Birmingham. Their October meeting in Marbella clashed with the 2007 UNA-USA Global Leadership Awards dinner at Cipriani-Wall Street, which I attended. There, Ted Turner presented Queen Rania of Jordan with an award in recognition of her philanthropic efforts.

That summer I gave a lecture on the use of Botox in the treatment of migraine to the Migraine Association of Ireland. The technique was adopted by both the Irish and UK regulatory authorities in 2010, and approved as a preventative treatment for chronic migraine headaches. It is estimated that over three quarters of a million people in the UK and Ireland are affected by chronic migraines and that this can adversely affect their lives.

In early September, the great humanitarian Luciano Pavarotti died of pancreatic cancer in Italy. He had lasted about the same length of time after diagnosis as my mother had. I had met Luciano on a few occasions and been enthralled by his talent and great spirit of humanitarianism; I attended his funeral in Modena's cathedral. There were many familiar faces at the ceremony including Romano Prodi, Kofi Annan and Bono.

In that year, I became a regular contributor on TV3's *Ireland AM*. The programme discussed, amongst other things, the rising tide of obesity, and it gave me an opportunity to explain to Irish people the differences among the many fat-removal techniques, including Vaser, Smartlipo and the fat-busting injection Lipodissolve.

In January 2008, I presented the results of a trial using Radiesse dermal filler for hand rejuvenation to IMCAS in Paris, and then left for Seefeld, Austria, to give the same lecture at the World Leaders Congress. I shared the podium with Florida dermatologists Mariano Busso and David Applebaum, and introduced a novel three-way-tap method of mixing anaesthetic into this compound.

Meanwhile, back in Ireland, the economy was worsening, presenting new challenges: Ailesbury was left exposed after failing to secure venture capital to build clinics planned for the Middle East.

Later that year, I witnessed student riots in Constitution Square, Athens, while attending the DHI Gala Dinner at the Hotel Grande Bretagne. This hotel had been used as the Nazi headquarters after Athens fell to Germany in 1941. For three years, Nazis leaders had lived in the hotel, with regular visits by Hermann Goering and Heinrich Himmler. From my balcony, I could see the lush vegetation on the side of Lycabettus Hill in the distance and remembered another night twenty-five years earlier, when Van Morrison had played a concert there. On that night, I had met Pat and we had gone on the last 'Turkey run'. My life had taken a lot of turns since then.

That summer, Ailesbury Clinic was named runner-up for the best aesthetic clinic in the UK and Ireland *Aesthetic Medicine* magazine awards. Julie joined me for the gala ball and updated me on her life in London. Later, we went to the House of Lords, where Rhodes Scholar Dr Edward de Bono lectured on 'a thinking evolution', designed to help change global attitudes to humanity. The event had been organised by Lord John Laird, who had invited leaders in various fields to use their creativity to generate ideas on how to bring about this change for a better world.

I visited the House of Lords again for a surreal event at which Taoiseach Bertie Ahern supped wine with members of the Orange

Order to the sound of two giant Lambeg drums crashing away. I shared a table with Princess Rima al-Sabbah from Kuwait and Lord Iveagh, a member of the Guinness family. During the night, the Irish prime minister said he was leaving office, but would like to have been around to deal with the problems. It was shameful to witness his lack of responsibility in causing Ireland's downfall. Within days, the Irish Stock Exchange fell to a fourteen-year low, and we were heading towards a deep recession and the biggest economic collapse since the formation of the Irish State.

In January 2009, I presented research on fractionalised lasers to IMCAS Paris, and a Radiesse vectoring technique to the seventh Anti-Ageing Medicine World Congress in Monaco. I was invited as main lecturer at the SOCEMMAM Euro-Mexican Congress of Aesthetic Medicine Conference in Mexico City.

Michael called sometime in February and said that Grace was no longer working with the family.

'I'm going to be in London soon for a series of concerts and we can soon meet up again in Dublin,' he said. 'Have you ever seen any of my concerts?'

Embarrassingly, I had to say that I hadn't, and he promised me some VIP tickets. There was no mention of Dr Conrad Murray, and I felt that Michael wanted somebody to look after his appearance while he was in Europe.

In March, Michael did indeed go to London, and he did a press conference at the O$_2$ Arena, stating that the 'This Is It' concerts would be performed during the summer of 2009, and would be his last. The response was immediate: nearly one million people submitted website registrations to purchase tickets the first day. Within days, the singer's agreement to do thirty concerts at the O$_2$ had been increased to fifty. Michael would be with us right into the early part of 2010, and I wondered whether he would stage the concert in Africa, as he had earlier promised.

June came, and news leaked that Michael was going to be returning to Ireland for further treatment, as part of his 'This Is It' tour. Paul Martin penned a story for the 8 June British *Daily Mirror* under the title 'Jacko Goes Green'. Although Michael had mentioned that he would be in this part of the world during the summer, I had kept his travel details secret, so I was interested in what the red-tops had to say. The *Daily Mirror* article said:

> Michael Jackson will make secret trips to Ireland for cosmetic surgery check-ups when he moves to London next month. The moonwalking star visited Dublin's Ailesbury Clinic a number of times when he lived in Ireland for a spell three years ago. Now the 50-year-old singing legend is planning to return after striking up a friendship with top cosmetic dermatologist Dr Patrick Treacy. A source revealed: "Michael has been there in the past but nobody has ever known about it. He has a great deal of admiration for Dr Treacy's work . . . Michael will fly over whenever he needs his skin treated and also for top-up treatments on surgery that he has had done in the past. He is always having his skin looked at because of his vitiligo, a condition that whitens his appearance."

The piece continued, saying that he felt 'comfortable at the Ailesbury because he doesn't get harassed by paparazzi there. All eyes will be on him so it's great that he can get away to Ireland when he needs to and be off the radar.' The article was interesting, as its source seemed to know as much as me about his impending visit and also seemed to quash other recent gossip: 'And despite rumours the star is too ill to perform at the 50 "sell-out" gigs the source added: "Michael is in good shape and has been leaving the younger dancers in the rehearsals in awe of him."' I later spoke to Paul Martin, who confirmed to me he had heard the rumour from a member of the singer's entourage.

Days passed, and I looked forward to Michael returning to Europe. He hadn't called in a while, and I wondered whether everything was OK. Meanwhile, he was attending Arnie Klein in Los Angeles, and if later reports are to be believed, received nearly $50,000 worth of medical services in the three-month period between 23 March and 22 June 2009. Some say he had over one hundred small procedures, probably to satisfy his body dysmorphic disorder. He allegedly also received quite a lot of Demerol in this period. Worse, what I didn't know was that Michael was suffering from insomnia and had employed the services of another doctor to provide him with the same propofol that we had used as anaesthesia in Dublin, as an infusion to get him to sleep.

I was at home in Ballsbridge when a breaking news report came on television: 'We've just learned that Michael Jackson was taken, by ambulance, to a hospital in Los Angeles . . . We're told it was cardiac arrest, and that paramedics administered CPR in the ambulance . . . It's looking bad.'

I stood in shocked silence listening to the horrific news. Over the next fifteen minutes the story developed. I shook my head in disbelief when the news bulletin said, 'We've just learned Michael Jackson has died. The fifty-year-old suffered a cardiac arrest earlier this afternoon at his Holmby Hills home, and paramedics were unable to revive him.'

I thought about his family, about Prince, Paris and Blanket, and how distraught and afraid they must have been at that moment. What life would they have without their father? Grace, their long-time nanny, had had a disagreement with Michael and I was some-what unsure if she was still in his employ, but I knew she was in London and therefore not available to offer them any kind of com-fort. Grace would be distraught. She had loved Michael. I knew she would contact me when she felt the time was right for her to do so.

The phone rang. I looked at my watch: it was 11.15 PM on 25 June 2009. TV3's *Ireland AM* wanted to do an interview with me the fol-lowing morning. I lay in bed that night thinking about the enormity of what had just happened. The world had not only lost a wonder-fully talented entertainer, a genius in his field, but also one of its greatest humanitarians. I thought about what we could have done together in Africa, building hospitals and helping children who had been orphaned when their parents had died with HIV. It would be nice to be able to continue this legacy, I thought. Michael had been misunderstood and often taken advantage of during his life, and now there would be nobody to protect his legacy; his children were just too young.

During the breakfast-television interview, I told the listening Irish audience about the side of the singer that I had witnessed, the enormous love between Michael and his children, and I defended his great humanitarian work. The interviewer, Mark Cagney, was very respectful of Michael's legacy and allowed me to tell the nation about the side of Michael that nobody really knew. I told some personal stories about how comical and intelligent he was. It was an honest appraisal of the person I had come to know.

Tom Prendeville interviewed me later that day for the *Evening Herald*, and I said that Michael had been the perfect embodiment of the rags-to-riches story, whose celebrity took him from gifted musical child to global superstar. Unfortunately it also took him back to America, to a place where he had endured painful lawsuits and unscrupulous people who took advantage of his good nature and kindness. I thought again about his words that night: 'I don't want to die another penniless black man while others benefit from me.' I wondered whether he had managed to fulfil his dream.

I decided to go to Michael's funeral and visit Neverland to pay my respects and say goodbye to him for the last time. The funeral was a very dignified affair, consisting of a private family service at Forest Lawn Memorial Park's Hall of Liberty, followed by a public memorial at the Staples Centre. Half a billion people flooded the Internet looking for tickets. Michael's casket was present during the memorial, which was broadcast live around the world and watched by up to one billion people. While there, I gave a television interview outside Neverland to Fox News, talking about Michael's great warmth and humanity. He had received so much negative press in America that I wanted to redress the balance in whatever way I could.

I was still in California when the *Irish Sun* ran a 'world exclusive' with my picture on its front page, headlined 'Irish Doc Fixed Jacko's Face'. The article told how Michael used to come to the clinic late at night and how he felt comfortable in Ireland away from the glare of the media. I wondered where they were getting their information.

In early July, William Bratton, chief of the Los Angeles Police Department (LAPD), indicated that the police were looking into whether Michael's death had been a homicide or an accidental overdose, but had to wait for the full toxicology reports from the coroner. In the days that followed, the LAPD grew increasingly concerned about the actions of Michael's personal physician, Dr Conrad Murray. Some articles stated that Michael had insisted that concert promoter AEG Live hire Murray to accompany him to England. I found this very odd, as he had never mentioned to me that Murray would be coming with him and, besides, Murray was not even registered to work in Britain. Michael knew that I *was* registered in England.

Murray became the primary focus of the LAPD investigation when they discovered he had administered propofol to Michael within twenty-four hours of the singer's death. I couldn't understand why someone who would not even use midazolam without an anaesthetist present would use a drug as powerful as propofol in his own home. The LAPD announced that they were referring the case to prosecutors, who might file criminal charges. In the media frenzy that ensued, there were reports about other drugs found at the scene, and that Michael had used aliases to procure prescription medications. Arnold Klein told CNN that Michael had had an anaesthesiologist administer propofol to help him sleep during the HIStory tour in Germany in 1997.

It almost seemed like they were talking about another person. It appeared to me that the media were being influenced by certain lawyers who had an agenda to make it seem like Michael Jackson was a drug addict who had killed himself. It was awful for me to know that, in my experience, Michael was not a drug addict, and to see his good name muddied once again on the world stage. I called Tom Mesereau, the attorney who had defended him during the child-molestation trial. Michael had spoken highly of Tom, whom *GQ* magazine had named one of its Men of the Year in 2005. He viewed him as a person of integrity, and I felt that Michael would want me to chat with him and help clear his name. When we talked a few days later, I found that he was exceptionally helpful. Tom asked me to contact Michael's brother, Randy, and the LAPD with information about some private documentation I had that might help clear Michael's name and preserve his legacy.

A few days later, a detective from the LAPD called me and took a long statement. The interview lasted thirty or forty minutes, and at the end of it, the detective mentioned that there was a list of nine or ten doctors who were under investigation, but that I was not one of them. They were subpoenaing medical records from these doctors, who had all treated Michael. The detective said I might be called as a witness when the trial started. The *Sunday Times* later published an article that said the police wanted to question thirty doctors, nurses and pharmacists, including Arnold Klein, who had said that he had occasionally given Michael Demerol. I felt sorry for Dr Klein, as he had always been professional whenever I had talked to him.

26.
DEVASTATION IN HAITI

The year 2010 had barely begun when a devastating 7.0-magnitude earthquake struck the Caribbean city of Port-au-Prince in Haiti, destroying everything from shantytown homes to national landmarks. Early reports said millions were likely to be displaced, with many tens of thousands feared dead. As darkness fell on Haiti's capital, crowds gathered in the streets and began to pray, as rescue teams from all over the world descended on the island.

Over the next few days, television showed horrific scenes of the shattered city. Corpses were piled up and lay on blood-stained sheets on the crumpled streets. Residents valiantly tried to prevent their loved ones from being eaten by gangs of prowling dogs. The scenes were almost too horrendous to contemplate. I decided that I had to go there and help.

The opportunity to visit Haiti arose after I was invited to a meeting in Miami that February. It had been organised to get the views of key opinion leaders from around the world, on where the field of aesthetics was heading. It was attended by some old friends of mine, Christopher Zachary and Bob Weiss from California, and Mariano Busso from Florida; Ravi Jain and I were the European representatives. Randy Waldman from Kentucky was also there, and he invited me to speak at the prestigious Las Vegas Cosmetic Surgery congress, which I've done almost every year since. Ireland was still in the depths of recession, and the meeting meant I had paid flights all the way to Miami, and the opportunity to give the bursary from the meeting to the victims of the earthquake.

Before I left Dublin for Miami, I had a meeting with my friends Peter Hanley and Peter Gannon, NGO volunteers who were keen to go to the island to try to help as much as possible. Gannon had visited the island in 2009, just before the earthquake, and while he was there he had met Bishop Pierre Dorcilien, who was from a Christian community involved in education. The bishop and his wife Gladys ran a primary-level school called the School of Miracles and Restoration. This school, like many others, had been destroyed during the earthquake, and we decided it would be our mission to help rebuild it.

God works in mysterious ways and, in early February, my friends and I were living in a small tent behind the collapsed school in Tabarre, Port au Prince. The bishop and his wife lived in a small hut on the premises and they made us feel very welcome. On the first evening, as darkness fell, we wandered with him around some nearby camps in Dumornay, where he provided spiritual assistance and talked to his people about their problems.

On the second morning, I took a taxi to see the devastated city of Port-au-Prince. It was distressing to hear stories of bodies being burnt in funeral pyres of old car tyres, and shopping trolleys being used to collect the dead when there was no more room in the cemeteries. The earthquake survivors told me how some of the injured had been cut from the rubble with butchers' knives or hacksaws, and how this caused problems later as the stumps, without skin flaps to cover them, became infected.

Peter Gannon and I visited Gena Heraty at St Damien's Paediatric Hospital, where she worked as the director of the special needs programme. She told me that the average life expectancy on the island was forty-four years, and the annual income was just over $650. I knew from working in disaster zones previously that the three things survivors immediately need are food, water and shelter. Next they need sanitation antibiotics and mosquito nets.

The next afternoon, we met with Richard Morse, owner of the famous Hotel Oloffson, which had been immortalised in Graham

Greene's novel *The Comedians*. At night, Richard played in a *rasin* band called RAM, his initials, which mixed elements of traditional Haitian voodoo ceremonial music with rock and roll. He told me not to fear the voodoo religion, explaining that it was just an extension of other, more familiar religions. He laughingly said: 'Protestants have God and the Trinity; Catholics have God, the Trinity and the saints; and Voodoo has God, the Trinity, the saints and the spirits.'

Later in the week, we met Hugh Brennan, a construction engineer working with Haven, an Irish philanthropic organisation, who promised to provide some sanitation for the shanty town we saw in Dumornay. Within a few days, Hugh had begun training twenty of the camp's inhabitants to make twenty-four toilets. He told me, 'These people require sanitation and our focus is to get them to help themselves. We have learned from the mistakes of the past and when you get a person to construct something themselves they are more willing to hold onto it.' It was good advice that I would later follow in Africa.

Many scores of NGO volunteers have participated in mission trips to the devastated island nation since the earthquake. They came of their own volition and, without their ongoing help, the story of Haiti would have been very different. Their goodwill mixed with the sweat of a courageous populace who laboured all day under the burning sun to try and rebuild their lives. I knew the best way we could help these people was to provide financial support and target specialist groups to rebuild their educational infrastructure. This was the only way to bring new hope for all those impoverished people in the huts and small villages of Haiti, struggling daily to break the bonds of poverty, which had largely been placed on them by others, mostly through slavery and trade embargos.

It took me a long time to get over the devastation I had seen in Haiti. In the months after my visit, I maintained Facebook contact with Bishop Dorcilien and his wife, and we formed the Haiti Leadership Foundation, which aimed at building a new Christian village, high in the Haitian mountains, to replace what had been lost. The village would be built in memory of the bishop's brother, Ned, who had been assassinated for political reasons some years before. The bishop had survived the attack, and still had the gunshot wounds to prove it.

The bishop and his wife came to Ireland to join the Doolough Famine Walk, which is held annually at Louisburgh, County Mayo, to commemorate local victims of the Irish Famine. On the night of 30 March 1849, one hundred people walked twelve miles to Delphi Lodge in the hope of receiving rations. It was a severely cold night, and it was reported shortly afterwards that the bodies of seven people, including women and children, were subsequently discovered on the roadside overlooking the shores of Doolough lake, and that nine more never reached their homes. Local folklore maintains that the total number who perished was far higher.

Irish radio stations and national newspapers interviewed the bishop and his wife about the progress after the Haitian earthquake. While on the walk, we rested by a monument in Doolough Valley, which had an insightful inscription from Mahatma Gandhi: 'How can men feel themselves honoured by the humiliation of their fellow beings?'

In 2012, the bishop moved some of his Tabarre community to a new village in Mirebalais, in the mountains about one hour's drive north of the earthquake's epicentre. I was glad to be influential in Irish entrepreneur Denis O'Brien's decision to fund a new school for the village.

★

In April, I was joined in Dublin by Grace Rwaramba, who was on the way to a wedding in the Middle East. She had found the days since Michael's passing very difficult, and was still devastated by his death. During the meeting, she expressed an interest in going down to Haiti to work as a volunteer. As yet, she hasn't visited the island, but we are still in contact.

On the first anniversary of Michael's death, I did an interview on *Ireland AM* with Aidan Cooney, during which I spoke about the singer's great humanitarian work. I was also invited to do an interview with Reverend Catherine Gross on a Chicago Internet radio show, and said that his body of artistic work carried a spiritual message relating to all the injustices of the human race: racism, inequality, disease, hunger and corruption.

In November, Jerry Biederman, executive producer of the Michael Jackson Tribute Portrait, invited me to Los Angeles to receive a dot in the pointillist painting by artist David Ilan. The portrait contained hundreds of thousands of dots: it had the blessing and support of members of Michael's family and those who were close to him, and was endorsed by Diana Ross. I was to be honoured with a dot in the area of Michael's heart, which was reserved for family and close friends.

Snow was falling over the Santa Clarita Valley when I arrived. I made a small speech for the media, saying that I was honoured to be given a place in Michael Jackson's heart, as his legacy as an artist often overshadowed the tremendous good he did in the world and the way he unselfishly supported many causes, often at financial cost to himself. He treated everybody equally, regardless of race, colour and creed. It was especially annoying to me that the media used against him a condition I was treating him for, I said.

While I was in Los Angeles, Dr Conrad Murray's preliminary hearing was taking place at the courthouse in Temple Street. There were some fans outside the courthouse with painted placards. I spoke with them and each had their own story to tell. In the circumstances, I thought it best not to mention to them that I had known Michael. After visiting the courthouse, I went to Forest Lawn Memorial Park to visit Michael's grave. Although it was not officially open to the public, it felt right to be in the presence of his spirit. I got as near as I could to his graveside and prayed for a while.

27.

THE TRIAL

I was invited to New York by the cable-TV host Aphrodite Jones to take part in her documentary series *True Crime with Aphrodite Jones*. Aphrodite and I had chatted on the phone a few times, and she had sent me a copy of her latest work, *Michael Jackson: Conspiracy*. The book examined how the American media had sensationalised the prosecution's case against the late pop star in the Santa Maria trial. Her writing had made the *New York Times* best-sellers list, and I admired her work.

During the interview, she asked whether I had ever prescribed anything to Michael for insomnia, or had seen needles or syringes in Michael's home. I told her, quite honestly, that I had never pre-scribed him any drugs for insomnia, and I'd never seen any drugs in his house. She delved deeper, stating that one of the theories pro-posed by the defence team was that Michael was very familiar with propofol and had the ability to inject himself. I assured her that any time he had received propofol in Ireland, it had been injected by an anaesthetist and that this had been done at his request.

We filmed for two hours, going over the same questions time and time again. It was almost like I was on trial, but I knew a lot of people in America would be listening to the programme when it aired, and I was keen to tell the truth. I felt that Michael's legacy was being tainted and, as a friend, this saddened me. Investigation Discovery channel posted some snippets from the interview on YouTube, which carried a disclaimer stating that they didn't share my views.

The *Irish Sun* carried a story on 8 May saying, 'Explosive claims by a top Irish surgeon about the mystery death of Michael Jackson have been banned from US TV.' The article claimed that defence lawyers had had the footage pulled as they fought manslaughter charges against Murray. It also said that the trial's start date had been put back, by four months, as they searched out new witnesses. News broke the next day that the trial would be rescheduled for the following September.

★

In June, Dr Randolph Waldman invited me to lecture about CO_2-fractionalised skin resurfacing at the 2010 Las Vegas Cosmetic Surgery meeting at the Bellagio. The conference attracted some of the top international aesthetic practitioners, and my lecture concerned laser resurfacing to the face and eyes. While in the United States, I was also invited to a give a talk to some students at Gardner Street Elementary School, in Hawthorn Avenue, Los Angeles, where Michael had once been a pupil.

Before my speech, I went to Santa Monica, where I met Grace Rwaramba. We spent a few happy hours strolling along Palisades Park, with its crumbling bluffs and views of the Pacific Ocean. She still seemed deeply troubled by the loss of Michael. When I asked why she had not gone down to Haiti as arranged, she told me that some of the Jackson family were accusing her of being involved in voodoo; she didn't want to visit Haiti because it might make it seem like they were right. We discussed some difficulties that she and Michael had had in Bahrain before arriving in Ireland, where he was happy and, she felt, should have stayed. In the end, Grace felt that it would be too distressing for her to visit Gardner Street and meet Principal Kenneth Urbina and the students.

The talk I gave was entitled 'What Would Michael Do?' and, thankfully, it got a standing ovation. I told the teachers and students how each of us owed a debt of gratitude to Michael, who had fought for those in need. 'Michael brought light where there was darkness, hope where there was despair; he never turned away from cruelty when he could give compassion,' I said. The speech borrowed heavily from Elie Wiesel, a Jewish Holocaust survivor, when it mentioned that we cannot be indifferent to the world around us, as that always benefits the aggressor – never the victim, whose pain is magnified when he or she feels forgotten.

During my speech, I also said:

Gratitude is what defines the humanity of the human being and that is what we owe to Michael Jackson, someone I am privileged to call my friend, somebody who often stood alone to fend for the children in the world, for the destitute, for the victims of disease and injustice. Michael was very troubled by the suffering he saw in the world and even more by the indifference to it. His first words to me when we met were, "Thank you so much for helping the people of Africa."

There were no airs and graces, no pomp and circumstance, and his only concern was for the lives of other people who lived on a different continent than the one on which either of us were born. I had been to Africa and seen the devastation of the plague of HIV at first hand and when we discussed it, there were tears in his eyes and he said we had to do something together for the people of Africa. He planned to hold a great concert in Rwanda and we would fly there together in his private plane and then go down to see his great friend, Nelson Mandela. Sadly, these events were not to happen and the world lost one of its great humanitarians.

While I was at Gardner Street, the teachers showed me a small desk in the music room, where Michael had once sat. They also showed me some memorabilia and said they would like to have a small area in the back of the classroom set up as a museum to honour their famous student. I took a guitar and sang the Neil Young song 'Out on the Weekend', which included a lyric about going to LA. Somehow, it just seemed appropriate at the time, as we had both once lived in that great city, and it reminded me of my time working with Carnival Cruise Lines some years before.

★

Conrad Murray's trial for the death of Michael Jackson eventually started on 7 September 2011. It was held in the Superior Court of Los Angeles County before Judge Pastor, and I was on the special witness list. During the opening days, I was interviewed by Dr Drew Pinsky, from CNN in Los Angeles, about whether Michael could have committed suicide by injecting himself with propofol. I was never called to testify.

On 7 November, Murray was found guilty of involuntary manslaughter. He was later sentenced to four years of incarceration. After the result, I was invited by TV3's *Midweek* programme to give my opinion. I said that while it was sad to see another doctor incarcerated, Dr Murray was guilty of not providing an adequate standard of medical care, and his reckless behaviour and neglectful actions had led directly to the death of another human being, who was also a father, brother and son – and my friend.

In the following days, I wrote a poem to Michael and posted it on my Facebook page. It was seen by many fans around the world, who felt that the words helped to heal their pain. The organisation Michael Jackson's Legacy invited me to become an honorary ambassador, to help preserve Michael's legacy. Their first project would have been close to Michael's heart: building the Everland Children's Home to provide a safe place for fifty children from the slums of Monrovia, Liberia. I was honoured to accept the position, and opened the orphanage there on Christmas Day 2012 with these words:

Michael Jackson felt the pain of the hungry children of Africa, often walking for miles with swollen bellies, dying without dignity in the night as the rest of the world emptied its supermarket food waste into the bins of New York, London and Dublin. He knew and felt deeply about a continent ravaged by civil war and pestilence, where children in this city were forced to hack off the limbs of their parents and eat the beating hearts of other humans. None of these children asked to become involved in an adult war, where man's inhumanity to each other is only outdone by the evil that lies within their hearts. There are times when we all feel that God has abandoned this world: the terrible earthquake in Haiti, the bloody streets of Northern Ireland, and when, at evening-time, shadows fall over the coffin makers in Nairobi, another HIV-infected child is put back into the earth from which they were born. Well, I say to you here today that there is a God who looks down on all of this wrong and he brought us an angel in the form of Michael Jackson to help solve it.

★

In June 2013, Michael Jackson's Legacy (MJL) started a second project: building an orphanage in Ned Dorcilien's Christian village in Mirebalais, Haiti. The building was to be called Everland Haiti. Bishop Dorcilien and MJL invited me there in January 2014 to open the new building for thirty children. It was built on the same ground as a new school, which had been completed with a generous donation of almost $350,000 from my friend Denis O'Brien, owner of Haiti's largest Telecom Company, Digicel.

It was wonderful to see my old friends the Dorciliens again after so many years. I stayed for a week in part of the building and was joined by Rachael Paulson, founder of Hands On the World Global. We slept amidst those same hills where Toussaint Louverture the 'the Father of Haiti' had got the rebel slaves to fight the armies of the English, which were supporting white colonialists opposed to the abolition of slavery, and then Napoleon too, to gain freedom for their nation.

During the opening ceremony for Everland Haiti, a great wind got up and blew the doors and windows of the building wide open. Everything was strewn from the tables across the floor. Many people there thought it was the spirit of Michael himself, supporting his legacy. In some ways I felt the same, and that it compensated for the concert he had wanted us to do together to help the children of Africa. Bishop Dorcilien and his wife were a little startled, but not keen to mention what had happened, as it may have been misinterpreted. They feared that orphan children might not have been brought to the village if there was any suspicion that outside forces or malevolent spirits were present there. After the doors had been closed, and some order restored, we resumed the ceremony.

When it was my turn to speak, I repeated some of Michael's words from his famous address to the Oxford Union in 2001. He had visited the university to promote his Heal the Kids initiative and to propose a universal bill of rights for children. I came close to tears at times during my speech, especially when talking about my memories of my discussion with Michael about his childhood and his relationship with his father. I also recalled Michael's proposal for what should be included in the children's bill of rights:

1. The right to be loved without having to earn it
2. The right to be protected without having to deserve it
3. The right to feel valuable, even if you came into the world with nothing
4. The right to be listened to without having to be interesting
5. The right to be read a bedtime story, without having to compete with the evening news
6. The right to an education without having to dodge bullets at school
7. The right to be thought of as adorable (even if you have a face only a mother could love)

★

When Nelson Mandela died later that year, the world lost another great humanitarian, and I fondly remembered the conversation that Michael and I had had with him about the concert in Africa. My brother was having brain surgery in London though, and I decided to stay with him rather than attend the funeral.

On the day Mandela was buried, his granddaughter said that he had run his last race. I thought of his words: 'To be free is not merely to cast off one's chains, but to live in a way that respects and enhances the freedom of others.'

AFTERWORD

I have just returned from seeing 'The Who Hits 50!' concert in the 3 Arena in Dublin. When they played 'Who Are You?' it brought me back to their concert in Wembley Stadium almost thirty-six years earlier, when I was just beginning my career in medicine.

So were am I now? I still live in Dublin, where I am the medical director of Ailesbury Clinic Worldwide, which has offices in London, India, Dubai and Saudi Arabia. I travel often, lecturing and visiting friends. I'm in touch with many of the people I've introduced you to in this book – my medical colleagues, my friends and the people I have met in my travels, from Garrison to Dublin, Germany to Turkey, Iraq to Miami, Kenya to Liberia.

Writing this book has given me a chance to remember so many people and places, and to reflect on my life, and think about how all the different strands have come together to form a colourful tapestry, woven over time by some unseen cosmic hand, the weft made up by my dreams and the warp by my destiny. What guides the weaver, or whether I can influence its actions in any way, no one can say for sure. The circumstances into which a person is born, the nation where one develops one's behaviour, the poverty and possibly also the grief that one experiences, all influence the final weave.

I don't know what will come next for me. I would like to raise a family, but I'm unsure if that will happen. All I know is that each day brings me new challenges and discoveries, and that I will do my best to meet the former and to enjoy the latter. It has been a long journey from Garrison, but it's not yet over.

—Patrick Treacy, Dublin, 23 June 2015